MOTHERLAND

L Todd Wood

Motherland
L. Todd Wood
ISBN: 978-1-943927-03-6
Library of Congress Control Number: 2016919050
Copyright © 2016 L. Todd Wood
All rights reserved worldwide,
Icebox Publishing, Westport, CT

No part of this publication may be reproduced, stored in a retrieval system or transmitted in any way by any means, electronic, mechanical, photocopy, recording or otherwise as provided by USA copyright law. This novel is a work of fiction. Names, places, descriptions, entities, and incidents included in the story are products of the author's imagination. Any resemblance to actual persons, places, events, entities, or incidents is entirely coincidental. The opinions expressed by the author are entirely his.

Cover Design by EBook Launch.

To the IDF girl in uniform I met on the bus from Tel Aviv to Jerusalem, and her grenade launcher.

"Our fatal troika dashes on in her headlong flight perhaps to destruction and in all Russia for long past men have stretched out imploring hands and called a halt to its furious reckless course."

Fyodor Dostoyevsky, The Brothers Karamazov

To me belongeth vengeance, and recompence; their foot shall slide in due time: for the day of their calamity is at hand, and the things that shall come upon them make haste.

Deuteronomy 32:35

Prologue

> The Northern Lights have seen queer sights,
> But the queerest they ever did see
> Was that night on the marge of Lake Lebarge
> I cremated Sam McGee.
> (Robert Service, "The Cremation of Sam McGee")

Captain Richards was tired and cold when he arrived at the squadron. It was a dark, winter night, and the moon reflected off the frozen ground as he shut off the jeep's engine and doused the headlights. It was the type of cold you could only experience in the Yukon, the type of cold that when married to the desolate wilderness seemed not only to chill a man but frighten him with loneliness. He sat for a moment in the warm air, pondering what the temperature was outside. *I wish I was in my bed...* In a few seconds, with no heater running inside the vehicle, the cold air attacked feverishly through the hardtop. *Time to get out?*

He was issued the vehicle a few days before—one of the perks of becoming a flight commander. The army was giving him more responsibility. He took it and asked for more. He had been in the Alaskan territory half a year now, although it seemed like much longer than that. Europe was far away in his memory. He was not sure if that was a good or bad thing.

Finally making up his mind, he exited the vehicle, pulling the parka hood over his head. Still, the wind allowed the cold to seep into his bones as he walked the short distance to the entrance of the wooden, military World War II structure that housed the fighter squadron, the same type of building he had seen at many other army posts around the world. The white stuff on the ground crunched under his mukluks. At least the snow had stopped a few hours before. The door slammed as he closed it behind him, and he allowed himself a few seconds to savor the warmth inside. The chill radiated off his army-issued parka but slowly faded away.

Earlier in the night, he had been in a deep, dead man's' sleep when the phone started ringing. Still drained from the previous day's brutal mission, he deserved the day off. But he could not say no to a full-bird colonel; even the famous Captain Richards, the war hero, could not do that. So he had dragged himself out of bed and put on a pot of coffee in the small kitchen provided in the Post Officers' Quarters.

He was not complaining, you understand. After a year fighting the Luftwaffe with the Royal Air Force in the United Kingdom, he appreciated the small comforts the army could give him. His own kitchen was definitely a perk, but he felt guilty about it. The faces of his long-dead friends at the hands of the Third Reich were still fresh in his mind. He hoped with time they would fade as well like the cold on his parka. The faces haunted him.

The squadron duty officer on the phone said it was urgent. Hell, things were always urgent in this war. *Hurry up and wait* was the soldier's mantra. Richards couldn't imagine what was so urgent that he had to be woken after flying for over fourteen hours back to Elmendorf Field in Alaska outside of Anchorage. But he was here, doing his duty. He always did his duty. The cold and the lack of sleep seemed inconsequential when compared to his comrades-in-arms still fighting on the Continent. No, Captain Richards wouldn't be complaining, not tonight. He would simply do what was asked of him. That's what soldiers do.

Warmed temporarily, Richards strolled purposefully through

MOTHERLAND

the hallway to the operations center, the boards in the floor creaking as he stepped on them. Maps of the local terrain adorned the walls along with pictures of wrecked aircraft. There were hundreds of wrecks in Alaska. Usually the hulks were left to rot in the tundra, which was dotted with these rusted remnants of flying machines, their stories long lost to the world. Richards could imagine the scene a hundred years from now, when some young pilot would fly over the carcass of a B-24 and wonder about the story behind it.

Soon he was facing the duty officer, a green second lieutenant who was lucky enough to get assigned here after being commissioned, rather than sent to the front in Europe or to some island, fighting the Japanese. He handed Richards a folded piece of paper. "Here are your orders," said the lieutenant. "The colonel says this mission is very sensitive and of the highest priority. This aircraft needs to get to Provideniya as soon as possible."

"That's it?" asked Richards. "Just another milk run to Provideniya? That's why the colonel got me up in the middle of the fucking night after a long mission yesterday? I guess he forgot about crew rest," Richards snarled sarcastically.

"No, I didn't forget," said a gruff voice behind him. "But this is war, and all the rules go out the window. Don't you know that, Captain?"

Richards turned. *Shit*, he thought to himself. "Good morning, sir! My apologies." Richards managed a crisp salute despite his fatigue. It was returned promptly.

"It's not a good morning, it's the middle of the fucking night," said the colonel. "And yes, it's urgent. This satchel has to be in Provideniya by close of business today. TODAY! You understand? Not tomorrow but fucking today!" He handed Richards a brown, leather, official-looking satchel. The briefcase was locked with a padlock containing a rotating dial key. "It's not me giving the orders on this one. This comes from way above my pay grade. It came from

Washington. So yes, I gather *it's rather important*, but I have no idea why. Just get it there today so they get off my ass about this one, okay Captain?"

Richards took the satchel and slung it over his shoulder. He unfolded the flight orders and scanned them quickly. "Looks straightforward enough, sir. I'll get this done and be back in no time."

"Thank you, Captain. That is all. I know I can count on you. That's why I woke you up." Richards saluted again. The colonel again returned the salute, smiled as he turned, and left the operations room.

The lieutenant spoke again. "Weather is waiting for you at the tower. I got them up for you as well. Yes, it looks like this should be a milk run. Only some cloud cover to deal with, sir,"

"Thanks, LT. Have a good night, whatever is left of it. I'll report in once I'm on my way." Richards left the room and walked back towards the entrance to the squadron and the cold. The wind bit him in the face as he made his way back to the jeep. *At least the heater is warmed up*, he thought to himself as he turned on the engine. He drove the short distance to the flight line and the aircraft parked not far away.

Elmendorf Field sat on the edge of Cook Inlet, the natural port that fed the Alaskan territory. It was an effectively protected harbor, and the town of Anchorage sat behind the inlet, snuggled up against the Chugach Mountains rising above it. The mountains were covered in snow. However, in a few months when spring broke, the snow line would move higher up the slope, leaving only the peaks covered in white. In the summer, the reverse happened. As winter approached, the snow would slowly move down the mountainside day by day. The locals called this phenomenon *termination dust*, heralding the approaching winter.

The aircraft were lined up along the runway, over twenty-five of them; a few of them had their shark-painted snouts snarling at the cold. Most of them, however, were devoid of more than just the basic markings, as if they were meant for someone other than the Army Air Corp, and they were. The Russians would of course repaint them when they were delivered.

The maintenance chief met him at the tail number that was selected. "She's fueled and ready to go, Captain," he stated nonchalantly as he arrived. The man completed this task hundreds of times a week. It was nothing special.

"Thanks, Frank. I appreciate you getting up in the middle of the night as well. Seems to be something about this run that's very important to someone."

"Yeah, that's what I heard. They wanted this plane ready to go and quick. I did my part. Now it's your turn, Captain. Have a good flight. I guess you'll be taking the DC-3 back again from Nome. Fly safe."

Richards returned the sergeant's salute and climbed into the cockpit, situated himself, started the engine, and taxied out to the runway. The massive rotary engine growled loudly at the night. It was comforting to him somehow. It seemed to him he was the only thing moving in the dead of winter. After receiving clearance for takeoff from the lone man in the tower, he gunned the throttle and shot down the runway.

A half hour later, he was approaching the Alaskan mountain range and Rainy Pass to the West. The tundra flew by beneath him, and he allowed himself some enjoyment flying two hundred feet off the ground as the dawn broke behind him and illuminated the world ahead. The caribou darted and jinked below him, attempting to get away from the strange, terrifying noise. A smile of peace crept across his face. To tell the absolute truth, he had fallen in love with Alaska. The vast wilderness, the wildlife, the freedom, they all captivated him. He was home. He could feel it.

The mountains surrounded Anchorage like a bowl and protected the small town from the more severe weather Alaska had to offer in the interior of the territory. Rainy Pass was a natural opening that wound through the peaks and provided a way to navigate through the chain without crossing over the top of the twelve-thousand-foot mountain range. Over the millennia, the river had cut somewhat of a canyon through the mountains.

Richards had stowed the satchel in the small, rear cargo compartment of the Curtiss P-40 Warhawk. The United States had been providing fighter and other types of aircraft to the Soviet Union for over a year now to fight the Nazi war machine, which had invaded Russia and threatened Moscow, although now the Soviets had begun to push them back. It was important to keep the pressure on the Nazis from both east and west.

The Lend-lease program had been very effective, enabling America to delay her entry into the conflict. The effort primarily aided the United Kingdom, but the Soviet Union benefited as well. American manufacturing provided over twenty percent of Soviet aircraft used on the Eastern Front. Ships, trucks, tanks, and other heavy equipment were all provided in massive quantities. At the end of the war, the material was supposed to be destroyed under American supervision, but only a small percentage was actually disposed of in this manner. Much of the equipment the Soviets would use for decades after Hitler was no longer among the living.

Richard's squadron's purpose, in addition to providing an air defense capability for the Alaskan territory, was to ferry these aircraft to Russia via the Bering Strait. Provideniya was the small village and military installation on the eastern coast of Siberia, where he landed the planes to deliver to the Russian Air Force.

The lieutenant was right, the weather was not bad. The only issue was a cloud layer at eight thousand feet. He would have to navigate beneath the cloud cover through the pass, as he didn't have

MOTHERLAND

oxygen available on this flight, and it was filed as a VFR, or visual flight rules, hop.

He enjoyed flying under the clouds through the mountains. It was like driving a Formula One through the narrow streets of some European city. Rainy Pass was the only one he had not flown since his arrival in Alaska. He had been offered and had accepted an initial orientation flight through each of the other passes, a daylight trial run with an instructor in a two-seater. However, Richards was a very experienced pilot and he was not worried. *Just a milk run*, he thought to himself.

He entered the throughway with plenty of space above him before the cloud cover thickened and created a dark ceiling, which he had no desire to penetrate. The clouds were ominous. The weather was actually slowly becoming worse than the boys at the field had forecast. There was ice in those clouds, ice that could seriously degrade the aerodynamics of his aircraft. Ice was dangerous in Alaska. If you allowed enough of the stuff to accumulate on the wings of your plane, you stopped flying. That was not a good thing to say the least. It was as simple as that. If you could avoid it, you did. *I'm not going near it*, Richards thought.

He focused again on making his way through the pass. Initially, the canyon was wide, and the walls on either side seemed far away and harmless. However, as he approached the halfway point through the mountain chain, the pass started to narrow and the cloud ceiling began to drop, providing him less room for error.

"Not such a milk run after all," Richards mumbled to no one as he twisted and turned through the tangled canyon. He had slowed the fighter plane to just above stall speed to give him more maneuverability to negotiate the now very small passageway through the ominous mountains on either side of him. Sweat dripped down his forehead, stinging his eyes. The turns were becoming quicker and

more dangerous; they required his utmost attention and skill.
I wish I'd had that orientation flight.
The visibility was dropping. The clouds above him were now emitting a thin veil of mist, which froze to his windshield. He continued to twist and turn and slowed the fighter even more, as much as he dared. The stall warning horn was buzzing in his ear. He wondered how much more time he had before he exited the mountain range on the other side and could relax on his way to Russia.
Where's that damn map? he thought to himself. His eyes quickly searched the cockpit, and he caught a glimpse of a sheet of paper on the floor under his left foot. The map had fallen down from where he had placed it on the left control panel. His aggressive flight maneuvers through the pass had seen to that. Richards took a chance and leaned down briefly to get the map, taking his eyes off the passage in front of him.
It was a mistake that cost him his life.
When he looked back up, his squadron commander's words came back to him with frightening clarity. "You've got to watch Rainy Pass; there is a twist halfway through that has killed many a skilled pilot. It's an S turn that is deadly if you're not careful."
The snow was falling hard now and the cloud cover was dropping fast.
As he glimpsed through the ice-covered windshield of the plane, Richard's heart skipped a beat when he saw the mountain passageway turn ninety degrees to the right and completely block his path. The adrenaline coursed through his veins as he jammed the stick to the rear, cut the throttle, and slammed the control to the right to slow the aircraft in hopes of executing a wingover maneuver back down into the pass to the right. He forced the stick against his thigh so hard he broke several blood vessels in the process as the chemicals in his body created superhuman strength in the face of death. The Warhawk pitched up, and then the right wing dipped and she sank back down

into the canyon. Out of the corner of his eye, he actually saw several carcasses of other aircraft lying in waste on the hillside that had made the same mistake. It was literally a graveyard of plane crashes.

He smiled as he thought he had made it and briefly imagined drinking vodka with the natives that evening at the local watering hole in Provideniya. However, as he banked harder to the right to fall faster back down into the pass, his right wingtip caught the mountainside and violently cartwheeled the aircraft down onto the boulder-strewn, granite slope. Mercifully, Richard's head impacted the left side of the cockpit with such force, he immediately lost consciousness.

The Warhawk made several flips before coming to rest in a small creek bed about two thousand feet above the floor of the pass meandering below.

In a few minutes, the snow covered any trace of tail number USSR-9328.

Chapter One

May 5, 1996
Rainy Pass
Alaskan Mountain Range
75 Miles West of Anchorage, Alaska

Captain Connor Murray tried to make out the herd of caribou bobbing and weaving a thousand feet beneath him through the chin bubble in the cockpit at his feet, the noise of the aircraft frightening them into desperate action. There were hundreds of the huge animals tromping over the lush, green tundra floor of the Alaskan wilderness. The calves tried to keep up with their mothers. The racks of the males stood out among the herd. The craggy, snow-covered peaks of the Alaskan mountain range rose on each side of him as he guided the HH-3E Jolly Green Giant through the pass on the way back to Elmendorf AFB, located on the outskirts of Alaska's largest city, Anchorage. The aircraft and crew were returning from ferrying supplies out to a forward operating, fighter alert base on the outskirts of the western coast, where the F-15s intercepted Russian bombers routinely trolling along the outskirts of the Alaskan Air Defense Zone, probing American air defenses.

"Lots of calves out here today, they must have just been born," said Airman Thomas, the PJ, or pararescueman, on board as he leaned over the open ramp at the rear of the aircraft. The only thing holding him inside the cabin was a webbed gunner's belt chained to the floor and fastened around his waist. "Too bad we don't have a sling and a water bucket today to have some fun. I'd love to try and drop a load of cold lake water on one of those big bucks!"

"I wish I had my rifle. One of those calves would feed my barbecue for a summer," added Master Sergeant Wolf, the flight engineer and the senior enlisted man on board. Instead, he picked up a high-powered camera and began snapping photos out of the starboard door in the cabin of the large helicopter.

"Now, now, Sergeant," Murray chided over the intercom from the cockpit, "the tree-huggers wouldn't like that so much, would they?"

"No but my wife would!" Wolf responded. "Heck, I might even get laid if I brought home that much meat to freeze for the winter."

Murray chuckled to himself.

"We can fit a calf in the back, can't we, Captain? I promise no one at the base will find out! I'll clean up the mess. And I'll invite you over for a steak this weekend!"

"No can do, Sergeant," replied the young captain in mock frustration. "Against squadron policy and every rule in the book, you know that!"

"But we can call it a relief stop, Captain! And I do really have to go! You can put her down somewhere on the meadow I see out the starboard side."

"Can't do, Wolf. I'd lose my wings. I just made aircraft commander for God's sake. I'm sure the relief tube in the back will do the trick just fine."

"I can't seem to find it, Captain! All I can find is your helmet bag!"

"Ha. And I was just looking for someone to sit rescue alert this weekend!"

"Okay, okay, you got me! I guess I'll just have to suffer with no game meat next winter. Geez, I've been through this pass a thousand times and I've never seen so much caribou. Bagging one would be like taking candy from a baby!"

Murray's thoughts returned to flying as he skillfully piloted the giant helicopter through the twists and turns of Rainy Pass. Ahead, the famous S turn in the canyon loomed. This was Murray's favorite part, and he slowed the aircraft about seventy knots to give himself more maneuver room through the tight passage.

"The ice is melting early this year," stated Airman Thomas. "You can see much more of the canyon walls. Man, there's a ton of Dall sheep out this year too. Look at them all over the rocky slopes."

"What the hell...what is that? Tally-ho!" Wolf suddenly shouted excitedly into the microphone in his helmet. "Target three o'clock low!"

"Whatcha got, Wolf?" Murray responded.

"There's a wreck down there I've never spotted before, and as I said, I've been through this pass a thousand times. Can you go back, Captain? Seventy-five percent was sticking out of the ice. One of the wings was broken off."

"I'll try, Wolf, but this better be good!" Murray pulled back hard on the stick, reduced the power to minimum, and the giant helicopter shot nose up into the sky. There was no cloud cover so Murray had plenty of room. Once the airspeed had bled off, Murray kicked the right pedal and pulled the cyclic towards the window, and the nose of the Jolly Green Giant pulled to the right and back down into the canyon, executing a perfect yet violent one-hundred-eighty-degree wingover turn.

"Jesus, Captain, remind me never to give you a hard right turn unless I mean it!" said Wolf as he held on to the cabin wall for dear life.

"There she is!" shouted Thomas. "Holy shit, that's a P-40 Warhawk. Man is this our lucky day!"

"And she's just decided to show herself after all of these years," added Wolf.

"You're sure she's a new wreck?" asked Murray from the cockpit.

"Yes, sir. I am very sure. I know this pass like the back of my hand. I've never seen her before," Wolf responded.

"Okay, then I'm going to report it to RCC. Heading up! Jeff, why don't you take her while I get the HF dialed in. You have the controls."

"Sure, Connor. I have the controls," stated the copilot.

"I'm marking her on the map," added Murray.

Jeff Raines, the copilot, took hold of the collective and pulled back on the cyclic and added power. The powerful machine bolted upwards into the thin air, as she was light on fuel. Ten minutes later, the Jolly Green Giant cleared the top of the mountain range at twelve thousand feet. In peacetime there was a ten-thousand-foot limit an aircrew could not pass without an emergency. A new wreck sighting, especially one from WWII, caused Murray to waive that regulation as the aircraft commander.

"We'll just stay up here long enough to make the call, since we don't have oxygen," stated Murray to the crew. The craggy summits of the mountains spread out below him. Murray marveled at the beauty. A wonderland of mountains, ice and snow carpeted the earth as far as the eye could see. He dialed in the correct frequency to the HF, or high-frequency, long-range radio, clicked the switch on the stick, and spoke into the microphone protruding from his helmet and touching his mouth. "RCC, this is Jolly 26. Do you read, over?" Nothing. He tried again. "RCC, Jolly 26." The Jolly Green call sign was a holdover from the Vietnam War, where the large, green aircraft made history retrieving pilots shot down over North Vietnam.

A few seconds later, there was a warbled response. The HF radio used only high frequencies as opposed to UHF (ultra high) or VHF (very high), and the quality of the transmission was usually poor; however, the range was much longer.

The RCC, or Rescue Coordination Center, was a unit located

MOTHERLAND

at Elmendorf Air Force Base in Anchorage, which coordinated rescue assets throughout the Alaskan theater. Located in the basement of one of the command buildings, the unit was responsible for also cataloguing all wrecks in the Alaskan territory so as to efficiently use government resources if a crash was reported. There was no need to send out a rescue crew to a site the RCC knew was a previously reported wreck. There were thousands of wrecks all over the UHAE, or Unique Harsh Arctic Environment, "yoo-hay" as the locals called it.

Major Jordan was leaning back in his chair, sleeping, when the HF call came in from Jolly 26. He was overweight, lazy, and really bored with his job. When things were slow, he typically took catnaps in his chair behind the radio console. The assistants on the row in front of him couldn't see him. At least that's what he told himself. But he knew they made fun of him. *Probably the reason I've been passed over for lieutenant colonel,* he thought to himself. *I just have two more years to make it to twenty and a cush retirement.* It took him a moment to focus on the situation. Duty in the RCC tended to be long periods of boredom sometimes broken by quick periods of excitement, like if a crash was reported and a rescue launched. Jordan's dreams of his young, female airman assistant were rudely doused as the radio blared.

"Jolly 26, this is RCC, go ahead, over," she responded.

"RCC, we have uncovered a new wreck. It seems to be of World War II vintage and appears to be a P-40 Warhawk carcass. It's slowly melting free from the ice. Coordinates are as follows." Murray reported the latitude and longitude of the crash site as the airman feverishly copied. Major Jordan sat up in his chair, now alert.

"Ask them to investigate," he told her.

"Jolly 26, request you investigate, over."

"Roger, RCC, WILCO. Jolly 26 out."

Captain Murray took in the situation and made a decision. The HH-3E was originally a naval helicopter; in fact, the fuselage

25

was shaped like a ship's hull for floating on the water if needed. The U.S. Air Force had adapted this machine for combat rescue missions in Vietnam a couple decades before, adding a ramp and air refueling capability. The problem was the engines on the Jolly Green Giant were not situated for high-altitude operations. They simply were not designed for hovering in the heat or where the air was thin. The good thing was that they were low on fuel, since they were almost at home base, having already drained the tip tanks on the long trek back from the Alaskan coast.

"Wolf, compute some power data for me. I want to see if we can hover over the site. The area looks relatively flat, so we should be in ground effect. I think the altitude is around two thousand feet. We are light, so I bet we're okay to go take a look."

"On it, sir!" Wolf responded. The flight engineer pulled out a metal-encased notebook and quickly made some calculations on a preprinted table and came to a positive conclusion. "You're right, Captain. We can hover. We'll even have some excess power. The bad thing is we'll only have about five minutes on station before bingo fuel back to base."

"Thanks, Wolf. Okay, crew, we're going down to take a look. You know the drill. If anyone sees anything dangerous, call a go-around. The escape path will be down and to the right into the canyon if we get into trouble, like losing an engine or something."

Hovering a helicopter was a delicate maneuver. Hovering an underpowered, twenty-thousand-pound helicopter at two thousand feet on a hot day was downright dangerous, a procedure not to be taken lightly. Murray set up the approach into the wind and left himself plenty of room to slide down into the canyon on the right if he had a power or control problem. Slowly, the huge machine reduced speed and lost altitude in a controlled manner. Three minutes later, they sat in a stable, fifty-foot hover to the right of the crashed aircraft. Murray concentrated on controlling the Jolly Green as the cabin crew

MOTHERLAND

scanned the crash site.

Wolf spoke first. "The left wing is visible as well as part of the rear fuselage. It's definitely a P-40, WWII vintage. Strange, none of the usual U.S. markings however. Just painted a dull green color. She's mostly intact. However, most of the right wing is still under the ice a ways back; must have broken off in the crash. Captain, can you slide back twenty? Maybe I can get a look at the tail number."

"Sure, Wolf, coming back slowly. Let me know when to stop." Murray eased back on the cyclic, added a little more power, and the giant helicopter moved backwards ever so carefully.

"Three, two, one, hold her there, Captain!" Murray did as instructed, all the while maintaining his reference to the ground through the chin bubble at his feet. "I got the tail number! It's USSR-6328. Shit, it's a damn lend-lease aircraft!"

Lieutenant Raines, the co-pilot, jotted the number down on his kneepad for future reference.

"We're bingo fuel, Captain, time to go!" said Wolf as he peeked into the cockpit between the pilots.

"Roger that, pulling power." Murray added power and dove off the side of the mountain to gather airspeed and to move from a hover into translational lift. Soon the power requirement was reduced as the airspeed over the rotor system increased, and he turned the aircraft back down towards the opening of the pass on the way to Anchorage. He could see the city's center buildings in the distance on the other side of the bowl, the Chugach Mountains rising behind them. Twenty minutes later, the HH-3E emerged from the western mountain pass and now was within range for normal VHF communication with Elmendorf.

"RCC, this is Jolly on Victor, can you read?"

"Roger, Jolly, what do you have for us?"

"We've got the tail number. I'll spell. Uniform, sierra, sierra, romeo, dash, niner, tree, two, eight." Murray spoke using the military phonetic pronunciation to prevent miscommunication over the airwaves, hence the strange pronunciation of three.

Major Jordan took the piece of paper with the tail number written on it from his female airman assistant, all the while noticing her slim waist and endowed chest. He smiled to himself at his coup of getting her assigned with him at the RCC. Jordan turned in his swivel chair to the computer console behind him. He brought up an internal search page and typed in the tail number and coordinates, expecting to see the crash site logged years before. The airmen jotted down the event into the daily logbook.

However, Major Jordan's attention was immediately fixated on the computer screen as the answer came back. He sat up straight as a board in his chair, and a low whistle escaped from his mouth.

IMMEDIATE OPSEC PRIORITY – NATIONAL SECURITY HIGHLY CLASSIFIED SITUATION. DO NOT COMMUNICATE ABOUT THIS INCIDENT OVER UNCLASSIFIED CHANNELS. IMMEDIATELY NOTIFY THEATER-LEVEL COMMAND UNITS. PREPARE TO SECURE CRASH SITE AS SOON AS POSSIBLE WITH TOP SECRET, SPECIAL COMPARTMENTAL CLEARANCE ONLY.

"Holy Mother of God!" Jordan muttered as he picked up the secure line to the wing commander.

Chapter Two

May 6, 1996

Anchorage, Alaska

Captain Connor Murray pushed the large lever above his head forward and applied the rotor brake. Noisily, sounding like a loud train hitting the brakes, the rotors of the giant helicopter slowed to a crawl and then eventually came to a full stop. As the brake brought the rotor system to a rest, the fuselage jerked in the opposite direction; the friction between the three tires and the asphalt prevented the helicopter from spinning on the tarmac, a scenario that happened occasionally in the icy Alaskan winter. *Well, now I've proven Newton's law works,* he thought. *There was an equal and opposite reaction.*

Connor was tired. It had been a very long day. His back ached from sitting in the armored seats of the combat rescue aircraft, designed and built to withstand ground fire while hoisting downed pilots from Asian jungles decades before. After he was confident the rotor and other systems on the aircraft were secure, and auxiliary power was applied, he pulled the throttles back on the two turbine engines sitting above his head. The decibel level dropped significantly. Even with earplugs and a helmet on, he knew he would not be able to hear in his older years. *Years of turbine engines running full blast for hours a few feet from your head will do that to you, I'm sure.*

He peeled himself out of the hard seat and struggled to lift his legs over the armored partitions and the controls of the helicopter, scanning the space all the while to retrieve his personal belongings. He left the cockpit and walked through the cabin and out the back ramp to the ground, stretching his legs and muscles as he walked. His body ached of fatigue. The rest of the crew had already exited the aircraft to secure her for the night. He grabbed his survival pack on the way down the ramp, mandatory equipment for the Alaskan theater. He could survive for a week in the bush, possibly longer, with what was inside. Far away to the west, the sun was slowly making its way down to the top of the Alaskan mountain range.

After he had radioed in the tail number of the downed aircraft, RCC and the base command center became really interested. *Too interested*, he thought. *Strangely so.* The high level of tension was apparent even over the radio waves. After returning to base the first time, he was ordered to hot refuel with the engines running then sent back to the site, along with several rather bookish-looking scientist types and a few more people, whom he had no idea what their purpose in life was.

His orders had been clear. They were to search the crash site and retrieve any remains, plus any other significant information or items they could find. Captain Murray was to accomplish whatever his new passengers asked of him. The trip back out to the mountains was tense, and the second time they arrived at the crash site, he landed near the historic aircraft on the ridge and shut down to only engines running while the search was completed, to conserve fuel. High on a mountain ridge was not the place to risk engines not starting. The search took about an hour. One of the men was a medical examiner, who traveled with an assistant. They removed whatever remains they could find in the cockpit of the P-40 and placed them into a black body bag. It seems the ice had preserved the man's body to a significant extent. Connor really didn't want to see or think about it. *They should just leave his body here. The man was at peace. But it's not my decision.*

His commander also came along for the ride and was especially interested in the aircraft search. The lieutenant colonel spent an inordinate amount of time combing through the compartments of the Warhawk. Eventually, he found something in the rear, exterior compartment that was partially exposed from the ice. It appeared to be a leather satchel, the kind WWII officers used to carry around. It was also remarkably intact. Connor watched him smile as he walked back to the helicopter. *Strange*, he thought to himself. Upon landing back at Elmendorf a second time, his commander had exited the Jolly Green Giant immediately and entered a waiting government sedan. *Again, rather strange*, thought Conner. *He's usually not the James Bond type. Anyway, it seems I do not have the need to know, so I won't ask.*

As he entered the crew quarters in the hangar, Connor attempted to forget about the whole day. It was time for some sleep. He dropped his gear inside the crew alert facility in the hanger, as he was still on alert for a few more days. Still in his flight suit, Connor then hopped on his Kawasaki motorcycle to take him off the air force base and back into Anchorage itself, where he lived.

Anchorage had grown over the centuries into a medium-sized city, protected from the severe cold of the interior by the Chugach and Alaska Mountains, which formed a bowl around the municipality on three sides. To the south, the Kenai Peninsula reached into the Cook Inlet. The area was famous for the Russian river, named after the original Russian settlers, and combat fishing when the salmon were running. The city had seen many migrations of gold miners, military, and hordes of fishermen, and just plain loners over the years. It was a sophisticated but rough jewel in the middle of the last great frontier. Connor loved it and he felt home here, like a long-lost, favorite place he had rediscovered.

Elmendorf Air Force Base extended westward away from the city; on the opposite side of Anchorage to the east snuggled the foothills of the mountain range. The old Elmendorf Army Air Corp facility boasted a large airfield, which dated back to World War II, and could handle any size aircraft. The base's main mission was to protect the Alaskan theater from Russian bombers. Native to the field were several fighter squadrons of F-15s and associated support aircraft.

C-130 airlift and HC-130 air refueling tankers were also domiciled at the base. There was also a gunnery range for the helicopters to practice firing their onboard machine guns and other pyrotechnics. In addition, located inside the base perimeter, was a hospital and large support community.

Even though it was still light outside, the time was after midnight, and the base streets were deserted. Connor exited the south gate and crossed the short bridge into the city. Soon he was coasting down the small hill along the waterfront of Cook Inlet to the tiny bungalow he called home. The beluga whales were diving in and out of the water. The sight was beautiful as the large group of stark white mammals moved up and down in the dark sea, gorging on fish as the tide rolled in. *There must be hundreds of them.*

Soon he had parked the bike behind his home and made his way to the porch of the old house overlooking the inlet, which he had made his home for the last year. It was almost one o'clock in the morning, and the sun was just now setting. The long Alaskan days could do a number on a person, completely screwing up their internal rhythm.

His favorite rocking chair was waiting for him, and he collapsed, relaxing for the first time in about twenty hours. The base command had even waived his crew rest requirements for the mission to search the P-40 Warhawk; they had flown much longer than the twelve-hour limit in peacetime. *Whatever was on that airplane must have been important.*

The pilot's remains had been transferred to the morgue. A security police detail had met them at the tarmac to retrieve the body bag with military honors. *Somebody's family will be happy they finally found out what happened to him,* Connor thought.

He had just lit a nice cigar, popped open a beer, and started to relax when he heard a sound in his driveway and noticed an SUV pull up the small, dirt alley between the next house and his. He recognized the vehicle. *Lieutenant Colonel Blackman?* Connor sat up. He saw his superior officer get out of the car and head to the back door. "Come on in, sir! It's open!" he yelled to the rear of the house. He heard the screen door open and close and footsteps approach his porch. Soon, his commander was standing next to him. "I don't know why you're here but can I offer you a cigar?" Connor asked. "Not the best, but they are smooth. I just lit this one."

"Sure, I'd like that," Lt. Colonel Blackman responded and sat next to Connor, who sliced off the end of the stogie and handed it to his boss along with the lighter. They sat silently for a while and enjoyed the beautiful scene of the inlet in the twilight as well as the flavor of the tobacco. The belugas frolicked in the setting sun. Connor decided to let the lieutenant colonel break the ice and speak, which he did a few minutes later.

"You did a great job out there today, Connor. I appreciate your professionalism. That was a difficult assignment, to keep all of those interested people happy and your crew performing at top speed. And, way past your crew rest I might add."

"Thank you, sir. I still don't really realize what happened out there. What was all the hullabaloo about?" The colonel hesitated to answer then spoke.

"The mission was highly classified. That's what I'm here to talk to you about. Did you see what I removed from the aircraft?"

"Yes, I did. It was a satchel of some kind."

Lt. Colonel Blackman turned toward him and leaned in close to Connor to make eye contact. "Let me be very clear," he started to speak then paused for effect. "You saw nothing. This was just a routine mission. The aircraft was just an old wreck and nothing else. Nothing important was seen, found, or otherwise. Do you understand what I am saying, Captain? Completely?"

"Yes, sir. I think I do."

"Good. But just in case, I have this form you need to sign. Your future in this man's air force depends on your being able to keep a secret." The senior officer pulled out a folder with a non-disclosure agreement inside.

Connor's eyes lit up. "Really? This is really serious, huh, sir?"

"Yes it is, Captain. I'm trying to make you understand this. This is *really* important. Capiche? Now read it and sign." Connor did as he was told. He and the lieutenant colonel finished their cigars in silence. Connor knew better than to ask anything else about the mission. The *need to know* was paramount in military circles, especially in national security issues, which he surmised this event was.

Soon after, his commander left and Connor downed a couple beers. He thought about how much he loved Alaska and the freedom it offered, as well as the isolation. He watched the wildlife frolic in the ocean, oblivious to the humans on shore. *I'll have to leave this place one day.* Connor fell asleep in his flight suit on the rocking chair in the Alaskan twilight, not to stir until the chill woke him in the Alaskan morning.

Chapter Three

Sderot, Israel
On Gaza Border

May 2018

Connor woke. He stared at the ceiling for some time, not wanting to move, wondering if he should get up. Natasha lay next to him, her naked, warm body clinging to him, entangled in his arms and legs like a hot pretzel. He smiled. He loved waking up to this woman. He would never leave her. That, he knew.

The heat was oppressive this morning, even though summer had yet to burst open—it was unseasonably hot. The sun had already burned off the cooler, night desert temperature. The sheet under him was damp with sweat. *I need to get up. I can't sleep anymore. My arm's numb and killing me.*

Connor slowly and carefully untangled himself from Natasha and swung his legs over the bed. The sun was pouring through the windows like a freight train, even at this early hour. *It's gonna be another blistering day,* he thought to himself. After regaining feeling in his arm, he decided to take an early morning walk out into the desert to clear his mind. He enjoyed this time of the day, when the sun was yet to make its full force known. He felt at peace early in the morning, when the environment was not yet awake. He felt more peace and contentment here than he had in years, decades even. He felt like he had come home in some strange, prehistoric way. It was a good thing. *I just hope it lasts.*

The Negev was calm this early in the day. There was no movement. Nothing stirred, except the vultures circling overhead, waiting on some poor creature to die. There was only peace and quiet. He glanced at the large, flying carnivores above him and then nervously at Gaza in the distance. *Kind of unnerving,* he thought.

However, the wall was still there. The terrorists were still at bay. *Nothing to worry about this morning. Just enjoy yourself,* he thought warily.

For weeks, the rockets had rained down on the small, Israeli village of Sderot, located outside the Gaza Strip, in the latest conflict between Hamas and Israel. This morning, however, the sky was quiet. The Iron Dome alarms had not gone off for almost twenty-four hours now. He felt safe enough to stroll away from the house in his shorts. The nearest neighbor was several hundred yards away, and the main town was to the east behind him in the distance. His small, covered garden outside the walled compound looked strong this morning. The plants stood erect in the sun, having been artificially fed and hydrated over the evening. The hydroponic system provided the nutrients needed for growth without the roots being enclosed in soil. Israelis were experts at hydroponic farming, and it was Connor's new passion. He beamed with pride at his vine tomatoes hanging from the top of the small greenhouse like they had thousands of years before in the Hanging Gardens of Babylon. *Maybe I will become a real farmer.*

After relocating to Sderot from Tel Aviv earlier in the year, as guests of the Israeli government, Connor and Natasha rebuilt their lives after the horrifying few months they had recently experienced. The two were introduced by former President Walker, who had been assassinated the previous year by forces unknown. All signs pointed to some type of internal hit, from inside the new administration that had succeeded Walker's, but nothing could be proven.

Natasha, a Russian citizen and the former girlfriend of the Russian president, was previously also an American spy. This fact did not go over too well with the Kremlin; they relentlessly pursued her upon her escape while on a business trip to New York sometime before.

MOTHERLAND

She was tracked for over a year by the Russian FSB, or national security police, formerly called the KGB. When the FSB finally obtained her whereabouts, she fled, all alone, leaving a secure life in the United States to protect Connor, who was battling leukemia. Eventually the two had reconnected at a safe house in Brazil but were discovered by Moscow. The resulting firefight saw them both secreted out of Brazil to Israel by the Israeli Mossad, who was working with them to find the Sultan, a powerful, anonymous, Islamic figure pulling the geopolitical strings in the Middle East. Now they were rebuilding their lives again, this time at the pleasure of the Israeli intelligence service. They had jointly chosen this location due to its relative isolation; the thought being it would be easier to protect, as anyone approaching the compound would be visible long before they arrived.

The dust from the previous, chaotic year had finally started to settle. Conner was enjoying being able to attempt to relax for a change. He was a former Wall Street bond trader, unhappily thrown into global geopolitical intrigue. Now in Israel, he had taken a position helping a local startup; tech companies run by the Mossad still require financing. He was a natural, since his finance career had ended only a couple years earlier. Connor dove into the challenge. Natasha put her talents to work helping the Mossad screen Russian Jews immigrating to Israel for possible connections that could be exploited. Many had important relationships back in the Russian Federation and could possibly be useful to Israel. Connor and Natasha both turned down any travel or fieldwork outside the country. They were content just to be together in a safe place, a place where they even discussed starting a family. It would be a long time before they traveled outside of their newfound home; it was just too dangerous.

Connor thought of all that had transpired as he walked out into the desert from the protected compound that housed the small dwelling he and Natasha called home. He waved at the three Israeli soldiers who sat inside the wall, playing some kind of board game.

They waved back. Connor had grabbed his M-16 just in case. It was a necessary precaution and was slung nonchalantly over his shoulder. Israelis were comfortable with weapons. It was a national pastime, an absolute necessity when dealing with thousands of people who wanted to kill any Israeli they could get their hands on if given the opportunity. It was not uncommon to see teachers, students, and young women with an automatic rifle slung over their shoulder like a school bag filled with books, or to sit next to an Israeli soldier on the bus carrying a grenade launcher.

The four Hamas, Palestinian terrorists had been waiting in the tunnel for hours, but they felt no apprehension or pain. They were well prepared, mentally and physically. They were trained in Hezbollah camps in formerly Syrian and Iraqi territory for eight weeks for this mission, dodging American airstrikes and Russian Hind helicopters that were still attempting to slow the Islamic State. Russia was still trying to support the Assad government while preventing jihadists from traveling up through the Caucasus, Russia's soft, vulnerable underbelly, all the while coordinating with their new Iranian allies to redraw the geopolitical map of the Middle East. Primarily, however, they wanted to keep the Assad regime in power, along with their Iranian ally.

America was now trying to destroy ISIS as a viable force altogether. The American withdrawal from Iraq and the Middle East had left the Levant and the Fertile Crescent a complete mess, a cauldron of competing ambitions, agendas, and quasi-governments.

Israel had even diffused multiple backpack nuclear weapons that were smuggled into Israel, the source of which remained unknown. Only the entrepreneurial, Israeli security establishment had saved the Jewish State with its radiation detection equipment that was installed after Iran announced it was soon to acquire a nuclear weapons capability in the coming years, despite an agreement signed some years before.

The tunnels were rebuilt over the recent period, after the powerful 2014 Israeli assault on Gaza had destroyed them almost completely. Obtaining the materials was the major roadblock. Israel had learned that cement allowed into Gaza was turned into tunnel support and the Israeli security services tried not to make the same mistake twice. However, over time, enough material was found and the tunnels into Israel were rebuilt. It was bound to happen, a question of when, not if. The digging stopped about a foot from the surface, to prevent anyone from identifying the tunnel from above. There was always the risk of new Israeli ground-penetrating radar discovering the tunnels, but every precaution was taken to prevent this from happening, as in digging the passageways deep underground until the exit point. Some were noticed and destroyed, but even the Israelis knew they could not get them all. So quietly, Hamas built the capability to send small teams under the border into Israel. Now Hamas had decided to test this new capability, for they had a target they wanted to capture very badly.

Connor returned slowly back to the compound. His brief, early morning walk in the desert had calmed his nerves as always. Even though he felt peace, he seemed to have a constant companion of anxiety tugging distantly at his mind since they had moved to the Negev. He had no idea why. It was as if something was not quite right, something was out of kilter. He couldn't put his finger on it. *Maybe it's because we both have been chased like wounded prey for the last couple of years?* He just knew something was wrong. He had always trusted his instincts, and his instincts were telling his body to be anxious, even subconsciously. The early morning walks helped. *Maybe it's post-traumatic stress syndrome.* However, the sun was rising now and the heat along with it. It was time to get back in the shade of the compound and into Natasha's arms. He was sure she was still asleep and could visualize her sprawled on the bed, the sheets in a ball. Connor smiled. He eyed the compound a couple hundred meters ahead of him and, with the thought of Natasha, quickened his walk.

The terrorists silently removed the remaining soil above them and exited the tunnel in the desert near the compound. The four men were dressed in camouflage fatigues to blend into the terrain and in the dawn light were almost invisible against the tan background. Once they emerged into the open, they sprinted toward the walled dwelling. Their intelligence was spot on, the commander recognized. He knew every inch of the structure and had studied the diagrams and satellite photos intensely for weeks. Failure was not an option. They did not make a sound as they approached their target, weapons at the ready. As they neared the wall surrounding the house, they slowed their advance and crept to the opening, which Connor had left forty minutes before.

The Israeli soldiers did not stand a chance. As the terrorists entered through the unguarded door, the three young, Jewish men died instantly as they were gunned down sitting around a gaming table. They had grown lax while attempting to while away the time and boredom they had experienced for the prior six months in guarding the compound. They did not expect an attack in broad daylight and had let their guard down. It cost them their lives. Once the terrorists cleared the outside of the structure, they put two bullets each in the soldiers' brains to finish them off, all quietly done with the aid of silencers. They then turned their attention to the occupants inside. At that moment, they heard an alarm sound inside the house.

Connor was walking back when suddenly he saw rapid

movement on the desert floor on the opposite side of the compound. At first, he couldn't believe what he was seeing, but then he realized it was all too real. Four armed men, obviously up to no good, had just emerged from a tunnel in the desert floor and were sprinting to his home, where his wife lay sleeping. Initially he froze, but a millisecond later, his training kicked in. They had rehearsed what to do in this type of emergency with the Mossad hundreds of times. He dug into his pocket and retrieved his specially altered cell phone and pressed a large, red button that protruded on the back side. Instantly, an alarm sounded inside the house via Natasha's phone. The message was also sent to the nearby Israeli Defense Force headquarters as a call for support and reinforcements.

Natasha awoke immediately at the sound of the alarm, rolled off the bed onto the floor, and grabbed her weapon under the bed. She hit a lever near the bottom of the nightstand, and the entrance to the house locked shut immediately with reinforced deadbolts. A loud claxon began to sound in the entire village area. She crawled to the bedroom window, which was complete with bulletproof glass, and looked quickly outside. The four terrorists stood highlighted against the dead bodies of the Israeli guards. *Connor! Shit! Where are you?* she wondered.

The lead terrorist saw Natasha peek out the window; he smiled and calmly raised his weapon and fired. They were not after her; however, her death would be a welcome outcome, a bonus if you will. *The Russians will pay.* He frowned as the bullets ricocheted off the hardened window. He pointed to the door and motioned to one of his subordinates. The man pulled demolition equipment out of a pouch and made his way to the door to rig it with explosives. *I'll show that bitch.* Then he heard another sound; it was a man yelling outside the compound walls.

"Natasha!" the voice screamed.

Murray! the lead terrorist thought smugly to himself. He yelled at his men to forget about the girl and deal with the threat outside. One of the men rushed out the door to intercept Connor, and Murray cut him down with a burst of automatic weapons fire. The lead terrorist climbed a guard post in the corner of the compound and raised his weapon towards Connor. The remaining Palestinians closed the compound door. Connor was exposed and locked out of the house. Natasha was inside, surrounded by the bad guys.

The leader fired a burst over Connor's head. Murray hit the dirt. "Put down your weapon. You are outgunned. Otherwise you and your wife will die," the leader screamed in fluent English. "We don't want her. We want you! Drop your weapon!"

Connor's heart sank. He was outgunned. *He's right. I really have no choice,* Connor thought to himself. He made a split-second decision and put his rifle to the desert floor beside him, stretched out, and put his hands above his head. *The IDF will be here soon. Maybe Natasha was able to secure the house, but that won't last long. I'm sure these idiots have equipment to get in the house, given enough time. But if I let them take me, then maybe they will leave her alone. Otherwise, if they are cornered, they will kill both of us.* "Alright! Alright! I've put my weapon down! Leave her alone!" Connor yelled back.

"As you wish!" the terrorist said as his two remaining soldiers quickly ran to Connor, tied his wrists behind his back, grabbed his weapon, and pulled him to his feet. The three terrorists then ran to the entrance to the tunnel, pushing Connor along ahead of them. They left their dead comrade behind. He couldn't talk now anyway. The IDF sirens wailed in the distance, alerting the town to the threat. They arrived two minutes later but it was too late for Connor. Natasha was left inside the house to greet them.

MOTHERLAND

The tunnel was large enough to stand up inside although just wide enough for one man's body. Connor was pushed forward with the muzzle of the gun. The terrorists were yelling, "Allahu Akbar, Allah is greater," and rejoicing, now that they knew their mission was successful and they weresafe. They anticipated, forty minutes later, emerging from the tunnel into a safe house in Gaza with their prize intact.

Chapter Four

Gaza

Connor felt himself being prodded down the tunnel, hands tied behind his back. A bag had been placed over his head, and he was having trouble breathing. They were moving so fast, he occasionally hit his head on some hard surface on the ceiling of the passageway. It hurt. He wondered if he was bleeding. Blood trickling into his eyes confirmed that fact. This seemed to go on forever. The ropes around his wrists cut into the skin, and he was frequently pushed up against the jagged rock walls of the tunnel, causing further shallow wounds. Finally, he felt the stifling air in the tunnel freshen, and he was brought up through some type of entrance. They walked for about fifty yards and then he was forced into a vehicle. The car abruptly started moving and must have drove for about ten minutes. He could hear the loud voices of many Arabs around him inside, screaming unintelligibly.

They ended up in a market or public gathering. Connor could feel the energy of the throng of people. Then he was hauled out of the vehicle and into some type of structure and forced into a chair. His hands were tied again behind his back to the piece of furniture. It was dark. "If you fall over, you die, painfully," one of the terrorists said sternly. Then Connor heard him leave the room and everything went quiet. He was left alone.

Connor sat this way for a long time. He had no idea how long. His wrists hurt and his arms ached and his head pounded. The blood had dried on his face and around his eyes. *The bleeding has stopped. At least Natasha is okay I think. Wrong time to take a walk in the desert I guess.* He chuckled out aloud. *This is not good.*

Connor fought to draw on his internal strength and control his fear. He was alone for hours, hours and hours it seemed. The darkness and the heat started to get to him. After a long time, he drifted in and out of consciousness over what must have been the length of a day. He had long since stopped being able to feel his arms or hands. The blood flow was severely restricted. He was thirsty. And he waited, and waited, and waited.

At some point, he felt as if someone was in the room with him, but he could not see in the blackness. Sounds of a door quietly opening and closing drifted through his mind. The hood restricted his breathing, and he sweated whatever fluids he had left in him through the pores in his head, soaking the fabric that kept out the light. He passed out.

He heard the sound again, the sound of a door opening, but he could not tell if it was real. *How long have I been here? How long before something happens? I'm so thirsty.*

His training from years before had already kicked in. As an Air Force pilot, Connor was required to take Survival, Evasion, Resistance, and Escape training, or SERE, before flight school. It was a grueling three weeks in the wilderness and then multiple days in a mock prisoner-of-war camp, so, he knew somewhat what to expect. He had been interrogated before but this was the real thing. He knew they were trying to soften him up to make him easier to break. But what did they want? Information on Israel? On Natasha? On his connections with the Mossad? *I'm not in a good situation. I know too much about too many things. This is not going to end well,* he thought. He knew everyone breaks eventually.

There was the sound again. He could almost hear someone breathing beside him. *I must be imagining things.* He drifted off into an uncomfortable sleep. Or, at least he thought he had; however, he was jerked back awake as he felt himself falling sideways. *I can't do this forever. Soon I'm gonna need some water badly.* He screamed for help. The small chair was hard and uncomfortable. It was also hard to keep straight up. He almost fell over several times. Connor didn't know it, but he had been sitting in the room for forty-eight hours with no real sleep. He also knew what sleep deprivation did to a body, and it didn't take long. He tried to stay alert to what was happening around him. But it was hard. He was slowly losing control.

Suddenly, he heard someone speak, someone very close to him. He thought he was dreaming at first but then he realized he wasn't. "You want to know who I am, don't you?" the voice said. Connor recognized the voice had a Farsi accent.

Connor didn't say anything. He tried to stay calm. *I wish I could warn Natasha. They know where we are.*

You're not going to talk to me? Don't worry. If I wanted you dead, you'd be dead already. And don't worry about your pretty little wife. We're not after her. Not *now* anyway. We got what we wanted. We wanted you."

Connor decided to speak. He tried to talk but his mouth was too dry. "Why?" he whispered.

The man saw his mouth moving through the black cloth but could not understand him. "I'm sure you don't know who I am, but I know who you are. We've been following and watching you for some time now. Your exploits in Brazil last year were quite impressive. Don't you think?"

Connor shook his head in the affirmative.

"Don't worry, that's not what you're here for. It was just business, I know. Killing a few assassins doesn't get me worked up. If I didn't respect you, you might not be alive right now, so let's say that's a good thing, yeah?" Connor tried to speak but no words came out.

"My name is Ahmad. That's all you need to know. Don't talk yet. You're not ready. We want to cook you a little more in here. You like the heat, yes? I'll be back in a while. Then we can talk, when you're good and ready." The man's voice became more evil. "And you will be ready, I assure you." Then the man left the room.

More hours passed. Connor gave up any hope of being alert. He dreamed. Then the blackness came. It was a welcome relief. How long he was passed out he didn't know. But eventually, the peace ended.

The hood was ripped off his head. Connor almost fainted from shock at the change. Then he gulped the new supply of air. For a moment he felt pleasure. Then the bright spotlights were turned on, aimed directly at his face. The light poured into his eyes like a million pieces of glass, stabbing him with pain. He screamed.

He seemed to sit like this for more hours, although it was only about thirty minutes. "What do you want?" he asked the lights. No one spoke for a while. Then he heard an answer.

"A new matter, rather urgent, has come to our attention. We want you to think back, Mr. Murray, way back. To a time when you were alone, flying up in Alaska. Do you remember this time?"

Connor thought. "Yes," he answered after some time, straining his parched throat to talk.

"Do you remember a certain mission in the mountains? Where you found a wrecked aircraft from the World War II?"

Connor was confused. What did this Iranian care about the crashed P-40 he found emerging from the glacier decades before? He remembered the document he was forced to sign for his commander, the one that said the entire mission was highly classified. Connor remained silent. He noticed his arm hurt, a lot. *The ropes must be cutting into my skin*, he thought to himself. Still, he said nothing to the terrorist.

"So you are not going to talk to me? Again, don't worry. We are not going to beat you. We have more sophisticated methods at our disposal these days. Let me explain if I might. You see, we want information about that crash. We know something was found there. We have hacked into your Rescue Coordination Center database, which was not so hard to do by the way, and we have discovered that a satchel was removed from the aircraft fuselage. We simply want to know what became of it and what the contents were. That is not so hard, is it? You see, we need the information. Last year, I received orders to just watch you and your pretty wife while you toiled with your little farm in Sderot. Now those orders have been amended. Now I don't care whether you live or die. What I care about, and what my superiors care about, is finding that satchel and the associated information. Do I make myself clear?"

Connor still said nothing as he suffered from the thirst and pain.

"Do you want some water?"

Connor shook his head yes.

"Aaah, I'm sure you are quite thirsty." Ahmad walked over to where Connor was sitting and lifted a bottle of water to his lips. The liquid stung his cracked skin and dribbled down his face. A relief washed over his body as the fluid of life entered his veins. The pain in his arm became more acute, and some feeling returned.

"So, once again. What can you tell me about the satchel?"

"I have no idea what you are talking about," answered Connor with newfound vigor.

"I know that is a lie. But like I said, I will not trouble you further. However, I do have something to tell you. You see, we know you remember this incident. We also know that there is no way you could know where the satchel is now or what was in it. We've talked to others you see. That fat RCC officer for one, he was willing to tell us a great deal. As much as he knew I think. It was sad that he had to have the accident. Car crashes can be so…dirty…of an affair, don't you think? But, we have an offer for you. As they say in your American gangster movies, an offer you can't refuse. We want you to find out where this satchel was placed and what was in it. You can do that for us, can't you?"

"And what if I don't?"

"I thought you might ask about that. Do you still feel the pain in your arm?"

"Yes. How did you know?" The bright lights still seared into the back of Connor's eyes. It was a different, intense, kind of pain he had not experienced before, but his arm hurt as well.

"I know because while you were passed out, we gave you some drugs to make you sleep for a while. Then we inserted a device under the skin into your upper arm, near your chest. That is the pain you feel."

"What kind of device?" Connor asked, now worried.

"A GPS tracker for one. You see, we will be tracking your progress in the quest we have given you. We also implanted a small bit of poison. It is not much but enough to kill you within thirty seconds. That is, IF we activate the capsule, which we can do anytime with this device." He held up a small transmitter so Connor could see. "Yes, Mr. Murray, we are going to release you soon, so that you can get more information for us. But, if you do not do as we ask, we will activate this device, and you will die, quickly but painfully I'm afraid. Oh, and another thing I should mention. If you try and remove the device, if it is exposed to air, it will activate immediately. We will be watching and following you. And another nice touch we programmed into the transmitter. If you come within five hundred meters of a U.S. or Israeli embassy, or military facility, the device will activate immediately and you will die, as I said, quickly but painfully."

Connor didn't know what to say, so he said nothing. His arm throbbed with pain.

MOTHERLAND

"So, now that you know what we want, we are going to let you go. Not here in Gaza of course. You're going to take a little ride on one of our boats. You will find out where to soon enough. We are going to give you another shot now. But don't worry, the effect will not be permanent. Oh, and one more thing. You will be provided with contact instructions on how to get the information we seek to us. We expect progress within two weeks, or else. We will be waiting. You will have a different identity. And don't try to contact any of your spook colleagues, or your pretty wife. That won't end very well for you." A different man came forward out of the light and stuck a needle into Connor's arm then there was only blackness.

Natasha waited but dared not leave the house, not until the cavalry arrived at least, which happened ten minutes later as several Israeli Defense Force (IDF) units roared up to the facility in their Humvees, fifty-caliber machine guns at the ready. A dozen soldiers dismounted immediately and secured the residence and compound. The bodies of the soldiers were put in body bags and taken away after a forensics team took pictures and preserved evidence of the raid.

Natasha, against her will, was then taken to a more secure facility at an unknown location within Israel, her location in Sderot obviously no longer a secret.

Chapter Five

Connor awoke. His arm hurt, but he realized he was able to move both his arms. He was no longer tied to the chair. It was light outside. *Was it a dream? Where's Natasha?* He was lying in a bed. He sat up, trying to understand where he was. It was afternoon. *My arm hurts. And so does my head.*

He looked to the left of the bed. There was water and some food on the table near the headboard. He ate ravenously and drank all the water available. He then lay back down to let his body recover from the recent experience and trauma. *Where am I? It wasn't a dream,* he thought.

Thirty minutes later, he sat up, alert, his strength recovering somewhat, and stood to look out the window. He saw olive trees, lots of them, and lots of artichoke plants. The countryside was green, in contrast to what he was used to. Then he felt pain in his arm and winced. There was blood coming through his shirt. He pulled away the cloth and saw the recent, two-inch-long wound stitched up, and he remembered. The cut was jagged and rough, like it was done in a hurry. *Great. I need to take care of this. It looks like it's getting infected.*

There was money by the bed also, lots of it, euros. In addition, there was a fake passport, a Russian one, and two credit cards. *Ivan Yaroslavovich. Nice Russian name. What have I gotten myself into?* There were also some clothes and a small satchel. He opened it. There was a phone inside and a note scrawled on a piece of paper. *Only use this phone. Believe me, your life depends on it.* "Nice," he said aloud. There was also a business card with just a phone number and email address written on it. *I guess that's how I contact them.*

Connor surmised he was in some type of hotel room. He walked into the bathroom and took a shower, cleansing the wound as best he could. The wound on his forehead and those on his arms and shoulders he also took care of. Then he got dressed in the new clothes, which fit surprisingly well.

He grabbed the travel document and the money, put everything in the satchel, and left the room. There was a key, which he used to lock the door. *Not sure I'll be back.*

He walked down the stairs and heard a woman talking on the phone. She was speaking Italian. *Phone! I need to contact Natasha. But should I? Not yet. I need to find out more of what is going on. And I guess I'll use the phone provided, for the time being at least.*

He exited the stairs and entered the lobby of a small guest house. A woman looked at him and said, "Buongiorno!"

"Grazie," he replied. There was a small sign in Italian near the computer on her desk. *I must be in Italy.*

He walked outside. There was a small market nearby. It said Brindisi on the front of the door. *Yes, I'm in Italy, on the coast.* He could smell the sea nearby. *Not a bad place to be if I wasn't in this situation. I wonder how I got here? But now, that doesn't matter. What to do?* He kept walking. Soon he ran into a small café overlooking an olive grove. The Adriatic coast was visible on the skyline. *As good a place as any to sit and think. Okay, I know where I am. It looks like I have plenty of money. I have IDs.* He looked down at the phone that was in the pouch. *I need to call Natasha and let her know what is going on. Or should I? Not now. I'll think of a way soon enough. I need to let her know I'm okay, at least for now.*

He ordered a coffee and something to eat, which was like moving heaven and earth in Italy in the afternoon. He was still starving. However, he felt better with something more in his stomach. *Now I need to figure out what I'm gonna do.* He picked up the smartphone and turned it on. It worked and soon connected to a network, and he felt not so alone. Immediately a message popped up on the screen.

MOTHERLAND

Keep your phone charged and on your person at all times. We'll be watching and listening.

Of course you are. Why would I think otherwise? He set the phone on the table. *I'm sure it's a listening device and will record everything I do.* Connor speculated for a moment then thought, *I have no choice.* He picked the phone back up and opened the browser. Soon he had logged into Facebook and searched for his old commander in Alaska, Lt. Colonel Blackman, although he remembered his friend had retired a while back as a full-bird-colonel. His picture soon popped up on the screen. The colonel hadn't posted for a long time, and there really was no clue as to where he was. Connor opened the messenger and started typing. *I've got to at least make them think I'm working on this and can get information they can't. That way, at least they will keep me alive.*

Col Blackman, It's been a long time. Was thinking about the Yukon a few days ago and thought of you. How are you?

Connor clicked send. *There, I did it.* He didn't expect a response any time soon. Connor finished his meal and then started walking back to the hotel. He entered the small market and bought some supplies, including something to disinfect his wounds. Soon he was back in the hotel room, and fatigue hit him again like a ton of bricks after the long ordeal. He locked the door and lay down in bed. Soon he was fast asleep.

The phone beeped and vibrated. Connor sat up in bed, remembering where he was. He looked at the phone. He had been asleep for an hour, his body attempting to recover. There was a Facebook message on the phone.

55

Connor, good to hear from you. I'm doing well and currently in Europe for some R&R. Stay in touch. Blackman.

Connor texted back.

Where in Europe?

I'm in Croatia. On the coast. It's beautiful here. Have you ever been?

No never. I'm sure it is lovely. But funny, I'm in Italy. Would love to hop over and have a beer.

Come on over! I've got some nice Cubans as well. I'll buy you dinner.

I'll take you up on that. How about tomorrow afternoon?

Deal. Message me when you're in-country. I'm in Hvar at the moment. Take the ferry.

Will do. See you tomorrow.

Well, that's done. Connor drifted off back to sleep.

He awoke sometime later, feeling rested. The effect of the drugs had worn off. *I must have slept for two hours.* He dressed and walked down to the lobby. The attendant was there as usual, talking on the phone.

"Excuse me," he said. "Can you have a taxi to the train station in thirty minutes?" She nodded her head in the affirmative, still chatting in Italian. "Thank you," Connor replied. She nodded again without missing a beat in her conversation. Soon Connor was on his way to Croatia.

Connor stepped off the ferry in Hvar, Croatia and mingled with the throng of tourists excitedly headed for the old city. He marveled at the ancient stones of the boardwalk and the obvious significant history of the town. The gulls swooped in off the water, desperate to find a scrap from the cafes along the promenade and the smell of the sea permeated the air.

It had been quite a long journey. He had taken the taxi to the local train station in Brindisi then boarded a ferry at Ancona across the Adriatic to Split, and then the ferry continued to the island of Hvar. The ten-hour boat trip to Croatia had evaporated overnight, as Connor rented a nice berth to sleep in for the ride. He now felt refreshed, strong, and himself again. *Now I can deal with this situation,* he thought. It did not take him long to rent a scooter at the docks and soon was on his way to the southern coastal highway. The ancient fortress of Hvar rose up the mountain beside him as he made his way through the twists and turns of the crowded port. Soon he left the urban area and was alone on the meandering highway along the blue waters of the Adriatic, the pleasant odor of the sea bathing his face.

Twenty minutes later, Connor slowed to a stop on the side of the highway at an overlook to get his bearings. The sea stretched out before him as the sun rose in the sky. The warm wind created a beautiful scene as the wild lavender thriving on the side of the mountain road added to the wonderful smell.

Hvar was an ancient island of the Greeks and the Romans. Its unique location in the Adriatic, off the Dalmatian coast, made it an important port to control trade in the region for centuries. The Greeks also developed the mountainous island into a terraced agricultural paradise for olives and other crops, and the field divisions were still visible and protected by UNESCO as a world heritage site. The island changed hands after the fall of Rome from a major Venetian naval base, to pirates, to the Ottomans, Napoleon, and then became part of the Austrian empire, where it enjoyed peace and prosperity, only to fall into decline in the twentieth century. Recently, however, tourism had rejuvenated the island's economy and now was a driving force for a more optimistic future.

Connor, having verified his position, now remounted the scooter and headed down the winding highway to the very small village below. He soon slowed and turned into a gravel driveway that led to a tiny community along the rocky beach. He parked the scooter and walked to the group of buildings on the cliff overlooking the water. He found Colonel Blackman sitting alone on a balcony, drinking a beer and smoking a fat cigar.

"Hello, my friend! It's been a long time," he bellowed as he wrapped Connor in a sincere bear hug. "It's really good to see you!" Blackman was a large man and still strong in middle age.

He must be over sixty now, Connor thought. He looked the same, just with gray hair and a few more pounds here or there but seemed to be in really good shape. "You haven't changed a bit!" Connor shot back. "It's good to see you as well."

"Have a seat and a drink," Blackman ordered. He then pulled out a similar cigar and handed it to Connor. "And one of these."

"I don't mind if I do." Connor sat and did as he was told. They chatted about the old times for a while then silently enjoyed the view. Soon lunch was served, and they ate their fill of local seafood and vegetables.

"If you don't mind me asking, what the hell did you do to your forehead?" Blackman asked as the lunch dishes were taken away.

MOTHERLAND

Connor was silent for a moment, not sure what to say. Connor's phone was tucked nicely in the satchel lying at his feet. He was sure that no one could hear what he was about to say. He looked Colonel Blackman in the eye. "I'm in trouble, Colonel."

"I thought so," said his former senior officer. "But I thought I'd let you bring it up first. And?"

"Do you remember the mission in Rainy Pass, from long ago? Where we found that WWII P-40 melting out of the glacier?"

"Yes, I sure do," said the colonel, sitting straighter in his seat, Connor having acquired his full attention.

"You found a satchel in the rear compartment. It was obviously a significant find. The entire air wing command structure was interested in the find. I need to know what was in the satchel. I need to know what we found." Connor quit speaking and looked out at the sea.

Colonel Blackman didn't say anything for a few seconds. Then he spoke. "Why do you need this?"

"I can't go into it right now. However, let's just say it's a matter of life and death. To be precise, my life or death."

"I see. Does that have anything to do with your forehead? And the blood dripping out of your upper arm?" Connor turned his head to look back at the colonel and then at his shirt, where a blood red circle had appeared. "Yes, I notice things like that."

"Yes, it does. You were always someone I knew I could trust. So I decided to talk to you."

"And you can't tell me any more than that?"

"Not at the moment. Maybe in time."

"That's extremely classified information you're asking about. You know that I presume. You remember what I had you sign?"

"Yes, I realize that. But I still need your help."

"Okay. Let me think on this for a few minutes." The colonel pulled out another cigar from his shirt pocket, removed the wrapper slowly, cut off the end, and lit the other end in a circle of flame. The fragrant smoke wafted out over the sea, creating an interesting contrast to the smell of the ocean life. Then he turned back to Connor and looked him in the eye with a serious look on his face.

"What I am about to tell you could get us both killed. It looks like it came close to getting you killed already. I've pretty much pushed it to the recesses of my mind since that episode twenty years ago, but it's obvious it can't stay there. I'll tell you what I know. Since I was the only one they could trust on the mission, who knew everything about rescue and was familiar with our search procedures, and I also was a senior officer with experience and judgment, they read me into the situation somewhat, so I would know what to look for." The colonel paused, took a draw on the cigar, and exhaled slowly, the smoke disappearing into the afternoon sky. He turned to Connor.

"Towards the end of World War II, the United States and Russia were both fighting Hitler in a match to the death. Nuclear weapons were being developed, and no one knew how far the Nazis were in their progress on such weapons. But this was not the end of the story. There were other weapons being developed, other technologies. At the same time, the U.S. was helping Russia through the lend-lease program, supplying aircraft and other machinery. The planes were flown to the Soviet Union through Alaska and across the Bering Strait. Apparently, the aircraft that crashed, that you discovered, was one of these planes to be delivered. However, there was more to the delivery than meets the eye. There was something on that plane as well to be delivered to the Russians. What it was? I don't know. But it was in the satchel that I found. They told me what to look for. I found it and turned it over to them. Any more than that, I don't know. This information remains Top Secret Compartmentalized. Does that help you?"

"Well, it sure makes a lot of sense and kind of fills in a lot of holes that I was wondering about. But I need to know more. Do you have any idea of how I could do that?" Connor asked.

Colonel Blackman leaned forward on his elbows across the table, looking Connor in the eyes. "I might. But why don't you tell me first what's really going on?"

"The trail goes back to the Americans," said the intelligence officer to the Israeli prime minister. "We have absolute proof of that. There can be no denying this." The officer let those words sink in as he studied the prime minister's face for some kind of cue as to whether to continue with the briefing or give him some time to digest what was just said.

Prime Minister Dahan stared silently out the window at the Syrian border from the location in the Golan Heights, having come to inspect the force structure on Israel's northern border on somewhat of a surprise inspection, the intelligence officer had traveled with him and scheduled a briefing. The prime minister didn't say anything for a long time. Then, when he spoke, he spoke as if he were alone, as if there were no one else in the room.

"I have feared this outcome. I hoped it wasn't true, but I have feared the answer to the question of who was behind the placement of the tactical nuclear warheads in Israel last year. That day has come. Israel is on her own. America has turned on her. At least the current government has anyway." Then he turned and faced the intelligence officer. "Continue with your briefing."

Natasha sat in the safe house in the middle of Tel Aviv. She was worried sick. They had told her nothing as of yet what had happened to Connor. That could not be good. The door to the room opened. Peter Quinn walked in and wrapped his arms around her. She buried her head in his shoulder and wept.

"I've spoken to the appropriate people. The good news is, we think he is still alive. The other news, good or bad depending on the way you look at it, is that we think he has been secretly taken out of the Gaza Strip on a freighter. We don't know to where. That's all I know."

Quinn was an old colleague of Connor's from way back, an energy analyst to be exact. Connor and Peter had been through a lot together over the decades on Wall Street and most recently with the activities in Brazil over the previous year that involved Natasha as well. The three of them had been spirited out of Brazil by the Israelis, and now he worked for the Mossad as well in an analytical capacity. Natasha trusted him completely.

"I'm going after him, Natasha."

"You can't, Peter, it's too risky. You'll be killed!"

"He saved my life once. He got me out of detention in the states when that corrupt DHS guy was after me. I owe him the favor, even if Connor wasn't my very best friend."

"Be careful. I want you both back." Peter gave her one last hug and left the room.

Chapter Six

Connor mounted the scooter and headed back up the mountain highway towards the main port of Hvar, the satchel hooked securely around his waist. The smell of fresh lavender still bathed the air in sweetness. The feeling of freedom was exhilarating, even if it wasn't real. The sharp pain in his arm brought that reality home.

It was difficult not to tell the colonel what was going on. He just said, "No, I can't tell you. I don't want to involve you," and left it at that. Colonel Blackman seemed to understand but was very concerned.

"I have someone for you to contact," he finally said before Connor left the bar. "Before I retired from the Air Force, as you know, special operations became quite the show, due to the events of 9/11. I made many contacts on the black side of things while working in counterterrorism. Many of them are not very nice people. But, you need these type of people when the shit hits the fan. One of them, I know, is currently in Moldova. He stays in the gray areas of the world. It suits him better. His name is Vitali. That's all I know him by. Here is an email address and a phone number. I'm sure he can help at least point you in the right direction. He owes me. Good luck, Connor. At least keep me in the loop, okay?" As Connor walked away from the bar, the colonel added, "Tell him Colonel Klink sent you. He'll like that."

I've got to get to Moldova. I need some help and I don't know who to turn to. I could contact the Mossad, but not yet. And I've only got thirteen days left before this thing goes off in my arm, and I'll never see Natasha again.

He drove the scooter back to the port terminal and caught a return ferry to Split. Then he bought a plane ticket to the former

Soviet nation of Moldova, the poorest country in Europe. The cab ride to the airport was fast. Soon he had left the European Union on his way to the east, his mind troubled as the water of the Adriatic drifted out of sight in the plane's window.

Prime Minister Dahan was back in Tel Aviv, and he was worried, very worried. Without American support, Israel was blowing like a leaf in the wind. And that support had definitely dried up. Arms shipments, money, logistical support, everything had dwindled to a trickle. It was obvious the American government had an alternate agenda as far as the Jewish State was concerned. *An alternate agenda indeed.*

At the same time, the Persian army and their Shia friends in Syria and Lebanon were massing. Russia had spent the last few years selling Iran every kind of weapon imaginable. Their air defense network was now tight. The S-400 and S-300 weapon systems were being deployed systematically throughout Iranian-controlled territory, even in Iraq and Syria under the watchful eye of the Revolutionary Guards.

I am responsible for this country. I have to find a way to ensure her survival. It is on my shoulders. I'm not going to go down in history as the man who lost the Jewish State for the Jewish people. He called his assistant. "Have the defense minister come to my briefing room right away!" *Maybe it's time to make friends with the Russians.*

Connor exited the airport in Chisinau, Moldova as Ivan Yaroslav. The trip was painless, except for his bleeding arm of course.

MOTHERLAND

He had managed to get the wound to stop seeping while in the lavatory on the plane. He even changed his shirt, no blood stains now to attract attention. He couldn't do anything about the wounds on his forehead. He'd bought a few things at the market in Hvar, before heading straight for the small airport to Split, switching planes in Kyiv, then Moldova. It was evening. The air was again warm. The passage through immigration control and customs was noneventful.

The difference between the East and West was striking. The buildings were all drab, Stalinist, concrete structures left over from the Soviet era. A few colorful establishments dotted the landscape from new construction. He boarded the small bus to the center of town, preferring to mix with the public and watch for a while, rather than attract attention in a taxi.

A large, older woman sat in the nearby seat and attempted to speak directly to him. She was speaking Romanian, which was the alternate language to Russian for Moldova. During Soviet times, all children had been taught Russian but Moldova was historically part of the Romanian region. She was obviously poor and barely surviving. Connor ascertained she was asking something about ticket prices but he just shrugged in disinterest. She then left him alone, chalking him up for just another selfish traveler, the kind that permeated Eastern Europe.

As he rode into the city, he noticed each apartment complex looked exactly the same, with similar small shops located in the base of the massive buildings, providing food and other supplies for the thousands of residents. The trip cost less than a cheap cup of coffee in the U.S. The Moldovan currency, the leu, had been devalued significantly, as the economy was in shambles. The party in power had shifted multiple times over the last decade, preventing a coherent economic policy from taking shape. Corruption was also rampant as with most former Soviet territories. The man on the street didn't have a chance. All he could hope for was basic survival.

Connor arrived outside the hotel a half hour later and strolled into the lobby. The entrance to the hotel gave off an ambiance of former Soviet glory and functionality. However, there was an obvious attempt to modernize the facility and compete with Western luxury. The attempt failed miserably.

As it was later in the day, people were starting to mill about the small bar located in the rear corner. Several attractive girls waited patiently for a possible client, for a trip upstairs to the patron's room for an hour of quick, sexual gratification. One of them stared at him, noticing he was a Westerner. Connor ignored her.

Check in was quick and no one gave him any problems. Soon he was alone in his small room.

The hotel was a study in the Soviet experience. *I'm definitely back in the U.S.S.R.*, he thought to himself. The room was functional but spartan. It seemed like everything in the hotel was original from the middle of the last century, but it was fine by Connor. One could blend right in to a place like this, drift into the woodwork, if you will. And that's what he wanted to do, find out what he needed without anyone finding out about him. The window looked out over the city as the sun sank finally below the horizon, outlining the buildings in an orange glow.

Connor took the piece of paper with the phone number and email address he was given in Hvar out of his pocket. He looked at the phone for a while, felt the hole in his arm with his fingers softly, and tried to make a decision. *Again, I have no choice.* Connor couldn't risk not using the phone, not yet. He picked it up and dialed the number.

"Da?" a voice answered.

"Yes, I need to meet with you. Colonel Klink sent me."

"Ha. Did he say that?" Silence. "Where are you?"

"Hotel Chisinau."

"A car will pick you up in thirty minutes. Be outside." The

line went dead.

Connor waited in the lobby at the bar, where he ordered and nursed a drink. The girls were gone, most likely having found some business. However, there were several businessmen at the bar; none paid any attention to him, which was just the way he liked it. At the right time, he walked outside, ignoring the doorman. Like clockwork, a late-model, dark red SUV pulled up, and the driver leaned over to open the passenger door. Connor jumped in and they sped off.

"Who are you?" Connor asked.

"None of your business. Let's just say I'm a friend of Vitali's. And no friend of yours," he added curtly.

"Fair enough," said Connor and remained quiet for the rest of the ride, casually looking out at the bland city passing by. The streets were wide and clean but devoid of a soul. The people looked worried, as if they were fighting for each meal on a daily basis, because they most likely were. It was a not a wealthy place but more one of barter and subsistence. Soon they pulled into a side street off the main boulevard into a small parking area surrounded by ancient office buildings. They were three-stories-high, made of brick, and looked very Stalinist. The man parked the car, got out, and came around to Connor's side of the vehicle. He opened the door.

"Follow me," he said. Connor did as he was told.

They descended into a stairway at the front of one of the old buildings that looked to be an entrance to some type of basement structure. The paint was peeling off the walls, but the walkway looked well used. There was a sign over the basement door. *Bacteria,* it read, in English. Connor followed the man inside to a small pub of some sort. Several men were at the bar, speaking to the very attractive bartender and her friend. The driver of the SUV pointed to a table in the corner. Connor walked over and sat down. The man left.

Several of the men looked at him occasionally but showed no interest. The bartender walked over and took his order. She was young and slim, obviously hired for her looks. He waited, and waited. An hour passed. Three drinks passed. The hour approached 2:00 a.m. and the crowd at the bar thickened.

Eventually, a Slavic man walked up to his table, pulled back the chair, and sat. He was approaching fifty, had salty gray hair, but was muscled and trim. He spoke with a Russian accent.

"Hello, Mr. Murray."

"Hello. Do I call you Vitali?"

"You may. I obviously know who you are. So why don't you tell me what you are doing here in Moldova of all places, looking for me. I'm extremely interested in the answer to this question."

"Yes, it is quite strange, isn't it? The answer is I need information. I was told you may be able to help me find it."

"It's possible. I guess it depends on the information you are looking for." The man stopped talking as the bartender arrived to ask for his order. Vitali resumed when she left. The bar was now crowded and noisy.

Connor pondered his situation at the bar. *Perfect for this espionage stuff. No one can hear a word we are saying. Much less the microphone in the phone in the satchel on my hip. That's a good thing.*

"Why don't you tell me what you're looking for," Vitali suggested calmly, staring him in the eyes.

Connor spoke. "A long time ago, I was a rescue helicopter pilot in Alaska. One day flying back from a milk run to the outer alert bases, we stumbled upon the carcass of a crashed P-40 Warhawk that had splashed in the mountains during WWII. We radioed our controller at Elmendorf Air Force Base, and they literally freaked out. All of a sudden, I had classified creeps crawling around my ass, trying to find something on the plane. I mean the thing wasn't even defrosted yet. To make a long story short, they did eventually find something. A leather satchel. I need to know what was in that satchel."

"Why did you come to me?" Vitali said incredulously with a look of disbelief on his face.

"Dave Blackman found the satchel." That shut Vitali up. He said nothing for a few moments. "Blackman said you could help," added Connor.

Vitali thought for a moment. "Yes, I possibly can. But it's going to take me a little time. I need to make some phone calls."

Connor leaned forward and stared at Vitali. "I don't have a little time. Do you understand? This is a matter of life and death."

Vitali sat back in his chair. "Okay. I get your point. Meet me here tomorrow. Same time. I'll have something for you. And by the way, I'm doing this because you're a friend of Blackman. I owe him. He pulled my ass out of the jungle, literally, a few years back. Just so you know." Vitali stood, walked out, and didn't look back.

Connor sat in the bar for another hour. *Where else am I going to go?* he thought. He was about to get up and leave when he felt the phone vibrate in his coat pocket. He pulled it out.

We need an update. Text us progress now.

Connor wrote back.

I'm working on some leads. Nothing to report as yet.

Just so you know we are not joking.
Connor felt a buzzing in his arm. The capsule was vibrating. He was hit with a wave of anxiety.

Don't worry. We are not going to kill you yet.

Great. Now I feel better. He left the bar and went back to the hotel.

Peter Quinn sat in the secure room at the safe house, surrounded by senior Israeli intelligence officers. The mood was somber and grim. "He's my friend. I'm willing to risk my life to find him, but I need your support," Peter declared firmly to the men at the table. "He's done a lot for Israel. He deserves your help."

"It's not that we don't want to help. It's that there are many other lives and covert operations to consider. We can't jeopardize these missions over the life of one man. Surely you can understand that?"

"Where has he been taken? What do they want?"

"Obviously they wanted him alive, or they would have just killed him. We don't know what they are after, other than a normal interrogation to see what intelligence they could get on our activities. And we know they wanted him specifically. The tunnel was recently dug, since Connor and Natasha were relocated there a few months back. They were after Connor and they wanted him alive. The problem is we really don't know why. As for where he has been taken? We know he has been taken out of Gaza. Beyond that, we can't say for sure, although we have our ideas. Does that answer your questions?"

"Yes, some of them. Thank you," Peter responded. "However, I'm still going after him. Unless, that is, you're going to try and stop me. If not, I need your support."

"You will have our support and *guidance*," the man who was

obviously in charge said. "We will have for you some documents as well as a new identity, money, and so on by tomorrow."

"Thank you," Peter replied heartily. "Where should I start looking?"

"Where else, but Italy of course!"

The Israeli defense minister entered the prime minister's briefing room in Tel Aviv. He had two staff officers with him. Soon the briefing slides sparkled to life on the viewing screen. He began to speak.

"As you well know, Mr. Prime Minister, the Russians have been selling Iran all sorts of weapons over the last twelve months. Most of the purchases have been for air defense, as Russia makes really good antiaircraft missile systems. The S-300, for example, is now being deployed throughout the Iraqi theater and parts of Syria with Iranian forces. The umbrella is very dangerous but not impenetrable. However, we would incur significant losses if we attempt to hit their nuclear facilities inside of Iran. In-country, if you will, nuclear processing continues as well as missile testing.

"We believe the Iranians are within days of having an operational nuclear weapon. We also believe they have miniaturized the technology and will have the ability to deliver a multiple-warhead strike on Israel within six months. Their missile inventory is now robust. We have also observed some preparations for this type of attack. Our intelligence leads us to believe that missile support production has been increased as well as production activity at multiple nuclear sites. There has been increased activity in the acquisition of nuclear, biological, and chemical protection equipment. Civilian defense drills have also increased. Many new command bunkers and deep-level bomb shelters are being constructed. Conventional force activity, including troop movements and weapons placement, has also increased dramatically, mostly along the Iraqi border. Mr. Prime Minister, this type of activity can only lead to one thing. We believe Iran is preparing to launch a nuclear strike on Israel."

Chapter Seven

Connor's phone buzzed. He glanced at the clock by the bed. Nine o'clock. *Damn. Overslept. I'm going to miss breakfast.* His head beat like a jackhammer from the alcohol the night before, and the bright sun streamed through the window. The mattress had a nice depression in the center from years of customers, and Connor really didn't want to leave it. *Maybe I can risk another few minutes of shut-eye.* Angrily, he reached for the phone, picked it up, and looked at the text, expecting another threat from his 'handlers,' but the message was from Vitali.

Coffeehouse down the street - 1 hour

Good, at least I have time to eat. He sat up grudgingly, his head pounding.

Connor threw some water on his face, dressed, and headed out the door to the elevator. The old, Soviet lift was moving slow this morning, but soon he entered the serving area on the second floor. The buffet breakfast was an assortment of Eastern European staples—buckwheat, yogurt, sausage, cheese, curd (an eastern cottage cheese), salads, and black bread. He devoured the food, which was either quite good, or he was really hungry, he didn't know which.

After quickly getting his fill, he asked the concierge in the lobby for directions to the nearest coffeehouse and was soon walking down the wide sidewalk on the busy main street outside the hotel, the drivers feverishly and aggressively honking at one another. For some reason, today this got on Connor's nerves. *Must be the stress. It's starting to get to me. I've got to figure out my next moves, get ahead of the game. Do something unpredictable to get out of this fix.* Connor looked around as he walked and wondered if he was being followed. *Are they tracking me? They must be. Is this whole threat for real, or can I just rip this thing out from my arm and be done with it? I don't know yet. That's the problem. I need to get an expert opinion. Soon.* Five minutes later, he arrived at his destination, a nondescript, quaint cafe; it was not one of the chains that permeated former Soviet cities. No expats were to be seen, only locals, and Connor found a small table in a dark corner, ordered a cappuccino, and waited. He was ten minutes early.

His phone vibrated in his pocket. He took it out and looked at the message displayed on the screen.

PUT THE PHONE ON THE TABLE. WE ARE WATCHING YOU.

Shit. Connor did as he was told, his anxiety shooting up by a factor of ten.

Vitali walked in at five after the hour. He nervously checked over his shoulder several times before spotting Connor then walked over and sat across from him, his back against the side wall and his eyes monitoring the door.

"You're quite a hot ticket, my friend."

"You don't say?" Connor replied.

"Everyone and their fucking mother is looking for you. To borrow a phrase from your Texas, they want you dead or alive, it seems."

"Well, that's comforting. So what do you have for me?"

Vitali nervously looked around one more time then started to talk softly. "It seems the information you have requested is highly classified, but I guess you already suspected that."

"I assumed so, yes."

"Here's the deal. The Americans and the Russians, as you know, cooperated during World War II. Mainly, the U.S. provided equipment, but that was not the whole story. The rest is more, shall we say, sordid. They were developing weapons together as well. No one knew how far along Hitler was with a nuclear bomb or other weapons of mass destruction. It was a different time back then, kill or be killed. People were scared on both sides, scared for their very existence as a nation, and a people.

"All I can tell you is that there was a weapons lab set up in Siberia that the U.S. was feeding information and technology to, in hopes that Russia could take down Hitler before he got the bomb. It seems the Soviets had a spy inside the German scientific community, deep inside, who knew all the secrets on WMD development. Somehow, the Soviets secreted him out of Berlin and set up the lab in Siberia. The deal with the U.S. was that they would share information. It was couriered back and forth via the Bering Strait in Alaska through the lend-lease program in disguise. You seem to have found one of the couriers frozen in the ice. Obviously, that's the kind of state secret Washington really wouldn't want to get out. And the results of that research would be something any rogue government or terrorist would love to get his hands on, no matter how old it is."

Connor let out a low whistle and sat back in his chair, silent for a moment. "I know who wants it," he murmured.

"Indeed, I'm sure you do," responded Vitali coldly. "I most definitely don't want to know. One more thing. I understand one of the Soviet WMD labs was in Provideniya, on the coast. This facilitated naval access and was about as far from Germany as possible; it was protected by the American navy as well. Maybe you can find some answers there." Vitali passed a small piece of paper across the table. Connor picked it up and flipped it over. There was a name scribbled on the opposite side.

"Who is this?" he asked.

"Start your search with him. He's still alive. In Provideniya that is. Good luck, mate. Don't call me again." With that, Vitali got up and left the cafe. Connor remained sitting in the dark corner, lost in thought. A few minutes later, his phone vibrated.

What is the name?

Connor typed the name, **Gennadi Ivanov** and hit send. He had no choice.

Peter Quinn was hot on the trail, Connor's trail that is, courtesy of the Mossad. He left the lobby of the small bed and breakfast in Brindisi, Italy and looked up at the clear, blue sky that covered the fields of olive trees. There was a comfort here that he would love to come back and enjoy at some point, hopefully with someone of the opposite sex. Connor, however, was nowhere to be found.

He spoke to the proprietor of the establishment and confirmed that Connor had been there for one night. He seemed to be in good health, but she had noticed blood on his forehead and arm. She admitted being somewhat concerned about that discovery. She said Connor seemed upset, worried, tense. She didn't have much more to offer. *At least he's alive, but, why isn't he contacting us? It doesn't make sense. And for God's sake where are you now, my friend? I can't help you if I can't find you.* Peter had no idea of where to look now. All he had was that Connor was headed towards the train station. He could have gone anywhere. Peter pulled his phone out of his sport coat pocket and dialed a number in Israel.

Connor was tired, tired of flying that is. He was in a sleepless daze after all he globetrotting over the last twenty-four hours. The vibration of the small prop plane kept him awake however. The droning seemed to be on a cycle, going up and down, like the handle of a water pump gyrating in ancient times. He didn't know how much longer he could take it. Hopefully it would all be over soon. He realized he now knew what Chinese water torture was like, the steady drip of an unacceptably annoying sound and vibration.

He had grabbed a quick flight from Moldova to Frankfurt and then a direct, long flight to Anchorage, Alaska. After arriving in the largest state in the union, there was the Boeing 737 to Nome, Alaska on the Bering Sea. Nome was a native Alaskan village that was completely isolated, dependent on air freight and barges from Anchorage for food and supplies, when the weather allowed. The natives supplemented this with centuries-old subsistence hunting, when they weren't drinking of course. Alcoholism and suicide were rampant.

He had enjoyed his brief return to Alaska. The scenery and the sweet smell of the air was as beautiful as he remembered from his tour with the Air Force decades before. Connor made a mental note to return to the frontier state once all of this commotion was over, hopefully with Natasha. *Alaska was once part of Russia anyway,* he thought to himself.

Now Connor was flying in a dual-engine turboprop and was approaching the Russian Siberian coast. His body didn't realize what time it was. All he knew was that he wanted to get out of the aircraft as soon as possible. Thankfully, he felt the aircraft begin to descend, and the droning changed octaves at least. His right leg was asleep from the vibration.

Soon Connor was flying low over the land along the coast, toward the airfield outside the town, which was backdropped by a range of snowy white mountains. The deepwater, military port of Provideniya loomed in the distance along the water. The town was situated at the mouth of a fjord and was protected from the brunt of the ocean's wrath by the mountains. Carcasses of old ships and industrial waste dotted the landscape from the occasional visits of the Soviet and now Russian navy.

Connor stared at the vast, desolate, snow-covered tundra passing beneath him as the sun headed for the horizon.

Peter Quinn walked the streets of Chisinau. He was out of leads. Looking around the barren streets, as much as he knew Connor, he could tell his friend would like the city. It was just nondescript enough that one could melt into the woodwork, although Westerners tended to stick out like a sore thumb. *There's no way I can fucking find him if I don't know where to look.* The Mossad had figured out through a Palestinian informant that Connor had traveled to Chisinau. They had someone deep inside of Hamas. "He is making quite a show over there. Go find him," they admonished. The source could not tell them any more at the moment regarding his whereabouts however. Peter was frustrated. He decided to duck in to a bar and have a drink and think. That's what Connor would expect him to do. He smiled, thinking of his friend.

Peter was alone in this endeavor. He felt naked, exposed, vulnerable. The Mossad had basically cut him loose. Connor was not their priority, although they offered to help Peter as best they could with support from afar. *Where are you, my friend?* He downed a shot of local vodka and asked for another. He needed to calm his nerves. *What was Connor looking for here in this place?*

The joint was about half full, and the ridiculously cute girls behind the bar were keeping the older customers happy with smiles, an occasional free drink, and letting them think they had a chance later, after the place closed, which of course none of them did, unless the price was right. Peter took in the scene and wondered what to do next. He could see through the window the sun was settling towards the horizon. After a while, the crowd started to thicken. *Do I stay here and drink? What to do?* A man sat next to him. Peter was lost in thought.

"Cheer up," the man next to him said after a while, in a Russian accent.

"What?" Peter said as he looked up at the man.

"I said cheer the fuck up. You look like someone killed your mother."

"Do I? Well, maybe they did," Peter replied, looking back down at his vodka.

"Don't worry, we'll find him."

"What did you say?"

"I said, don't fucking worry, we'll find him."

Peter was astonished. "I don't know who you are, friend, but you'd better start fucking talking."

"Or what?" The man smiled.

Peter looked at the man for the first time, focused this time. This guy didn't look like someone he wanted to mess with, so he let the man take the first move. "Why don't you tell me what's going on?" he said in a more friendly manner.

"That's better," the man said. "Why don't we take a walk?"

Peter got up and walked outside. The man followed. When they had left the bar and walked a hundred yards or so, the man spoke. "My name's Vitali. We are on the same team. Your friends in Israel contacted me. I met with your friend a few days ago. He's okay but he is scared. Something or someone is leaning on him big-time."

"How did you know to find me?"

"They told me when you were coming. They told me to help you. I'm being compensated, handsomely. So, like I said, we are on the same team. At least for now."

"So you've been following me?"

"Ever since you left the airport."

"Jesus Christ. So what do we do now?"

Vitali stopped Peter under a tree and they stepped into the shadows. The people were milling around the many food stands that were set up along the avenue. The girls, decked in high heels and miniskirts, were flaunting their stuff, hoping for Mr. Oligarch to notice them. Once he was certain no one was listening, Vitali started talking. "Look, let's get one thing straight. I'm no patriot. All I am is a mercenary. But I'm being paid quite well to help you out. So, you asked, what do we do next?"

"Yes, what do we do?" Peter replied. "And how the fuck do I know you are for real?"

"One second," Vitali ordered. He pulled out his phone and hastily typed a text.

Thirty seconds later, Peter's phone buzzed. He looked at the screen. All it said was, Trust him. It was from his contact at the Mossad.

Peter looked up at Vitali. "I guess you're legit. What's the next move?"

"I don't think we try to follow him. That's a waste of time. I think we try and contact him and find out what is going on." Vitali held up his phone in the air in front of Peter's face. "I have his phone number."

Sergei was amused when Vitali came into the picture. He recognized him from the many photos he had seen. Vitali was a wanted man, in Russia anyway. He put down the powerful field glasses he was using to watch Peter from across the square and smiled. *Well, well, my old friend Vitali. Nice to see you again.* He had been tracking Peter since he left Israel, and now Vitali presented an unexpected target of opportunity.

Peter didn't know it, but he and Sergei went way back, to Brazil, the previous year in fact. While attempting to kill Connor, Natasha, and Peter at the behest of his Russian superiors, the entire operation was interrupted by the Mossad at the last moment. Peter had led Sergei to Connor and Natasha's safe house near Bahia, Brazil. Sergei hadn't anticipated the Jews showing up, killing the rest of his hired team, and then spiriting his three targets out of Brazil and into Tel Aviv.

Sergei had been waiting patiently for the day when the three of them would leave Israel so he could complete his original mission, to kill them. *How did his superior officer say it? Make them feel pain, and then kill them. Yes, that was it.* Sergei picked up the glasses again to survey the two men and attempt to discern what their next move was. They were still talking.

The Russian agent had no idea where Murray was; all he knew was that some group in Gaza had kidnapped him and then spirited him out of the territory. *This Peter chap can tell me where he is for sure,* Sergei thought.

He had hoped Peter would again lead him to the target, like a moth to a flame. But now, Vitali's entering the picture changed everything.

Vitali was a Russian traitor, a former FSB officer and a double agent. He had helped the Americans and other Western governments for some time now and for much money. He was very much wanted dead by the Kremlin. The Motherland didn't let double agents live. *Yes this is an unexpected development indeed.*

Sergei made up his mind. Vitali would die, now. Then he would take Peter and interrogate him, find out where Murray had run off to. Slowly, a plan came together in Sergei's mind.

He put down the glasses and started the vehicle he was sitting in, across the expansive square from Peter and the other Russian. The engine in the old, Soviet-built, Lada roared to life with all the gusto of a go-cart. *She'll have to do the trick,* Sergei thought.

He put the car in drive and looked both ways across the square. Peter and Vitali were still across the way, talking under a tree with their backs to him. Vitali was smoking a cigarette. They had no idea Sergei was even there. Many other citizens of Chisinau walked nonchalantly about their daily lives, unaware that a murder was about to take place.

Sergei eased out of his position of concealment—he was parked between two other vehicles—and turned towards his two targets. He pressed the accelerator and moved forward, attempting to blend in to the other traffic while getting as close to his two victims as possible. When he was about twenty-five yards away, Sergei smiled and stomped on the gas pedal. The Lada shot forward.

Killing Vitali would bring him much adulation from his comrades in the security services as well as most likely a promotion. Vitali was that much of a high-value target. He would take his trophy back to Moscow and maybe even be stationed back in his favorite home city. Sergei thought briefly of the girls he would meet and take advantage of. Moscow had thousands of young, beautiful girls just waiting to meet a man of power and means. He would have both for killing this traitor to the Motherland.

Vitali heard the noise first and instantly recognized the danger. His hand went immediately to inside his sport coat flap and came out with a powerful pistol. He was trained for this type of situation. *Such a dumbass I am. I let my guard down.* He spun on a dime and raised the pistol to fire at the car he knew would be approaching. As he made eye contact with the driver, he could see the smile on Sergei's face. Vitali instantly realized who his attacker was. He squeezed off two shots before the bumper of the Lada crashed into his waist and propelled him in the air into the wall behind him. He died instantly.

Peter didn't even have time to take in the scene before the Lada brushed by him, spinning him around and knocking him to the earth. As he lay on the ground, Peter saw the Lada continue forward and crash into the same wall that Vitali had hit. He couldn't believe his eyes and fought to regain control of his senses. Peter got up as pain shot through his hip. He tried to ignore the discomfort and limped over to where Vitali was lying in a pool of blood. He then looked inside the vehicle.

The driver was dead, one of the rounds having blown out his eye socket. Peter then reached down and felt Vitali's pulse. Nothing. He was gone.

Vitali's words rang through Peter's mind. *I have his phone number.* He reached down and rifled his dead friend's pockets, pulling out a cell phone as well as the weapon from his hand and a spare magazine. Peter got up immediately and looked around. The people were approaching. He heard a siren off in the distance. Someone must have called the police.

Peter started running. He ran and ran until he couldn't run anymore then he ducked inside a small theater, bought a ticket, and sat down in the back of the establishment to think. *Jesus, what the fuck to do now?*

Chapter Eight

Connor finally stepped out of the small, twin-engine turboprop onto the hard pavement at the airstrip in Provideniya. The warm air was gliding off the Pacific Ocean into the mountains surrounding the port. He glanced around at the buildings of the town, and his first reaction was a feeling of extreme loneliness. The nondescript, Soviet, concrete apartment structures were like every other former Soviet city, except here, contrasted against the empty hills behind them, they looked even more forlorn. The residents had attempted to cheer them up by painting them in pastel colors to mimic some of the Dutch islands in the Caribbean, but the attempt was weak. *It doesn't work,* he thought to himself.

There was not a tree in sight. In fact, there was barely anything alive visible at all. Nothing but gray clouds, gray concrete, and gray mountains. *It must be a really tough life out here, amongst the nothingness of the Bering Sea.* He finally saw a few residents milling around the small terminal building. *Emptiness. Nothingness. For days and days and years and years. Yes, a tough life indeed.*

Completely alone himself, Connor started walking. He carried only a small bag over his shoulder, traveling light as usual. All his earthly belongings currently were in that satchel, including the money and the identity the terrorists had given him. He didn't know where he was going, just that he felt the need to walk, to blend in, to experience the town for himself, to decide on a plan to get out of this freaking mess! He reached up and felt the bump in his upper arm, where the device was implanted. The incision had started to heal, and he would have to get the stitches out soon. *Or should I leave them in? Will removing them trigger the device?*

Soon he had walked up the small incline from the airstrip to the main road leading into town. His aircraft loaded quickly and took off once again. There was no reason to hang around this godforsaken place. Rusting shipping containers lined the shoreline, left to rot in the sea spray and hot sun. Connor could see the Orthodox crosses of a cemetery on the top of the hillside looking over town. It was complete desolation. *I wonder how many souls have lived and died here in the middle of literally nowhere, cut off from the rest of the world.*

After walking a half mile, Connor heard several cars coming down the road behind him. He stuck out his hand flat, pointed to the ground, and immediately one of the vehicles traveling into town stopped to pick him up. It was the universal Russian signal for hitchhiking and worked everywhere in the former Soviet Union. The driver was an old member of one of the native Eskimo tribes that were split between the Russian and Alaskan sides of the Bering Sea. He looked ancient; his dark skin wrinkled with the ages, but his reflexes were sharp and there was a twinkle in his eye.

"Hello, stranger, I've never seen you in these parts," he said in fluent English.

"Yes, it's my first time here. How did you know I speak English?"

"Because it's obvious you don't speak Russian," he said with a smile. "And you also don't speak Yupik. So, you must be American? Da?"

Connor smiled and said nothing.

"Where should I take you in town?" the man asked.

"I'm not really sure. I guess I need a place to stay. Is there a hotel?"

"Well, it's not really a hotel, kind of a guest house. But don't worry, they have plenty of rooms available. Might I suggest we start somewhere else? After all, you're going to need a guide tonight, right? Because you really have no idea what you're doing, right?"

Connor smiled again. The man was perceptive in his old age.

"Okay, you got me. Where do we start?"

"Why the bar of course."

"Take me to your leader," Connor quipped. The man chuckled.

Soon they arrived at a building on the outskirts of town. It really wasn't a building in Connor's opinion; it was more of a cinder block shack. Once he walked inside, he realized the structure had a charm of its own. The winters were so brutal here that the residents didn't spend much time on the outside; however, the inside was warmly decorated. Several customers sat at the bar while others lingered at tables. There was a small stage in the corner of the room. Connor followed the man to the bar and sat beside him. Before the bartender approached, he leaned over and asked, "What's your name?"

"People call me Sam. I've long forgotten what my real Yupik name is. I suppose if I thought about it long enough, I could remember it, but what's the point? Like I said, people know me as Sam."

"Thanks for the lift into town."

"Don't worry about it. I could tell you weren't from around here. So why don't you tell me what you're looking for?"

Connor reached into his pocket and pulled out the card with the name written on the back that Vitali had given him. *Gennadi Ivanov.* He showed it to his new friend. "I'm looking for this guy. Do you know him?"

Sam's eyes widened. Then he smiled. "Yes, I know him."

"Can you take me to him?"

"I can. But let's sit here and drink for a while. You are in no hurry, are you? It's rude to leave a new friend in such a short time. Have another drink!"

"Okay, my new friend, if you say so. I'm in your hands."

Connor had to admit, he rather enjoyed the old man's company. He told Connor of life in Provideniya over the last decades since the Great Patriotic War. He told of the changes he had seen and the things that had not changed at all, like the barrenness and the silence. Connor could see the pain in his eyes as he spoke of loneliness and the alcoholism the people faced on a daily basis.

"How do you survive all of this time?" Connor asked.

"We cling to our traditions. We help each other. In fact, you will see some of our traditions soon. Tonight we are drumming."

"Drumming?"

"You will see. Just wait."

Connor and the man talked for another hour or so then Connor noticed several of the men get up from their tables or leave the bar and head to the stage in the back corner. They each pulled up a chair on the platform, and then someone brought a large kettledrum and placed it in the center of the circle of sitting men. Then the drumming started as the men used large sticks with covered ends to create the sounds. It was slow at first but then progressed to a loud, pulsing, rhythmic beat. Soon the men added a native chant to the beats of the drum. Connor sat listening, mesmerized. After about ten minutes, Sam looked at Connor and waved him to an empty seat next to him. *Why not?* Connor thought. He got up and joined the drumming and the chanting. The festivities continued into the night.

The Yupik tribes had settled the area long before the Russians or Americans arrived and they flourished on both sides of the Bering Sea. Regular flights had reunited families after the fall of the Soviet Union. The traditions were very similar in Nome as they were in Provideniya.

At some point, Connor didn't really remember when, the drumming stopped, and the men drunkenly wandered back to their tables or out into the night air. Connor found himself back at the bar with Sam. "Quite an unexpected night," he said.

"Yes, I'm sure it must be for you. For us, it is normal. It is how we survive. Our traditions keep us sane. Come, I want you to meet someone." Sam stood up from the bar and walked over to a corner table where one of the old men who had been drumming was sitting quietly, smoking a hand-rolled cigarette, the harsh smell wafting throughout the building and adding to the ambiance. He looked even more ancient than Sam, with deep crevices in his face; his skin was more fair and his beard full and gray. Connor and Sam walked up and asked to sit. The man looked at Connor with small slits of eyes as he agreed to the request with a slight, almost imperceptible nod.

"Connor," said Sam. "Meet Gennadi Ivanov."

Connor's face lit up. "I've travelled here to meet you, Mr. Ivanov." Connor then realized he didn't know if the man spoke English. He looked at Sam for help with that question.

"He can understand you but would prefer Russian, or German."

"Well, my Russian is not the best. Maybe you could translate." Sam proceeded to interpret the conversation.

"What do you want?" asked Gennadi in Russian.

"I want to know about the weapons lab in Provideniya during the Great Patriotic War, and what became of it and its personnel."

"You want too much," replied the Russian. "I no longer speak of those things."

"Why?"

"Because the work was evil."

"In what way?"

"You must already know why it was evil."

"All I know is that it was concerning weapons of mass destruction. What was your role in the process? Did you work at the lab?"

"Yes, I worked at the lab, until it was moved farther into Siberia once the war was over. I was very young at the time. Now I am old. However, I remember it clearly. Still very clearly. One day I will pay for the sin of helping to create those weapons." The man seemed to drift off to another place. Connor fumbled for a way to move the conversation forward.

"Did you know the spy the Soviets had in Berlin? Did you know of his research efforts and the information he brought back to the Soviet Union?"

The man turned to look at Connor and seemed surprised. "Yes, I knew him. He is my brother."

Connor let out a slow whistle and sat back in his chair and looked at Sam, who had a concerned look on his face. He looked at his old friend Gennadi and said something incomprehensible. Gennadi waved off his concern with a hand.

Connor looked at Gennadi closely. He had to be over ninety years of age but still somewhat strong and alert.

"Where is he? Can I talk to him?"

"I haven't seen him in over sixty years. The Soviets moved the lab away from the exposure of the coast and into the heartland of Siberia. They wanted to continue the research. My brother agreed and moved with them. I wanted nothing more to do with the research. I left the project and refused to be involved anymore. As I said, it was evil."

"What was so evil about the research?"

"The Soviets were pushing the development of nuclear and chemical weapon research. But this was something different. It was against God. It was a weapon of mass destruction alright. It wasn't just a biological weapon that could kill someone if they became infected. It was a weapon to destroy a whole race of people, based on their DNA. The Soviets were very advanced with this research. Much more than the rest of the world realized. The work was done in an extremely secretive manner."

"And the Americans were helping?"

"They helped in the beginning, with scientific help and the like. But after the war ended, all the cooperation stopped of course. We saw each other as enemies."

"So you are telling me that the weapon being developed was a way to kill an entire race?"

"Yes, one could release a virus into the open that would only attack certain DNA. You could make it very specific. For instance, to only attack those of German blood. Or Jewish, or whomever you wanted to exterminate forever from the face of the planet. As I said, it was evil. I wanted nothing more to do with it."

"Where do you think your brother is?"

"I have an idea. But I don't desire to reach him. And I'm sure he doesn't want to talk to me. He thinks I am a traitor to the Russian cause. Or so I have heard, over the years."

"Let me ask you another way. If you could help stop the spread of this weapon, would you get involved? Help me contact your brother?"

"Why do you ask me that?"

"Because someone very evil is trying to obtain the weapon. They want to rule the world. They want to use this weapon. I am sure of it. I think they want to wipe out the Jewish race once and for all. They are trying to find out information about how developed it is, where the information is located, et cetera."

Gennadi seemed to drift off again. His eyes grew glassy, and he seemed to slump into a depression that was written all over his face. "I have feared this for many years. Now the time has come." Connor didn't push him anymore but let him think in silence. Finally, he answered Connor's question.

"Yes, I will help you. But I cannot protect you. This road is very dangerous. I am old and it doesn't matter if it destroys me.

However, you are young. Are you prepared to find out what is behind the door? Are you prepared to take this where it leads you?"

"I have no choice in the matter it seems. And yes, I am ready to take this where it leads me."

"Then I will help you find him."

With that, the man's strength seemed to ebb. It was getting very late and Sam helped him to the door. Gennadi refused any more help and slowly walked out into the night to his home.

Sam escorted Connor to the guest house in town, and they agreed to meet in the morning.

The next day, Connor woke early and decided to take a walk through the middle of the desolate town. He strolled down the wide, empty streets. He decided the buildings couldn't be designed to be any more devoid of soul. They were functional at a bare minimum level but lacked any type of artistic detail whatsoever. They were also dirty and run-down. Unless painted, everything was a dead color of gray, only the shading changed. The pavement was cracked and potholed. The grass grew wherever it could; no effort was taken to landscape or make the area more aesthetic. On the buildings that were colored, the paint was peeling off the walls. The geometric patterns painted on the outside of the walls of the apartment buildings were meant to be artistic but served only to highlight the ridiculousness and the lack of purpose of the town's existence. In the distance, a smokestack belched waste from the local power plant. Dangerous crevices on the side of the road carried the water runoff away from the street. Connor was saddened just to be here. His phone rang.

"Are you making progress?" the voice menacingly asked.

"Yes, I have found a connection to the scientist from the weapons lab that was located here. I'm trying to track him down."

"Good. You are running out of time. Keep us posted." Click.

MOTHERLAND

I had almost forgot about these assholes. I've got to figure out a way forward. Something will come to me. A plan. Something.

Connor met Sam for breakfast at one of the few restaurants in town. It was an extended kitchen more than anything, located off one of the lobbies of an apartment block in the center of town. Connor was hungry and enjoyed the local food complete with whale blubber and fish oil. If he didn't understand one of the dishes offered, Sam explained it to him.

"I've never in my life heard Gennadi talk of such things. I had no idea."

"Thank you for introducing me to him," Connor replied. "He is an interesting man. A good man, I can tell."

"Yes, he is a good person. But an old one. I'm not sure how he can help you. He is supposed to meet us here soon to get something to eat and talk further with you."

Two hours later, Sam and Connor were still waiting for Gennadi. "I'm going to go check on him," Sam said in frustration.

"I'm going with you."

The two men made their way to Gennadi's flat on the twelfth floor on one of the apartment blocks via the tiny, creaking elevator, and soon were standing outside his door and knocked. The smell of food cooking in someone's kitchen permeated the hallway. There was no reply to their repeated knocking.

Sam turned the latch, and the two of them walked in slowly to the apartment. They found Gennadi sitting in a lounge chair in the middle of the main room, lifeless. A bottle of sleeping pills sat on the table next to the chair. Sam felt his neck. The body was cold. "He's been like this for a long time, probably from last night."

"I upset him," said Connor. "He couldn't deal with the thought of being involved in that project, even though it was so long ago. I resurrected some old demons."

Connor reached down and picked up a piece of paper that was lying next to the bottle of pills. There was something in bad English scribbled on one side. It was a name of a person and also a town. Then the words, "Destroy the evil. I'm sorry."

"Must be his brother's contact information."

"He was my friend. Rest in peace Gennadi," said Sam mournfully.

Sam then picked up the phone and called the police. Once they arrived, the police took the two men's statements and then they were free to go. With an air of sadness, Connor and Sam went back to the bar where they planned to celebrate Gennadi's life.

Chapter Nine

The Israeli prime minister walked up to the long, wooden, polished table, reached down, and pulled back a chair then sat in the plush padding. He slowly raised his eyes and met the gaze of the man across from him. This was a man whom he had distrusted from the beginning, when they first met. It was a gut instinct, but he never dreamed that the evil could be so complete. Here was the man who had attempted to destroy his country, Israel. Well, maybe he wasn't completely in charge of the operation, but he let it happen. He had wanted it to happen. The prime minister was certain. That was bad enough. Prime Minister Dahan just knew the man was complicit in some manner, up to his eyeballs. And here he sat across from him, smiling, thinking the prime minister knew nothing. It was all he could do to maintain his composure, not to act in a way that was entirely unbecoming for a head of state at an international event.

Two tactical nuclear weapons had been smuggled into Israel via an aid convoy for the Palestinians and on board a ship that eventually docked at the port of Jaffa. Only the incredible work of the Shin Bet, the Israeli security force, to find and disarm the weapons via nuclear detection devices invented in Israel had prevented Armageddon for his country. This bland result must have bothered the man sitting across from him. To have his evil goal within sight but then to have it snatched from him at the last minute. Prime Minister Dahan smiled as he thought of the instant the president of the United States knew his diabolical plan had been foiled. The prime minister made a mental note to ask his intelligence personnel if they had heard of any reaction from the White House that raised any suspicions Israel knew who was behind the attempted attack. He doubted there was any evidence to be found. President Chahine was very good at his charade. He hid his tracks for quite some time, that is, until Israel discovered who he really was.

Israel had been chasing and attempting to find out who the Sultan was for some time before his identity was discovered. This sometimes mythical person, who controlled the Middle East and was bent on destroying Israel, was now all too real. The Mossad had tracked him for years, until finally one day, they put the pieces together.

It was Reshma Nadir, an Arab Israeli agent, who discovered the cold trail that led them to unmasking this villain. She worked tirelessly to uncover the Sultan. The prime minister was grateful to her for that. An Arab had saved the Jewish State. If only the world knew the irony.

The prime minister was jerked back from his deep thoughts when the president spoke. It was as if they were here to plan a party or something, rather than discuss an issue that was existential to Israel.

"Thank you for coming to Camp David, Mr. Prime Minister. I hope the parties here can come to some agreement for peace for all of your people."

The prime minister looked around the table. They were all here, Israel's enemies. Hamas, the Palestinian Authority, Hezbollah, Iran, the entire terrorist clan. They all smiled. They knew Israel was backed into a corner, and they smiled and acted like peacemakers. Nothing could be further from the truth.

"I am glad to be here to make peace, Mr. President. But, only a real peace, if that can be achieved. Frankly, I am doubtful."

The prime minister could see a faint flicker of anger cross the president's face. *Yes, I am sure you are angry I don't bend over like a whore for you, Mr. President,* the prime minister thought to himself. *Israel is not dead yet, not by a long shot.*

The Iranian president spoke, "We are here to make a real

peace, Mr. Prime Minister, but we agree, the peace has to be fair and long-lasting."

The only peace you want is one where Israel no longer exists and Iran is the nuclear hegemon in the region, the Prime Minister again thought to himself. "We will honestly consider your terms, Mr. President," he said to the Iranian head of state.

The meeting was set up by the American administration, with the goal of solving the Palestinian question and peace in the Middle East once and for all. The problem was that the solution the American president was proposing was for Israel to go back to the 1967 borders proposed by the United Nations. This was suicide for Israel and everyone in the room knew it. Without the territories Israel annexed from the Arab armies that attacked her, the country would be reduced to a small strip of land barely one-mile-wide at some points. It was a non-defensible footprint, and that was why everyone in the room was attempting to force the Jewish leader to accept this trade. *Land for peace,* they thought. It was a ridiculous proposal.

The prime minister scanned the table full of monsters and then looked the twice-elected American leader in the eye. "Let's get started, Mr. President," he said tersely.

The old, Russian man was tired. He read the letter of his brother's suicide with extreme sadness as he sat at his desk. He glanced at a photo of them together, years ago, still hanging loosely on his wall. His brother had been such a weak man. A man afraid of doing what needed to be done to save his people. Yes, *his* people, their people. Why didn't his brother ever realize that the ends justified the means? Why didn't he realize that things had to be done, bad things, but necessary things?

Anatoly sighed. It had been a long day, and he was very tired. He barely even remembered what his brother was like. It was that long since he last saw him. He walked over and took the faded, framed picture off the wall and put it in a drawer in the next room. *Enough of him. I need to finish my work.*

Anatoly thought back to the days when he was a spy in the Nazi government for the Soviets. He spoke German then and still did mostly now. It was his original tongue that his parents taught him. He thought in German.

He worked hard for the Soviets once he was back in Russia, after being secreted out of Berlin and into the Soviet Union, to work in Stalin's laboratories, continuing work on the weapon to end all weapons. During that time, life in Provideniya was actually much tougher than it was now. They didn't have the creature comforts or the direct communication with the outside world that existed today. Of course the communist overseers would arrive regularly via the airstrip to check on their progress. They were extremely interested in the weapon they were developing, as were the Americans. They provided much help, and there was regular communication via flights from the Alaskan territory to the lab in Provideniya. Once the war ended, that cooperation ended of course.

In the end, the process of development took much longer than anyone expected. The research needed was not completely solved until decades later, when computing power became more readily available. His lab discovered and mapped human DNA much earlier than anyone thought, anyone on the outside that is.

Later, after fall of the U.S.S.R., the lab was moved further into the interior of the country, in Siberia. His brother did not follow him. He said he had a problem with the evil nature of the research. *Such small-mindedness.*

Even in this late stage of his life, Anatoly still managed his laboratory and the project. It was his life's work. He would not stop until he stopped breathing. His people had to be protected.

He walked to the window and looked outside at the mountainous landscape. It was necessary to move his project here. Leaving was the right thing to do. They had achieved much success in the last couple decades. The weapon was almost operational. It had to be perfected so that it did not cause mass death but only a targeted effectiveness. That was the key. *We are so close. So close to protecting the Motherland against all enemies. I will not fail. I will succeed, or I will die trying.*

Peter Quinn didn't go back to his hotel room; it was too risky and he was scared. Thankfully he had travelled light and left very little there that was important. He had his passport and money. That was all he needed.

Peter didn't know if he had been followed, or if Vitali had for that matter. It really didn't make a difference. He couldn't take any chances. He had to assume someone knew he was there and going back to the room would be suicide.

But the man in the car was after Vitali, not him. At least, not initially. *I'll never know what he was really after, but he obviously wanted Vitali dead.* The man looked Russian. It seemed that Vitali recognized him for an instant before he was killed. *Maybe he and Vitali went way back. Maybe they had old scores to settle. Anyway, time to move on.*

Peter had found a small, rundown hotel across town. After the incident, he jumped on the nearby trolleybus and just rode for several hours, trying to decide what to do. Eventually he got off at a lower rent part of town, checked in to the hotel, and secreted himself in his room. He now sat on the bed, pondering the situation as the traffic blared outside the establishment in the middle of the night. Finally, he reached over and grabbed Vitali's phone. Looking through the numbers, he eventually found one that didn't match and was listed as CM. *Must be Connor,* thought Peter. *Well, here goes nothing.* He dialed the number.

Connor was on the train, heading into Siberia. He was running out of time per his captor's instructions. This was no way to live. He wasn't sleeping and hardly eating. The stress was too great. He was lying on the top bunk in the black silence of the four-passenger compartment as the train rambled through the Siberian wilderness, wondering if he was going to live or die. An old, Soviet blanket was thrown across him to keep out the night dampness. It was dark outside and no lights were on inside the compartment. The other three passengers in the cabin were silent as well, two asleep, one on her iPhone.

He tried to fit in with the Russian passengers as best he could. However, they knew he was American. It was obvious. They distrusted him. Connor wondered if they had alerted the authorities. Not many people were authorized to be in this area, in spite of his Russian passport. He was taking a big chance but he had no other choice.

Connor wondered how he had ended up here, in this desolate place, with really no idea how to move forward. He was just running on instinct now and was losing faith that he would make it out of this predicament alive. The terrorists' phone was in his pocket. He never let it get away from him, as he was afraid of the consequences. The incision in his arm was throbbing and had maybe grown infected. *This is not good,* he thought.

The trip to the interior went easy enough, so far. He had

boarded the train in Provideniya for the five-hundred-mile journey to the small city in the interior. It was not even marked on some maps. *That was probably intentional,* he thought. *A weapons lab and all.* The pleasant, rhythmic rocking of the train back and forth should have been comforting, especially to someone who wanted to get some sleep. But for Connor it was no use.

Connor didn't know what to expect. He was looking forward to meeting Anatoly. Although he had a number from his brother that he assumed was for Anatoly, he didn't dare call. He didn't want to warn the authorities, whom he was sure the old man would alert if he tried to contact him before arriving. So Connor took a chance. He decided to just show up in town and try to talk to Anatoly. It was his only lead and his only hope. He was running on fumes now.

Soon the sun started to peek over the horizon of the Siberian countryside. The burly stewardess brought hot water and instant coffee a few minutes later. Connor managed to pay without causing too much trouble. The Russian he studied long ago in college came in handy. The other passengers in the cabin started to stir. The person under him was a young woman in her early twenties. She left the cabin dressed in sweats with her hair up, once it was obvious people were waking. She returned twenty minutes later appearing as a different person, having changed and applied makeup and combed her hair. *She's actually quite attractive,* Connor thought. *Actually stunning! I'm not in Kansas anymore.* She did not speak to him, but he caught several glances out of the corner of his eye. She was definitely interested in who he was. *Maybe I can use that to my advantage in this situation,* he thought.

Connor tried to think of enough Russian words to carry on a conversation about nothing. Then his phone rang. His adrenaline shot up. *It must be the terrorists. How am I going to talk here?* He jumped off the top bunk and quickly opened the cabin door and entered the hallway outside in an attempt to find a little bit of privacy.

The countryside flew by outside the train window in the pink soft glow of the early sunlight. Connor didn't notice, he was too worried about who was calling.

"Yes?" he answered firmly but softly, as many people were still not fully awake and he didn't want them to hear the conversation anyway.

"Connor! It's Peter."

Chapter Ten

President Chahine sat in the Oval Office, alone. He was angry but he didn't quite know why. He shouldn't be angry. Things were going his way. But he was angry all the same.

He sat at the Resolute desk and looked out the window, trying to collect his thoughts. He tried to tamp down the anger and think clearly. *Keep the goal in mind*, he thought to himself. *It is God's will. Nothing can stop the final outcome. It's just a bump in the road.*

The rain was coming down hard now into the White House grounds, slamming against the window. He enjoyed the rain. It brought him a depressing clarity that he loved. Slowly, his anger began to subside.

It was that damned Jewish Prime Minister. *He really gets under my fucking skin for some Goddamned reason.* He closed his eyes and tried to calm himself in the silence. *He sees right through me. I wonder what he knows. I'm sure he is aware of my agenda but he may not know the scope of what we are doing to ensure Israel comes out with the short end of the stick in all this; hopefully it won't come out of this at all.* He smiled to himself at that last statement. *It really doesn't matter what he knows. He cannot change the final outcome. Things cannot go on as they exist today. It is in Allah's hands now.*

His mind drifted back to when he was a child in Egypt and he closed his eyes. Instantly the smells of the market were everywhere like they had never left. Visions of being with his family and visiting the mosque with his father floated across his memory. The Muslim call to prayer drifting over the city was such a sweet sound.

He had left the Middle East as a child and immigrated to America. It had been hard on him. Those memories were not pleasant. *How I wish I could go back to when I was happy, when I was with my parents and at peace.* Slowly the responsibilities of his title and position came back to him and soon he was back in reality. The weight of his role in the world weighed on his psyche. Being president was easy enough. No, he was thinking of his real, secret role, as Sultan, savior of Islam, destroyer of the Jews. He still had much yet to do and accomplish.

    The President had been busy after the events of the last year in Israel. The Shin Bet diffusing the tactical nuclear weapons he planted to destroy the Jewish State was a setback, for sure. The establishment of the caliphate from the Levant to Tehran was paramount for Islam to regain its rightful place of power in the world, and the destruction of Israel was a must to achieve that goal. *Palestine must belong to Allah. Not just a portion but all of it! From the Jordanian desert to the Mediterranean. But I can't think about that now. It is water under the bridge. I have to think of the process at hand. The 'peace process.'* He smiled again at the obvious subterfuge in that statement. *We will force Israel economically, and shame them, into giving back land to return to the '67 borders. The country will then be indefensible. Then the final battle can begin.* The Sultan pulled out his rug, turned to Mecca, and knelt to pray.

    Connor didn't understand what was going on. "Peter, what the fuck. Why are you on this phone. Don't say anything for God's sake. Are you okay?"

    "Yeah, I'm okay. Why wouldn't I be okay? Why shouldn't I say anything? Are you okay? Connor, what the Hell is going on?"

    "Don't...say anymore. Stay out of this. For your own good. It's like high yield again, Peter. Goodbye." Connor hung up.

    The phone immediately rang afterwards. "Who was that?" the terrorist asked. "Tell me exactly who that was and how they got your number or I will kill you right now. And, I would enjoy doing it."

The tension once again arose inside of Connor. *I can't take much more of this!*

"It was an old friend from inside Israel. I don't know how he got the number. That is the truth." There was a silence on the phone for several seconds and then the line went dead, the caller apparently somewhat unsettled.

Peter racked his brain after the line had disconnected. *What did Connor mean was like high yield?* Peter was an energy analyst on Wall Street when he and Connor met. Connor had been running the fixed income trading operations of the firm while Peter had been digging up juicy high yield bonds for his traders to score big profits from. High yield was almost like trading a stock, the securities moved more with the fundamentals of the company rather than with macroeconomic rates like normal bonds. It had been a very profitable time for the two of them; that is until the housing crisis in the latter part of the first decade of the 21st century.

Then Peter remembered. The two of them had been discussing moving their operations to another firm for a big check. They were far down the road on this idea, in negotiations with another large investment bank, when the crisis happened, so the move never materialized. However, they did not communicate over landlines about this move for the obvious reasons. They used an obscure set of emails that no one else knew about to bounce ideas back and forth about how to move the business. *That's what Connor is talking about. He wants to communicate the same way. Now, if I can just remember the damn email address.*

The Russian general walked into the conference room at the Kremlin in Moscow and smiled as he saw his guest sitting at the long, ornate table. The man stood up immediately to greet him. He strolled up to the man and embraced him in a tight, bear hug. Then turned to sit across from him and waited for the man to start the negotiations.

This was a tenuous point in the discussion. The Russian knew very well why the Iranian representative was here. The Iranians wanted more weapons, a lot of them. They wanted even more sophisticated air defense systems, on top of the point defense systems they had already purchased. They wanted tanks. They wanted frontline Russian fighters. They wanted help with their nuclear program. And Iran had a *lot* of money coming through the door these days, hundreds of billions of dollars. The end of the United Nations sanctions had seen to that. Also, the Iranian oil fields were pumping once again and even though the price of oil was in a historically low range, it still was a boon for the Iranian treasury. So, the Iranians decided to go shopping.

"Good afternoon, General Kursk, my old friend. Thank you for taking the time to meet with me."

"Of course, Minister Javadi. Russia and Iran are now very good friends. It would be wrong not to meet with you, per your embassy's request. Russia is always ready to meet with anyone to further the cause of peace in the Middle East. What can I do for you? Would you like some tea? We have a nice British green tea that I am sure you will find delightful! Straight from the queen herself!"

"That would be most gracious of you General Kursk." The Russian signaled for tea to be brought in the room and the Iranian waited until it had been served, and the servant had left before he spoke.

"General Kursk. I think you realize my country has come into a great deal of money in the past year. Due to this good fortune, by the grace of Allah, we now have funds that we can use for certain additional needs that we have." The Iranian let those word sink in, knowing full well the Russian knew exactly what he meant.

"Go on, Minister," the Russian said softly, his face growing more sincere as he slowly drank his dark tea and watched the Iranian intensely. *Yes, I know what you are here for you Persian bastard, but I want to hear you say it,* he thought.

"We need more weapons General. Your country makes the best in the world for our needs, especially since we can't buy from the Americans or the West. Of course, the price needs to be right. But I think we can do some very good business for both our nations if we work together." He then took a folder from his briefcase very slowly and slid it across the table to the Russian general for him to review.

General Kursk took the folder, opened it, and didn't say a word as he viewed the list of weapons desired by the Iranian representative. He smiled to himself, although he didn't show it, as he mentally did a calculation to add up the sum total of the weapons buy the Iranians were presenting. It was a huge purchase, magnificent actually. It would ensure his family's wealth for the next generation. Of that, he was sure.

An order of this size would also have a marked effect on the Russian treasury, for money was something the Kremlin needed desperately. Russia did not export many things but they made really good armaments. Marketing those arms to needy regimes around the world was a priority for Moscow. Iran becoming a large customer would be a fantastic marketing point. Russia sold them the weapons for top dollar, as they were in high demand for those nations that did not want to buy from the Americans or the Europeans, of which there were many.

He prolonged his examination for a few more minutes just

for effect. Then he closed the folder and put it back on the table and spoke. "This can be arranged, Minister. The cost will be competitive; but, we will of course not give them away."

"As I said, General, we have plenty of money at the moment and will pay you handsomely. We want your technology. We still have this little problem of the Israelis, you understand. They have a very advanced military capability. We want to close this gap as fast as possible and actually surpass the Jews in the very near future. Our goal, as you know, is to eventually destroy the American puppets."

"We will not talk of such things publicly Minister. You only need to pay for the weapons. What you do with them is none of our business. I will have our technicians contact your government to start the acquisition process. Russia thanks you for your business and we look forward to conducting a great deal more over the coming years." The General began to stand but the Iranian stayed sitting in an expression of having another topic to discuss.

"There is one more issue I would like to raise with you General, if I may."

"Of course, Minister," said General Kursk, regaining his seat.

"We have information that your government has been developing for some time a very special type of, shall we say, capability." He let those words sink in as he watched the face of the Russian general. Then the Minister, sensing no reaction, continued speaking.

"This capability would of course be considered a weapon of mass destruction. We have heard that you can target certain genetic traits, for lack of a better way to say it, 'extreme prejudice'. Of course this would be helpful in our great contest with the Zionist state."

"I do not have any idea what you are speaking of, Minister. Of course we have had experiments in the past but we are not developing such weapons at the current time. We have signed treaties against it."

"Since when do Russians worry about treaties, General?"

The Russian's face once again became stern. "We are not developing such weapons, Minister. And, even if we were, we would not sell them to your government. You don't have the best history with, shall we say, restraint. I don't think you are to be trusted with such a powerful capability, to be honest."

The Iranians face became taut with anger. "I thought we had a partnership," he said curtly.

"Yes, but some things would necessarily be off limits, even if we had them for sale, which we do not." General Kursk responded.

"Very well. I think we have concluded our business here. We look forward to starting the process to acquire your armaments. Please have your people act without delay. Iran wants to rebuild its military capability as quickly as possible."

"You have my word, Minister." The general stood and shook the minister's hand. The cordiality had grown more frosty once the conversation turned to genocide.

The Iranian was led from the room to a waiting car, to return him to the Iranian embassy in Moscow. As he drove along the Moscow River, he enjoyed the scenery of the people out and about and the beautiful boats on the waterway. Gorky Park was alive with activity and bursting with flowers as the landscapers had been busy.

One day my country will be as beautiful as this once again. We will have this weapon. The general so much as confirmed its existence today in what he didn't say. Yes, it exists. And we will obtain it. We are patient. We have almost achieved all of our goals. All that is left is to annihilate the Jews. The minister smiled as the doors swung open to the Iranian embassy and his car was cleared through the gates.

General Kursk walked down the hall to the Russian president's office. He was in a quandary. The news of the substantial Iranian weapons buy, larger than anyone had predicted, was very good news and he was sure that the president would reward him and his family handsomely. However, the conversation at the end of the discussion still rang in his ears. *We have heard that you can target certain genetic traits for extreme prejudice.* How had this Iranian dog heard of Russia's research in this area? This was an extremely troubling development. The general was not really in the mood to pass this unfortunate news on to the president, at least not yet anyway. *No, I will have to think about this news. I will decide how to handle this in due time. For now, I will just bask in the success of the Iranian treasure coming our way.* He reached for his phone to call his new mistress. They would enjoy a nice evening together. Svetlana was nothing if not very talented. The thought of this possibility quickened his walk.

Chapter Eleven

The lumbering train slowed to a crawl with a loud groan as they approached the station in the forgotten, Siberian town. The metal-on-metal squeal of the brakes was louder that it should have been as the passenger car came to a violent halt. The large, modern facility seemed out of place with the rest of the industrial landscape. Large smokestacks in the distance belched black particles and gave away the position of one of the armament factories. It was now past sunrise and the sun was beginning to beat down on the concrete wasteland. Any type of artistry or soul seemed to be absent from the downtown area, even the trees seemed gray instead of green as they should be in the middle of summer. The only splotches of color were the shawls a few old women were wearing to cover their hair as they ventured out into the polluted air.

Connor climbed down from the top bunk in the passenger cabin, grabbed his satchel, and stretched his legs and arms to regain feeling after the excruciatingly long ride. The young girl below him, now fully decked out in Prada and Louis Vuitton, waited in line outside the cabin portal for the main door to the passenger car to open and release the riders to the outside world once again.

She turned to Connor and smiled as he joined the line. "Do you speak English?" he asked.

"Yes, a little," she responded.

"You look out of place here. You look like you belong in Moscow, not out in an industrial town in Siberia." She smiled a wider smile and Connor couldn't help but smile back. She was very attractive, with a firm, toned body.

"I'm here for work," she responded with a heavy accent.

"Well, I have to ask, what do you do for work here in this

Godforsaken place?"

"I'm a ballet dancer."

Connor's jaw dropped incredulously. "Here?" he asked.

"Well, I dance all over the world. But, when I'm not traveling, I come here to teach Vasilovich's children. How do you say in English? A governess?"

"Really? Well, I'd love to be one of his sons. Having a very attractive governess would be quite a treat!" She smiled wider with a confident air that she knew she was gorgeous. It was obviously not the first time someone had told her that. It was almost a patronizing smile. "What's your name?" he asked.

"Sofiya."

"Aaah, beautiful name," responded Connor. His compliments were genuine. The more he looked at her the more he realized how beautiful she really was.

"And what is you name?" she said in broken English.

"I'm here on business as well." Connor was hoping to find out a little about the town. At the moment, she was the only person he knew here. He was taking quite a chance and obviously stood out like a sore thumb. He needed to blend in. *I think she can help me,* he thought.

"What business?" she asked inquisitively.

Connor thought quickly. He instantly realized he should have already anticipated this question and had an answer ready. He said the first thing that popped into his mind. "I'm a journalist." He immediately regretted his answer as he noticed the concern rapidly cloud her face. Connor tried to rectify the situation. "I'm doing a story on the positive impact the defense industry is having on the Russian economy." Her face brightened somewhat.

Desperate to connect with someone for information, Connor took a chance. "Why don't we friend each other on Facebook? I'd love to follow your dancing!"

MOTHERLAND

Sofiya blossomed and pulled out her phone. Connor gave her his Facebook page and she sent a friend request. "I did it!" she said as the doors of the train started to open and the passengers began filing out. Connor's phone pinged in his pocket as the connection was made. She made her way out of the sleeper car and disappeared out into the throng of people milling about the train station. She was gone.

Connor drifted into the crowd embracing their loved ones as they left the train car. He really didn't have a plan. He was completely winging it now. *How am I going to find anyone in this godforsaken Siberian town? Much less Anatoly?* He flagged down a taxi and in broken Russia asked to be taken to the nearest gastinitsa, or hotel. Soon he was sitting in his room with no plan, no way forward, at the only hotel in town. *I need to reconnect with Sofiya.* Connor picked up his phone and opened the messaging app. *I guess the terrorists will have to get this. I have no other choice.* He typed.

Hi, It's Connor from the train. Can I meet you for a drink somewhere tonight? I need to find out about the town. You're the only one I know. I'm staying at the local hotel.

A few minutes later she responded.

Sure, I'm free tonight. There is a bar in the lobby. I'll meet you there in an hour.

Connor was waiting for her as she strolled into the somewhat empty bar about ten minutes late. The only people there were a couple of security guards having a few vodkas after the end of their shift, their AK-47s casually laid on the bar as they downed shot after shot.

113

"Thanks for meeting me," Connor said as she approached his table.

"Sure, you didn't tell me your name until your text. Hello Connor," She said with a deadly sexy accent.

"Can I buy you something to eat? Drink?"

"I'll just have tea, green." Connor waved to the bartender and ordered the tea and a glass of wine for himself. "What do you want to know?" she asked.

"Who are the power brokers here in town?" asked Connor.

"That's easy, my chief, Vasilovich. He runs the town. Nothing goes on here without him giving approval. That's the right word in English right? Approval?"

"Yes, it's the right word." Connor thought a moment, then continued speaking. "I want to meet him. Can you arrange?"

"No one just *meets* Vasilovich. Why would he want to meet you? Just some terribly dressed American?"

"Is it that bad?" Connor asked. "Sorry, it's been a rough week, believe me."

"You need a stylist. You should hire me."

"I'd love to. But some first things first. Can you arrange a meeting or not?"

"Yes, I can arrange. I'll let you know tomorrow. I have a meeting with him in the morning to discuss the children."

"That would be very helpful." They made small talk for another fifteen minutes before she rose to leave.

"Thank you. I appreciate your assistance as I know you don't have to. I will try and repay you some way if I can."

"Just get some nice clothes. That will make me happy! I'll talk to you tomorrow Connor," she said teasingly and quickly left the bar.

As she left his phone buzzed. He looked at the screen.

MOTHERLAND

We heard everything. You have one more week before you die. You had better work faster. We want to know about the weapon. Find this Anatoly and make him give you the information. Make him talk.

Connor had another glass of wine, went back to his room, and then passed out in the very comfortable bed after the long train ride.

"The weapons transfers are going as planned Mr. President," said the aid as President Chahine sifted through the morning intelligence briefing in the Oval Office. "The S-300 systems bought last year are now fully operational in multiple nuclear sites throughout the Iranian Islamic Republic and beyond. Iran has now fully paid for these purchases. Next on the list is the additional acquisition of the longer-range S-400 components from Russia. Since the S-400 is a much more powerful and deadly system for Western fighter aircraft, the transfer is a little more sensitive. However, we do believe these weapons sales will go through as well. Russia desperately needs the foreign currency and Iran really wants the capability these sophisticated systems can give them. It's a match made in heaven. Israel will have an almost impossible task now to destroy the Iranian nuclear effort. We don't believe Israel has the capability alone to defeat Iran's air defense net once the S-400 is in place. That is, without our help." The aid stopped talking for a moment to allow the words to sink in. He thought he detected the hint of a smile on the president's lips.

"Thank you William. That will be all for this morning." The president closed the briefing folder. "Leave these with me. I'll review further after a few phone calls." The intelligence community aid smartly understood the president wanted to be alone and immediately exited the Oval Office through a side door. The president sat by himself and pondered the situation.

The noose is tightening, he thought to himself. It was time again to pray.

Connor was in deep REM state when the door was kicked in. It took him a few seconds to realize someone was in his room. Not just someone, several very large men. They dragged him out of bed before he had time to react and threw him against the wall. At that point, he became wide awake.

"Who the hell are you?" he managed to get out as the punch hit him in the gut. He doubled over. As the lights came on in the room, he eventually made out four men, dressed in leather jackets and jeans. They were not the welcome party. Another punch landed in his abdomen and he fell to the floor.

"Get dressed!" they ordered in broken English. Connor slowly climbed off the floor and did as he was told. Soon they were 'escorting' him out the door and into a waiting SUV. The proprietor of the hotel behind the desk in the lobby did his best to ignore the entire episode. The vehicle sped off down the road in the middle of the dark night. Connor was sandwiched in between several very large thugs. Nobody said a word.

Eventually the SUV entered the gates of a large estate. The guard checked the occupants of the vehicle and waved them through. It was quite a long drive to the main house. However, the vehicle kept driving past the residence to some type of barn which was a few hundred yards to the rear of the compound. There were armed guards everywhere. Connor was pulled out of the vehicle and taken into the barn where his hands were tied together above a large crossbeam. His shirt was ripped off. Several of the men took turns punching him in the gut a few more times, in a way that would not leave a mark of course, at least not yet. Connor felt himself pass out. When he awoke, the barn was dark and he was alone. However, he was sure his tormentors were just outside. He could hear them laughing.

What the fuck have I got myself into now? He thought as he strained to see in the darkness. The rope that bound his wrists dug into his flesh. The weight of his body partially held up by the beam which put additional pressure on his arms. It was extremely painful. *These fuckers know what they're doing alright. I guess I'm not the first person that's enjoyed their hospitality.* He waited, for the additional pain that was sure to come. *It might be over this time.*

At some point, the lights were turned back on and someone entered the room. He was an older man, around fifty, heavy set and very mean looking. He pulled up a chair and sat down in front of Connor as he stared at him, inquisitively. Connor could see the stubble of his thick beard that was smeared with something he had been eating. He reeked of alcohol, as older, Russian men often do. He was an enforcer. He was not the brains of the outfit, whatever outfit that was.

"What is your name?" he asked in a thick Russian accent. Connor gave his Russian name given by the terrorists. The man seemed to think on this for a moment and then said, "Don't lie to me. We have found that passport. It is a forgery. Tell me your real name." Connor was quiet.

"Let me explain something to you," the man continued. "You are an American who has been found snooping around a Russian, Siberian weapons plant. You have fake documents. You're lying about your true identity. I think you are a spy. Spies can be shot on sight." He let that sink in for a moment. Connor was still quiet.

"In addition, you are out at a bar in the middle of the night with the mistress of the man who controls this entire area. A woman he has not seen in a month. Yet, she goes to the bar to see you first. Why is that? Either you are stupid and ignorant, or you are simply a truly incompetent spy. Which is it?"

Connor finally spoke. "I am neither."

"What happened to your arm?"

Connor looked at his upper forearm where the wound had torn open and blood was dripping down his chest. With all of the other pain he had not even noticed. The wound looked nasty and infected. He decided to tell the truth. He had nothing against the Russians, although he was sure they had something against him. It was probably all over now anyway. No one knew where he was, nor could anyone could help him. And, he was going to die in a few days by the Iranians whether or not the Russians killed him. "My name is Connor Murray. Yes, I am an American. Believe it or not, I am not a spy. At least, not in the normal sense. I came here because I was forced to, because in this wound on my arm there is a capsule full of poison, and if I don't give them what they want they will kill me."

"Who will kill you?"

"Some fucking Iranian terrorists, I think anyway."

"What are you looking for?"

"I am looking for Anatoly. I need to find information on the bio weapon." With that comment, the man's eyes widened. He immediately jumped up, knocking over the chair, and left the barn, slamming the door behind him. Connor was going nowhere.

The Iranian operative Ahmed had left Gaza and now was back in Tehran. His superiors were happy with the operation so far but were impatient for results. He had gone out on a limb in starting this effort on his own. The success or failure of the operation would alone determine his future, whether he lived, or died.

MOTHERLAND

His team was monitoring the whereabouts of the phone they had given the American, and therefore his current location. They were doing the best they could to garner as much as possible from the audio and other sensors on the device and from smaller tracking devices planted in the materials given to Murray. However, several hours before, there had been some unexpected commotion and noise picked up by the phone and now all the signals had gone dead. The operation may have turned into a failure. This would not be good for his future. Ahmed's thoughts now turned to how to salvage the operation. They had gained a lot of information and now knew the location of the Russian scientist who was working on the weapon. Or, at least they knew where Murray thought he was in Siberia. Soon Ahmed would have to activate the poison in Murray's arm. He could not let the Russians know that Iran had sent someone into their interior to spy on their weapons complex. Yes, he would have to kill Murray soon. However, he still held out some hope that communication could be reestablished. "A few more hours," Ahmed said aloud. "I will give my future a little more time."

The lights came on again full blaze in the barn. Connor had lost feeling in his arms but his shoulders burned with pain. *I'm sure my rotator cuffs are ripped for good,* he thought. He tried to make out the person who had walked in with several bulky bodyguards behind him. The man focused on Connor for about a minute, studying his face. He was dressed in an expensive suit along with a very expensive gold watch. He was well groomed and obviously powerful. He was a small man but a man that carried with him much authority and stature. That was obvious by the attentiveness by the guards to his every word.

"Cut him down! And then leave us!" the man ordered. The

group of bodyguards swiftly followed instructions and soon Connor was sitting in a chair across from the man, drinking a bottle of water. The fluid drained down his cracked throat. They were alone.

"Mr. Murray, my name is Andrei Vasilovich. I run this town. Nobody tells me what to do, not Moscow, not anyone. Do you understand me?"

"Yes," Connor said dryly as the fluid slowly brought him back to life. The wound on his arm had long ceases bleeding as he was seriously dehydrated. "I understand you."

"You are a very lucky man. I say this because you are lucky I found you and not the Russian intelligence services. They would like you dead you see. Shacking up with the Russian president's ex-girlfriend is not a way to ingratiate yourself to the Kremlin. Yes, I have done some research on you with some comrades in very sensitive areas of the government. However, the FSB does not even know you are here. The factories you see all around you as you drive into the city, they are all mine. I guess I am what you would call an oligarch." A thin smile creased his lips.

"What happened to your arm. Tell me the truth. I mean you no harm. You see, we have some of the same certain *friends,* in the Negev. I am a Jew. Yes, I am a Russian patriot but I am also a friend of Israel. That is between you and I you must understand. So I know who you are and what you have been up against and what you are trying to do. You can fill in the details for me later but I am here to help you. You need to trust me or you will die." Connor decided to do exactly that and told him the story of the last few weeks. He had no choice.

Vasilovich listened attentively and then finally spoke. "Well, we will fix your little problem. My scientists will see to that. Then we will talk in the morning, after you've had some rest. Do not try to escape, you will be shot immediately. That is all I have to say for now." Vasilovich got up and left the barn. Immediately the burly men came back in but with an entirely new, pleasant attitude.

Soon Connor was transported to a facility several kilometers away and whisked into a secure area of some type of laboratory. Several men met him and examined the wound. They asked questions in English which Connor answered truthfully.

"The issue with the capsule is keeping it in similar surroundings. We need to get it out immediately, as you are no longer in contact with those who put it there and they may try to activate the poison at any moment. I have seen this type of operation before, so I know what to expect. We are going to submerge your arm in a gelatinous liquid which simulates human tissue, and remove the capsule. Hopefully there will be no problems with the extraction. However, just in case, please write down any final thoughts on this paper and we will see they get delivered.

The last comment shocked Connor but he did as he was told, writing a short but moving letter to Natasha, with instructions on how to handle certain financial affairs. It was a strange thing to do, a morbid undertaking. *Natasha, my wife. I haven't had the time to think of her very much lately. I hope she is okay. If I do not make it out of this, I hope she can move on, find someone else. I miss her.*

A few moments later, Connor was entering his arm into a vat of liquid inside another one of the laboratories under the roof of the large facility. There was a divider so he could not see what was happening. He felt the anesthetic shots go in and then some tugging on the wound. It should have been the most stressful moment of his life but he remained calm. *What is meant to be is meant to be.* The procedure took all of about five minutes.

"There, it's out," said the Russian scientist in English. Connor felt a wave of relief wash over him. His optimism returned immediately. Now all he wanted to do was contact Natasha.

Chapter Twelve

Connor sat next to Sofiya in the SUV as it sped towards the local airport outside of the town with no name. She was dressed in a fashionable jacket with tight pants. Connor had to admit she looked really good. However, the only thing on his mind was getting back to Natasha. He just wanted to hear her voice on the phone, to hear she was okay. He missed her. They had been together through thick and thin over the last few years. He hadn't realized how much she meant to him until now, now that he had his life and his future back.

A private jet awaited them. A body guard was driving along with another in the front seat, guns bulging from underneath their dark jackets. Another black Mercedes SUV followed closely behind, also filled with large Russian men with weapons. This SUV darted back and forth erratically behind Connor's vehicle to ensure no other vehicle could even get close. He felt like he was in Chicago during the 1920s, riding with Al Capone. As they shot around a sharp turn in the road, Sofiya tumbled into him. They made eye contact. She looked away sheepishly and picked up her phone to make a call.

Connor was tense. He wanted to contact Natasha but all of them decided it was too risky to call from inside the Russian Federation. Now that the device was out of his body he was impatient to return to his normal life, whatever that was. At least he would see his friend Peter again soon. Vasilovich had instructed Sofiya to accompany Connor enroute to Moldova, to smooth out any problems that might arise with the Russian authorities. The oligarch had one of his men call Peter in Moldova with the number Connor provided and set up the reunion at a predetermined spot in Chisinau. The only hurdle was to clear Moldovan immigration. No one even checked Vasilovich's plane as it departed from the small Russian airstrip outside the weapons factories. *It's nice to have almost unlimited power,* thought Connor as the wheels retracted into the aircraft and they climbed high above Siberia. *The Russian authorities would never mess with Vasilovich as long as he turns out outstanding weapons and brings the Kremlin lots of hard foreign currency. That was plainly obvious.*

Connor had discussed with the oligarch the bio weapons program and his target, Anatoly, before they had left the facility enroute to the airport. Connor had rested well overnight and his arm was sewn back up professionally this time. They also gave him antibiotics for the infection that had raged over the last week. He felt better than he had since he had been so rudely forced to leave Israel and Natasha. His arm was now just very sore and the infection was wilting.

"Anatoly is gone," Vasilovich had said when Connor asked about the whereabouts of the old scientist. "He was kidnapped. It happened several years ago. I don't know where he is. So, your trip here was a waste. But not entirely, at least I got rid of that little device in your arm for you."

"Yes, thank you for that. I mean that sincerely. But, who took him? And where do you think he is?" asked Connor.

"We don't know. It was a *big* problem. Maybe it was the Islamic State, or some variant of it. They desperately want these weapons of mass destruction to use on Russia as well as the West. The fact that security was lax enough that he was exposed shook the foundations of the Kremlin. Heads definitely rolled. I'm lucky to still be here; but, as you say, I have friends in *high* places. We had FSB all over the place for months, digging into everything we do here. But they found nothing. The Russian government hushed the entire episode up. They don't want anyone to know he is gone or that they have made significant progress on the bio weapon. To have the ability to target a certain race or one individual with a bespoke virus is the ultimate assassination tool.

MOTHERLAND

"Now the weapons development continues, but without its leader. It set the effort back years. He was the driving force behind its research, even at his advanced age. He truly believed in the research and the effort, to protect the Motherland. Russia is still some time away from developing such a weapon, but not for lack of trying."

Connor sat on the private jet and stared out the window, returning to the present and pondering the events of the last week of his life as he remembered the oligarch's comments.

But what of the weapon? He was intrigued with the idea of investigating it further, for the world's sake! *Who would be after such a capability?* The Shia theocracy of Iran supported the Islamic State in Egypt, or when ISIS terror furthered their own agenda, but opposed them in Syria, where the Shia, Sunni civil war raged. Iran was also supporting Hamas in the Israeli territories, sheltering ISIS commanders in Gaza from the Egyptians wrath. *I'm sure Iran would love to get hold of this technology. That's why they did this to me. A weapon that could target a specific race or person; obviously they want to kill all the Jews. They somehow found out about the crash in Alaska. But how? They must have been following this trail for quite some time and also have friends in some very high places, American places.*

This would finally enable them to destroy Israel completely. The world cannot let that happen. Nor can it be allowed to fall into other evil hands. They got very close through me. It is my duty to stop them. I must find out where Anatoly is. I must stop this weapon from getting into the wrong hands. No one knows where I am right now. I am the perfect rogue agent if you will. And, rogue operatives can be dangerous.

Connor looked at Sofiya. She was quietly typing on her laptop, connected to the plane's WI-FI. She's definitely more than a ballet dancer or a mistress. *She's a fixer, for Vasilovich. She knows much more than she lets on. I'm sure her looks open many doors that he may not be able to.*

"What are you doing?" Connor asked after he stared at her for a while.

Sofiya looked up and noticed he was focused on her at the moment. He thought he detected a slight blush. "I'm contacting some of our clients. I communicate a great deal for Vasili. He is a very busy man and trusts me completely to do certain things."

"I'm no expert, but I noticed your accent is slightly different than most Russians I have heard. Where are you from?"

"Aaah, most astute of you Mr. Murray. I am actually Ukrainian. It gives me an edge in dealing with both sides in the conflict, war, whatever you want to call it in Donbass. Many of my people are dying there. I guess you could consider me a half-breed, Russian and Ukrainian. So I can see both sides."

"Interesting," said Connor. "Who do you think abducted Anatoly?"

This time he could see her face darken. "I don't know. It was very disturbing that this could happen under our very noses. Our friends in Israel are very worried about who now has access to this research and technology." Sofiya smiled at the look on Connor's face. "Yes, I am Jewish as well. I'm a member of the tribe, the diaspora. I am a friend of Israel, as are many Russians. Does that surprise you?"

"Nothing surprises me now after the last couple weeks." Suddenly Connor felt a wave of fatigue wash over him as his body took account of the last several days stressful occurrences and forced him to shut down for repairs. He drifted off to sleep.

The Iranian, Ahmed, was now sure the operation was dead. Of Murray's situation and whereabouts, he had no idea; he was not getting contact with any of the tracking devices they had installed. It was time to close off the loose ends. He pulled the small remote control device from his pocket and entered a detailed code to start the sequence to activate the poison he thought was still in Connor's arm. There, that's finished, he thought as the confirmation appeared on the screen. At least he won't be able to talk if he was still alive. In any event, he'll be dead soon. *We came close to the heart of the weapons project but now once again we have hit a dead end. However, at least we have confirmation it exists and that the Russians are working on such a weapon. Now we have to develop a plan to find out more. We have made much progress, but, there is much more to be done.* "It is imperative we find a way to continue this effort for my family's sake. The Mullah's can be very harsh on failure," he said aloud. The Iranian operative threw the remote control device on his desk in Tehran, sat back in his chair, and closed his eyes to think. *But how do we find out more? I must find a way!*

President Chahine sat again at his desk in the Oval Office, alone, deep in thought. The 'peace process' negotiations were going as planned. Extreme pressure was being brought to bear on the Jewish State. Even the Europeans were starting to ban Jewish goods. The Israeli economy would soon collapse under the weight of new sanctions being planned by the United Nations and the European Union. The narrative that everything was Israel's fault as the rockets rained down from Gaza was working quite well. His friends in the media did their propaganda job with panache. The U.S. would abstain and the U.N. would let the vote move forward, all the while deploring their former ally's actions. He would see to that. Israel could not last much longer.

The phone on his desk buzzed. He glanced at the red flashing light. His assistant wanted his attention. The president debated breaking his concentration. It was when he was alone and had time to think that he made progress with his plans. He felt the past weigh on his shoulders. All of the Muslims who had been killed by the Crusaders, the Europeans, the Jews. *I will avenge them.*

President Chahine picked up the phone and spoke quietly, "Yes?"

"Sir, the Iranian Supreme Leader is on the line. It is an unscheduled communication. Do you wish to take the call?"

The president thought about it, then said, "I do. Put him through."

A few seconds later he heard the line connect, an older man speak in Farsi, and the interpreter on the other end of the line began to translate the Leader's words.

"Mr. President. I wanted to thank you for *arranging* our situation with the Jewish pigs. We will continue to apply pressure in the occupied territories, with our foreign fighters, Hezbollah, and with our allies in the Assad regime. The Russians will turn a blind eye. They don't care about an American ally, even if there are many Russian citizens there. They bombed their own soldiers and civilians in the war against the Nazis when it was in their interest to do so. So, we are moving forward, everything is going according to our plans. The Russian weapons are arriving in force. Soon we will be in a position to act. Israel cannot do anything now. The Iranian Islamic Republic is too strong. We await your word, my Sultan to launch the attack! Islam will bathe in glory and we will have our revenge! Allahu Akbar!"

President Chahine hung up the phone without saying a word. He sat back and smiled. It was time again to pray. *God was truly great!*

MOTHERLAND

The Russian S-400 weapon systems were now being delivered to Iran in force. The range of this sophisticated anti-aircraft missile system had been increased to well over 400 km. The radar element could track and engage multiple targets from very low to very high altitude. The Iranian Supreme Leader was right when he bragged that Israel was now prevented from stopping the Iranian Islamic Republic from going nuclear in a very short period of time. Israel simply did not have the firepower or the technology to penetrate this integrated air defense system. The Americans had been slow about delivering the F-35s the IAF had ordered. It was on purpose of course. The Sultan could not allow this capability to be delivered to the Jewish State. He had to destroy Israel first.

The Israeli prime minister listened to the briefing from his national security staff deep in the secure bunker in Tel Aviv. It was a depressing afternoon. He had ran on a platform of security, of protecting his people. The government had purposefully not told the public the truth as to what was happening as they tried to defuse the situation. With this latest intelligence information, that would have to change. He would have to go on national TV and tell Israelis what was happening. They would have to begin preparing for war. He could not delay this action any longer.

His options were extremely limited concerning the Iranians. His choices now simply consisted of going to war immediately and hoping for the best under very bad circumstances, or allowing the Iranians to get stronger and stronger. With every missile system delivery, every Iranian pilot that was trained in Moscow, every Sukhoi that was delivered to Tehran, Iran became that much more capable. Time was not on Israel's side.

Hezbollah was preparing for another assault on northern Israel and the Golan. That was obvious from the intelligence gathered recently. Hamas was stirring up another Intifada in the territories. Scores of rockets were landing on Israeli towns every day from Gaza.

What really concerned the prime minister were reports of Iranian troop and missilbattery units deploying into now Shia controlled Iraq.

The noose was tightening. *I have to act soon.*

Chapter Thirteen

Vasilovich's jet landed at Chisinau and was directed to a secure hanger away from the public terminal. The building was old and there were carcasses of ancient Soviet era aircraft parked nearby, decaying in the hot sun. Sofiya and Connor deplaned and were rushed through immigration and customs with no problems. *It's nice to be important. I could get used to this*, Connor thought.

He was relieved. Although he had been provided with new documents and identification, and money, he still did not feel quite comfortable with his new found friends. However, at this point, he could not quibble with the situation. He had to take what he was given and make the best of it. That meant trusting Sofiya and Vasili, at least to a certain point. *They want something. Or, they would not be helping me out as they are doing. They probably want to find Anatoly as much as I do. After all, he was the brains behind their bio weapons program.*

The two of them were put in the back of another black SUV and again sped away from the airport with bodyguards in tow. *Here we go again.* They drove for thirty minutes through the gauntlet of old Soviet high rise dwellings and soon were in the center of town. There were now colorful signs interspersed with the drab architecture. However, the place really looked very similar to how it did decades before under the Soviet system. *The old Soviet cities almost all look the same,* thought Connor as they pulled up in front of a restaurant which occupied the bottom floor of a structure that was at least a hundred years old. Connor and Sofiya were led by the guards to an upstairs private dining room. The depressing, gray paint was peeling off the walls and the typical Soviet iron hand rails adorned the stairwell. There were even old signs to a long gone, communist, administrative unit that had once occupied the space above the restaurant. No one had bothered to remove them.

Upon reaching the upper floor, one of the guards opened the door to the space and then both of the bodyguards stood by the opening, guarding the entrance. Connor walked in, not sure what to expect.

"Connor!" he heard his good friend yell. Peter jumped up from one of the tables and bounded over to give him a bear hug that embarrassed him somewhat. However, he was glad to see Peter as well, and returned the embrace. "It's good to see you alive my friend!" Peter exclaimed. "Very good to know you're okay!"

"I'm glad I'm alive myself, Peter!" said Connor rather sheepishly. He hadn't thought about all the pain his loved ones and friends must have been going through. "I need to call Natasha!" Connor blurted out, his priority getting in the way of the festivities.

"Of course," Peter stammered and reached for his phone, dialed and handed the phone to Connor."

"You can go in here," one of the body guards said and pointed to another, less formal dining room off the main area. Connor took the phone and walked into the smaller room and closed the door behind him. There was no other way out.

"Hello," she answered.

"Hi Babe, it's me," Connor said softly. "I miss you!"

Connor could hear Natasha gasp on the other end of the line. "Connor! Is that you?"

"Yes, Love! It's me! I'm okay, alive, breathing. I'm okay!"

"Oh Connor…" Natasha broke down on the phone.

"Natasha, it's going to be alright."

"Enough!" demanded the bodyguard. Connor turned to see the large man holding his hand out for the phone. "Too many people are listening here. You need to end the call now!" he said in rather good English.

Connor looked at him in shock but then realized he was right.

"Natasha, I've got to go. I'll call you again very soon. I'm okay and I'll be home before you know it. I love you! Bye, my Love." He hung up the call and handed back the phone to the large man in the black suit.

Connor walked back in the larger room and locked eyes with Sofiya. "Why don't you tell me what's going on here Sofiya? I think I deserve to know." Then he turned to face Peter. "How did you get here?"

"I found out you were here but was a few days behind you. I ran into your Russian friend, Vitali. However, he met an untimely death, right in front of my eyes actually. That pretty much freaked me out. I was scared and on the run, laying low. I called you with his phone, but obviously you couldn't talk. Then somewhat later I was contacted by Sofiya. She arranged for someone to pick me up and bring me here. I did not know you would be here. I didn't know what the hell was going on with you! All I was told was that I was to find out some information about your whereabouts from a friend. That is all. So, I took a chance. I had to do something. Then you walked in the fucking door! This is all a little bit too much James fucking Bond for my taste. It seems to follow you like a black cloud my friend. So, I'd love to know what's been going on with you. And, so would our friends back in Tel Aviv."

"No one will be learning of your situation or whereabouts just yet," said a female voice as Sofiya chimed into the conversation. "Yes, we need to talk Connor," she added as she looked back at Connor and locked eyes. "No one knows the two of you are here. The Mossad may have an idea, but they do not know for sure of your whereabouts. Yes, they are our friends but we do not work for them. We work for Vasili, who works for Russia but also works for himself. The FSB does not know you are here." She let that sink in for a minute, looked around at everyone in the room, and then resumed talking.

"We need to find out where Anatoly is. We have an idea. But, we want your help." She turned again to Connor. "We have helped you when you should have been shot as a spy. You owe us. You owe Russia. Russia did nothing but help you, not harm you."

"What could you possibly want from us that you don't already have?" asked Connor.

"You are not Russian. You are American, Israeli, whatever you choose to be. You have a natural cover. You can be useful. We have an idea of where Anatoly is. However, we need someone who is not going to be suspect to help us close in on his location and bring him back to Russia."

"Why would I help Russia finish development of this terrible weapon?"

"Because we will be responsible with it. You are very aware of the alternative. The people who just did this to you cannot be allowed to access the technology. There are also many other groups who want this bio weapon. They must be stopped. We are somewhat friendly with Iran but do not trust them, nor anyone else in the Middle East. And they do not trust us. We only trust Russia. We did not know about this little stunt they were pulling to try and find out more about our research. Now we know their true intentions and agenda. Anatoly must be found and brought back to Russia. Mr. Murray, you can help save the world. You can help save the Motherland, as well as your own country. You will be compensated believe me. Think it over Connor, you as well, Peter."

Connor pondered everything for a second as the wheels turned in his head. Then a light flashed in his eyes. "Why were you in the same cabin on the train with me Sofiya?" he asked suddenly.

She smiled. "Because we knew you were coming. We wanted to make contact. We did not know your situation but we had been following you since you arrived in Provideniya. People notice when an unknown American with a Russian passport arrives out of thin air. You did not think an amateur could operate freely in the former Soviet Union, asking about weapons programs, without raising suspicion did you? We have friends *everywhere* Connor. We made you tell us what you knew so we could gauge your knowledge level of the situation. But, we already knew who you were. So, yes, I was on the train to meet you.

A Russian FSB agent here in Chisinau, Sergei, was following you, Peter as well, before he was so rudely killed by our old comrade, Vitali. You were running around town like a bull in a China shop, Peter. Someone couldn't help but notice you.

"So, you can see why we do not want the Israelis involved. The less anyone outside our team knows about this, the better. Connor, you have told your wife you are alive. That is enough for now. There will be time for more festivities. However, in the short run, you work for us. If you want to leave, you can, right now with no recriminations. However, we will not be able to help you any further. I think in your heart, you know I am right. Our scientist must be found and returned, for the good of mankind."

Connor turned and walked towards the window and looked out over the city, lost in thought. The people were busily running around trying to survive, oblivious to the danger brewing around them as the world hurtled towards destruction. He stood there for perhaps a minute, then Sofiya spoke again. "By the way, you should know, they activated the device. The poison was released safely in our laboratory. If you were not here with us, you would be dead."

Connor listened as he stared out into the nothingness of the gray city bustling beneath him. Then suddenly, he turned, walked to the bodyguard, reached out his hand and said, "Give me my phone."

The guard looked at Sofiya, she nodded in approval. Connor took the phone and began typing a message, then he hit send and threw the phone over to the chair next to Sofiya. She picked it up and read the text to the Iranian terrorist Ahmed.

I am alive and I am going to kill you.

Prime Minister Dahan had a decision to make. Israel was facing an existential threat, possibly the most dangerous one since her founding after World War II. A nuclear armed Iran could 'wipe Israel off the map' as it had threatened to do for some time. *I am not going to go down in history as the man who failed the Jewish people, not after all we have been through over the millennia.*

It was not that Israel was defenseless. The Jewish State was the first nation to become a nuclear power several decades before but Israel never admitted to that capability. She followed a strict policy of *nuclear opacity*. In other words, she kept the world guessing. Israel had an arsenal of ground-launched ballistic missiles, submarine-launched missiles, and aircraft-delivered gravity bombs. No Muslim country would be able to touch her in this regard for some time. However, the Russian air defense systems being purchased by the Islamic Republic changed the game altogether. Dahan of course knew this was the Sultan's plan all along. He prevented and delayed Israel from destroying Iran's nuclear capability long enough for them to acquire enough funds through his 'nuclear deal' to purchase a sophisticated, integrated, air-defense system from Moscow. This umbrella would not totally prevent Israel from attacking Iran with nuclear weapons. However, it could target ballistic missiles and hostile aircraft and would inject into the calculation just enough doubt as to whether a first strike, even nuclear, would be successful enough to prevent Iran from returning nuclear fire. In this sense, the Sultan had accomplished his goal. He had put together a scenario which would allow Israel to be destroyed.

Prime Minister Dahan had no doubt this was the Sultan's goal from the start, all the while slamming Israel for preventing peace by not accepting the return to the 1967 borders which would ensure her demise. The Iranian nuclear 'deal' was never about preventing Iran from obtaining nuclear weapons. The agreement's only purpose was to enable Iran to obtain such a nuclear capability while at the same time providing the resources for Iran to almost completely defend itself against Israeli attack.

The Prime Minister had been provided an update on Iranian troop movements, as well as Hezbollah and Syria, strengthened from Assad's victory in the civil war, with Russia's help of course. The Shia terrorist army now had access to Russian weapons depots inside Syrian territory. They had also acquired a large number of armored vehicles from American-backed forces as well as those captured in the fight against the Islamic State.

Dahan was also provided updated information on the ongoing process Iran was following to encircle its nuclear facilities with the Russian air defense umbrella.

He had to admit, the S-400 was good. It was scary good. It could track and attack well over one hundred targets at once at low to high altitudes. The range of the system was over 400 kilometers. It could defend Iran against high-speed, low flying, Israeli aircraft, as well as her ground and sea-launched ballistic missiles. It wasn't perfect but it was good enough. *I have to make a decision.*

The prime minister stared out across the Golan, remembering all of the other Jewish leaders since before the Egyptians who had faced the destruction of his people. After a few minutes of deep, silent thought, he picked up his phone and called an emergency meeting of his cabinet. *Decision made.*

President Chahine walked down the hall to the podium for the news conference. *How I hate doing these,* he thought to himself as he smiled confidently to his aides lining the hallway, offering him last minute tidbits of advice. His strategy was working perfectly, in spite of the delays and small setbacks Mr. Murray and his friends had caused him over the last year. *Soon, this formality will not be necessary. All I need is to fool the majority of the American people a little while longer.*

The Sultan smiled in front of the cameras and began to speak. "My fellow Americans, as you know my administration has worked tirelessly to bring peace to the Middle East. We have made some progress, as with our Iranian nuclear deal. This deal will ensure a nuclear free Middle East, prevent an arms race in the region, and ensure the security of our ally, Israel.

However, there has been one obstacle to peace that we cannot overcome. That obstacle being the State of Israel. Israel continues to illegally occupy the territories of the West Bank, portions of the Golan, and Gaza, and continues to prevent peace from thriving in the region. Today, I want to outline to the American people how they are preventing peace and pressure them to come to the table and agree to our common sense solution of returning to the 1967 borders which were approved by all humanity in the United Nations...

Chapter Fourteen

The plane's wheels touched down on the Swiss runway with a screech. Connor jerked forward in his seat as the thrust reversers were applied. The aircraft slowed violently, momentarily worrying him that they would veer off the runway into the grass. However, soon they were taxiing to another private hanger, this one much more modern and luxurious. He peered out the window of the private jet and noticed the looming, dark green mountains on both sides of the airfield, framing the smooth, glassy lake reaching its finger in to Geneva from the north. The snow-capped peaks completed the picture beautifully. They did not have time to enjoy the scenery as they were immediately passed through a bespoke immigration process and guided to a waiting vehicle.

Vasilovich had provided the three of them new documents and financial resources, all properly identified and legal. Connor, Sofiya, and Peter were the only occupants of the plane besides the pilots and one cabin crew member. Connor and Peter were promised a large sum of money to help in the operation. They both refused. They did not want to be seen as bought and paid for by the Russians. *Besides, we both have enough money. That's not the issue.* Doing the right thing is the issue. Connor wasn't even sure what he would do when he found the scientist, that is if they did find him. But he did know for sure he wanted to know what was going on, who had the weapon's program and what were their intentions. *I've got to see this one through.*

Sofiya had informed Connor and Peter, after they agreed to work with her temporarily, that Anatoly had a long-term close friend who lived in the north of France. She informed them he was elderly and his mind was not as bright as Anatoly's, who still thought as clear as an alpine lake and worked harder than most fifty year olds. The man called Irving, lived in a small, ancient castle on Lake Annecy in the French Alps, about thirty-five kilometers south of Geneva. "He most likely has been in touch with Anatoly, that is, if he is still alive and able, or allowed, to communicate at all," remarked Sofiya as they boarded the jet for the flight from Chisinau. "We're flying to Geneva," she said. "Then we will go to his location by car. The area is quite mountainous and inaccessible by plane. The train also does not suit our purposes. It is a half an hour car ride."

Once again, Connor and Sofiya, and this time Peter as well, were in a dark SUV that was speeding along the winding Swiss highway on the way to the French border. The countryside was dotted with bright, golden fields as farmers cashed in on the lucrative rapeseed crop that could be converted into vegetable oil or biodiesel fuel in the rush find alternatives to hydrocarbons. It looked like a giant jigsaw puzzle with the pieces painted either bright green or a smashingly vibrant yellow. The Swiss penchant for orderliness was on full display as even the high-speed motorways were perfectly constructed with not a speck of graffiti or trash anywhere, not even a pothole or a crack in the pavement.

Twenty minutes later they approached the border crossing which turned out to be a non-event. The guards simply waved them through, although they did have to stop and pay a small toll. Soon they were inside French territory and crossing the final miles to the village of Annecy on the lake of the same name.

As they arrived into the village, Connor immediately noticed the sparkling blue, perfectly still lake in the distance abutting one of the large, grand hotels in the town. The water was surrounded by sharp relief as the terrain jutted skywards, leaving room only for the road along the shore around the body of alpine water. The rocky cliffs were dotted with ancient castles and other exotic dwellings that literally had been there for a millennia. Annecy, nicknamed the

MOTHERLAND

'Pearl of the French Alps,' had changed hands multiple times over the centuries between the Counts of Geneva and the Counts of Savoy, and many other owners, including the Nazis.

They drove through the village, past the castle that had sheltered priests during the Catholic Reformation, past the winding canals of the French Venice, and past the colorful shops and cafes that were sprinkled throughout the pristine community. *It's like a fairy tale,* thought Connor. *I have to remember to bring Natasha here one day.* Eventually they turned left and uphill through one of the few valleys that dotted the mountainous landscape. Connor could see in the distance a small castle that was nested near a creek and surrounding pasture dotted with cows. It was complete with a moat and accompanying wall, along with towers at the corners of the fortress. "Wow, this is the real deal," Connor remarked as the closed in on the ancient structure. A guard at the gate waved them inside and soon they were walking up to the massive wooden doors that gave away the castle's age.

Another servant let them inside. They were greeted by a stone space with a soaring, curved ceiling that resembled a half circle and ended at the floor on both sides. Large chandeliers hung from the high, wooden rafters that crossed the upper area of the room. The light was dim and candles flickered along the walls to provide a perfectly medieval sense of being. In front of them was a large, elongated wooden table that looked like it could have seated the King of France back in the day. At the end of the table, seated in front of a massive, unlit fireplace, sat a very elderly man with hair white as snow. He was a very small figure, having shrunk to about half of his original size in his old age. He seemed not to notice he had visitors.

A gray haired woman, not so young herself, sat by his side. She looked about seventy. The group was led in and seated across from the two older residents of the castle and Connor waited for Sofiya to speak.

"Hello, Irving," she finally said in German. "Do you remember me? I'm a friend of Anatoly's. We met a couple years ago, here in the castle at a party."

The old man turned to look at her, seeming to have comprehended what she said. The woman to his side, probably his daughter, held his hand as he peered into Sofiya's eyes and into his memory to try and pull out the details of their last meeting. Suddenly his eyes lit up and he replied, "Yes! I remember! It is so nice to see you again my sweet girl! How is your friend Vasili?"

"He is fine and sends his regards. He would have liked to come but he is very busy," Sofiya continued in German, the man's native tongue.

"Just as well, you are much prettier to look at!" the man exclaimed, his yellow, aged teeth showing in the dim light.

"You are too kind!" Sofiya responded and reached out to hold his other hand. "Irving," she said after a short silence. "We came here to ask you something." She looked at Peter and Connor who said nothing but smiled. Turning back to Irving, she continued, "We are worried about Anatoly. No one has seen or heard from him in a long time. We were wondering if you could tell us where he is. Have you heard from him recently?"

The old man slumped back in his chair, the subject having changed from his obvious interest in Sofiya's beauty to the issue of the whereabouts of a friend.

"I don't think I will ever see Anatoly again," the man finally said after pondering the question for some time. The older woman squeezed his hand and patted rubbed his arm to comfort him. The thought of his friend obviously disturbed him.

"Why not?" asked Peter, who was fluent in German as well.

Irving looked at him and spoke, "Because he is far away now. We are both too old for that long of a trip anymore. Neither one of us have much time left. No, I don't think I will see my good friend

Anatoly again."

"Where did he go, Irving?" Sofiya asked calmly and patiently. "Where is it that is so far away?"

Irving turned to look at the older woman for approval before he spoke, she nodded her head that it was ok. "He's in Argentina."

Sofiya was shocked. "Why do you say that? Did he tell you that?"

"No, I could just tell. We used to spend time there often, cooking meat out under the stars and enjoying the rustic countryside, the dancing, beautiful women, the peace of it all."

"How could you tell?" asked Peter.

"Because I heard the cows. I heard them in the background and I knew he was there. He meant for me to hear them. And, he told me he was home. He couldn't tell me really where he was but I knew what he meant. They wouldn't let him tell me."

"Who wouldn't let him tell you?" asked Sofiya.

"I don't know. Like I said, he couldn't talk. But he called to tell me where he was and that he was okay. He also told me we would never see each other again, without saying so. My good friend." The old man broke down at this point, his emotions getting the better of him. Sofiya squeezed his hand and the older women motioned that that was enough. Irving looked up once last time and said, "He called to say goodbye."

The Sultan was meditating in the Oval Office, which was one of his favorite past times. There was a chime on his phone. "Yes?" he answered as his eyes remained closed.

"Sir, it's Johnson. We just received a message from one of our Iranian intelligence contacts. They thought they had lost Murray. In fact they thought he was dead. But they may have picked his signal up again. They hid an ultra-thin RFID tracking device in one of the pieces of currency initially given to him. They just got an unexpected hit and it came from France, near the Swiss border. We have the location. They thought the devices were all dead but I guess not. Should we proceed with our earlier plan?"

"Yes," said the president. "Now leave me alone."

"They were very close and did much research together for the Soviet Union," said Sofiya as the three of them sat outside on the piazza of a large hotel anchored on the side of the cliffs overlooking Lake Annecy. The waitress had just brought a round of drinks and they were alone, no one could hear their conversation. "I believe Irving was telling us the truth, or at least what he thought was the truth about Anatoly's whereabouts. I could see the emotion in his face. He meant what he said."

"But, why the hell would someone take him to Argentina?" asked Peter.

"That's the question," Sofiya answered. "The two of them loved to vacation there. But, there was another reason for their trips to Buenos Aires and beyond." She let that sink in to the two of them.

"Well," said Connor. "Are you going to fill us in on this little secret?"

"As you know Anatoly was connected at first to the Nazi regime and learned his craft from others in Berlin during the war as they researched new and different types of weapons of mass destruction. Anatoly was taken out of Berlin by Russian intelligence as you have been told. Many of the other scientists were secreted out of Germany by other powers, such as the Americans. They were sent to hide out of sight in South America, mainly Argentina. A few of them are still alive. Anatoly and Irving occasionally went to Argentina to collaborate with these evil minds. Russia had full knowledge of the situation and even encouraged it, although it was kept quiet with the utmost secrecy. We needed the information on what was possible for the weapons. The Americans grew tired of the old Nazis. But, not the Russians, not us. And they were quite useful, until they became too feeble. Some of them we had killed to destroy the evidence."

"Jesus!" said Peter.

"Yes, Jesus would not have approved of our working with these evil men. That is for sure." She smiled. "However, the protection of the Motherland required it in the view of the Kremlin."

"So, we just have to go to Argentina and find the remaining Nazis and we will find Anatoly and whoever is building the bio weapon?"

"Yes, something like that." She smiled again. Connor sat back in his chair and looked out over the lake down below. It was calm as a piece of glass and an incredibly beautiful sight, nestled in between the mountains towering above on each side. The deep blue against the deep green was striking.

"Here we are discussing the end of the world in this place of beauty. It doesn't seem right," he said as the sun sunk past the horizon and the day began to come to an end.

"I think that is why Irving came to live here. He was trying to escape this evil once and for all," remarked Sofiya.

Connor heard it first. It was like something from the dark recesses of his mind. A sound he was intimately familiar with but couldn't immediately place. Then he felt the vibration in the seat of his chair and he immediately knew. He was instantly taken back to flight school, sitting on the bench in the hangar, waiting on his aircraft to be released from maintenance and be ready for a ride.

The helicopters returning to the airfield. It was a distinct sound, a low rumble that was hard to misplace. He looked up, trying to spot them. The sound of a rotor system was distinct. Bell aircraft had the trademark wop wop sound that was unmistakable. The Sikorsky's were a smooth beat. This one was something else. *It must be European,* he thought. *I'm not used to the sound.*

Connor stood up in his chair. "We've got company," he said firmly. "There!" he pointed towards the valley they just left and spotted two aircraft hurtling towards them. "Sofiya!" take cover!" he screamed as he dived towards the retaining wall around the piazza. Peter was moving fast also. Sofiya was on the other side of the table and had a longer distance to cross to get to cover. Connor looked over his shoulder at her as she sprinted towards the same wall he was about to crouch behind. Connor saw a small red dot illuminate her forehead. "No!" he shouted.

It was too late. Her head jerked back as the high-speed bullet penetrated her brain. She collapsed on the stone floor. Connor looked at the helicopters now breaking the border of the hotel property. Snipers were hanging outside of the aircraft doors with very high-powered weapons. They moved their sights to him next. He had to move.

"Peter! Over the edge! It's the only chance we've got!"

"Go!" screamed Peter. "I'm right behind you!" Connor and Peter ran towards the outer guard rail of the piazza and jumped. They never looked back. Bullets ricocheted off the stone wall around them, sending chunks of rock in every direction. Seconds later, they splashed into the water many meters below.

The icy, cold, mountain water was a shock to both of them. Connor took off his shoes under water and began to swim towards the shore, not breaking the surface. His shoulders screamed in pain from the beating they had taken at Vasili's barn and the wound in his arm throbbed. Peter followed. Luckily they landed near one another and Peter was able to see him under the surface as the light from the day dimmed above. They came up briefly for air and resubmerged immediately. Soon they were near the shore and Connor noticed a natural grotto cut out of the rock along the water. He pointed to the area so Peter could see and they submerged again, surfacing only inside the eroded cutout in the rocky cliff. *At least we have some protection here,* thought Connor. *But not for long. They won't give up so easily. They are professionals, here to do a job, to kill all of us.*

Peter burst out of the surface of the water, heaving for breath. He reached onto the rocky ledge and attempted to rest. "Jesus, who the fuck are they?"

"I don't know. But we need to break up. If we are together, then we're easier to eliminate. I don't hear them anymore but they could be circling back." He looked at Peter. "Peter, I want you to go back to Israel, to my wife. Tell her what is happening. Tell her to wait for me. I will get word to you guys as soon as possible."

"You're going to Argentina?"

"You're damn right I am. I'm going to find out what is really going on. I've been put here into this mess and now I'm the one to end it, this weapon, once and for all. I can at least expose what is happening, who has it, and maybe prevent it from being used."

"Okay Connor. But I have one question. How did they find us?"

"I've been thinking the same thing. I have a few things that the terrorists gave me, money, a pouch, and such. There must be some tracking device there. I'm stupid for bringing it. It cost Sofiya her life." Connor pulled out the small pouch he still had connected around his waist and threw it into the water in the grotto.

"I still have what Vasili gave us. That will have to do for now. Contact me in a few days via our internet channel. No one knows about that. I may need you to send money or something. I have a passport. I'll make do."

"Take care my friend. I'll take care of Natasha. You take care of yourself. So how do we get out of this little predicament we are in?"

"We split up. I'm going up the shoreline under water to the north. You head south. Don't surface unless you absolutely have to. Maybe we will get lucky and they didn't bring any heat sensing equipment and we can evade them. I'm sure they have night vision though so stay underwater until you find some type of cover. It's dark enough. Good luck my friend."

"Too bad about Sofiya, I liked her."

"Yea, me too, but now we have to save ourselves. She knew she was living on the edge. In fact I think she liked it there. She died young, but lived fully. Take care of yourself Peter." Connor embraced his friend, took a deep breath, and then slipped back under water, swimming out of the grotto and up the shoreline to the left. Peter followed immediately and went the opposite direction.

Chapter Fifteen

Connor broke the surface and quickly looked around. This time, he didn't hear anything, at least not the signature sound of a helicopter beating the air into submission. He had been swimming for some time. The lake and the valley were quiet. *They've left. Maybe they thought they killed me and Peter. I hope he gets out alive. I want Natasha to know I'm alive.* He resubmerged just in case and continued swimming up the lake around twenty meters from the shoreline, coming up from time to time for air. The sun had set and the twilight was growing dim. *That's really just fine with me at this point,* Connor thought to himself as he broke the surface again and scanned the shoreline for concealment. *Damn this water is cold,* he allowed himself to feel now that his life was not in immediate danger.

As he treaded water he noticed he was next to a luxurious home that extended to the edge of the lake and was several stories high. The lights were not on inside the structure. *No one is home. This is it. It's now or never.* Connor moved quickly and silently out of the water and rapidly hid under the pylons holding up the porch that extended to the water's edge. He tried to remove as much water as possible from his clothing and then scampered up the embankment next to the foundation of the home and soon was protected in the side yard of the house, crouched beneath the wooden fence. He looked one more time around the skyline for a sign of the heliborne attackers—nothing. Connor then scanned the house for a way to get in. *I don't hear anything. Nothing. They're gone.*

He noticed on the second floor that one of the windows was open with just the screen deployed to keep out the insects. He immediately made a decision. *That's my way in,* he thought. Connor then searched quickly around the yard for something to hoist himself up to the opening above him. Soon he spotted a wrought iron bench sitting in the corner next to a sculpted bird bath and fountain, surrounded by landscaping. He quickly ran to the bench, lifted it, and carried it to the side of the house, putting one end on the ground and leaning the object against the cedar siding. He was able to quickly climb up the makeshift ladder, stepping on the ribs of the back support, and soon was noisily ripping the screen away from the window and hoisting himself inside. He worked quickly as he did not know when the residents might return. It's early evening, they could just be out for dinner for all I know.

Connor searched the house rapidly for the bedroom and soon found the master closet, complete with men's clothes. He quickly undressed and put on some dry pants, shirt, shoes, and a sport coat. It will have to do. He looked in the full length mirror in the closet. A little big but not bad. It will work until I can buy my own. Connor grabbed a hat from the closet as well and made his way back to the window in the hallway from which he entered. Soon he was back outside, cautiously walking along the road, a small distance inside the tree line along the local highway that ran around the lake. It was dark now and there was no way he would be seen by anyone on the road driving by.

He felt his pockets. Connor still had his travel documents along with the credit cards and cash that were provided to him by Vasili's team. He also had the phone Sofiya had given him. It looked waterproof. Connor pulled out the device and dialed one of the preset numbers. A man answered. A voice he did not recognize. A Russian voice.

"This is Murray," he said. "Sofiya is dead. We've been blown. I'm on my own now. Tell the man thank you and I will let him know what I find." Connor hung up the call. Memorized the number and threw the phone in the grass. No one will be able to track me now. I really am on my own and that is a good thing. And after all I've been through, I'm no longer an amateur.

Ahmed was alone. He sat in the chair in his office, filled with rage. The text had been received from the American. The entire intelligence staff of his unit knew about it. He was humiliated. Ahmed had gone out on a limb to prosecute this mission. Now, he was exposed, possibly marginalized inside the Revolutionary Guards. The damn, hunted American has become the hunter.

Somehow the operation was blown. He just didn't know how. The last time they picked up a location on Murray he was in the Russian town. What happened? How did he survive? Who helped him? Was it the Russians? They know nothing about this. Or do they?

If they are on to this operation then I have serious problems of my own. This was my op, my idea. No one wants Moscow angry at Iran. "Damn that American pig," he said aloud to no one. "I will have to kill him with my own hands."

Every time I get close to being on top in life, something happens. Why is that? Is Allah angry with me? What have I done to disappoint him? Ahmed thought back to when he was a child, when his father used to beat him, repeatedly, then sexually abuse him. Should I feel shame? Yes, I feel shame. Was it my fault? Why did Allah allow this to happen to me? I was just a child. Memories of his father climbing into bed with him and the horror that followed. Ahmed never slept well. Images of the evil man's face always followed him to bed. It is no use. I am cursed. Allah is angry with me. I should feel shame. I am the one that evil man desired. It was my fault! Forgive me, Allah!

At that point the call to prayer drifted over the Iranian evening as the sun returned to its hiding spot for the night. Ahmed tried to calm himself and left his office for the mosque. There I will find some peace, some direction, some resolve on how to kill Mr. Murray. It is in Allah's hands now.

The Sultan was on Marine One, on his way to Camp David for a relaxing weekend, when the call came through. It was his national security advisor. "Mr. President, our Agency tactical team was able to terminate Murray and two other unidentified targets with a heliborne assault into the French alpine town, Annecy, near the Swiss border. Once they were airborne enroute to his location, they were able to pick up the signal from the Iranian tracking device that was inside Murray's belongings. From then on it was a straight shot into his coordinates for the hit. A woman was terminated on the plaza of a restaurant and Murray and the other male were hit as they tried to escape over the railing into the surrounding lake. The snipers were pretty adamant about the results sir, but nothing is completely positive without an on the ground confirmation which we obviously couldn't do in this situation and with such short notice."

"Go on," said the Sultan.

"The two aircraft egressed safely back to their point of origin without detection. We believe that due to the mountainous terrain, the French, or the Swiss, radars would have not picked up the incident, or detected the helicopter's flight path. We believe there is a 95% confidence Murray was terminated. As for the other two, we do not know their identities. There is a high likelihood they were Russian nationals as our Iranian friends have confirmed Murray's location in Siberia before they had lost contact temporarily.

"You think the FSB was involved with getting Murray to France? And what were they doing there?"

"That is a good question sir, and one we don't have the answer to at the moment. We are working on that. The location where Murray was confirmed in Siberia was near the Russian weapons plant that housed a Russian scientist Anatoly Ivanov, which Iranian intelligence says Murray informed them was connected to the bio weapon development. That is all we know at the moment. We obviously don't have a lot of resources in that area. We are checking signals intelligence for any connections or intercepts we can validate for this issue.

"Inform me immediately if there are any developments in this situation. Highest priority please. I want confirmation Murray is dead and I want to know who was involved and what the Russians know. We need to wrap up the loose ends here. And get from the Iranians everything they learned from their little 'mission.' We need to know the status of this weapons development and who has the technology. Our capability in the area is decades behind as we stopped research in this area some time ago per our treaty obligations."

"Yes, Mr. President. We will do as you direct. I will update you when we have more."

The Sultan terminated the call and slammed down the phone. I don't like being outmaneuvered. Murray may be dead but if he's alive he knows something I don't know. I need to know this man is dead. He's been a pain in my ass. I can't have him screwing up my plans again. The caliphate for the next thousand years is just too important. Nothing will stand in my way of its creation.

The Sultan picked up the phone again and rang one of his assistants in the White House on a secure line. "I want an update on the Iranian nuclear plans immediately upon landing at Camp David," he ordered.

"Yes, Mr. President. We will arrange."

The Sultan hung up the phone again and looked out over the Virginia countryside as the Sikorsky aircraft smoothly carried him away from the District. No, I will not fail this time to destroy the Jewish State.

Peter sat in the back of the train heading to Tel Aviv from Ben Gurion airport. The man seated next to him was an IDF soldier, in uniform. Ever since arriving in Israel Peter had been fascinated with the country's comfort with weapons of all kinds. The soldier seated to his left had his M-16 with attached grenade launcher across his lap. The barrel pointed absentmindedly at anyone that walked by. You wouldn't see that in America, he thought. Peter thought about taking a picture. Here is my friend and his grenade launcher. Peter chuckled to himself. Several rows up were a half dozen female IDF soldiers, weapons also nonchalantly laid across their legs. He studied each one of them. Each were young and very beautiful. Israel's army of supermodels. Fascinating.

He thought back over the events of the last couple days.

Upon separating from Connor, he had swam towards the city of Annecy from the location of the grotto, occasionally stopping to surface and survey his surroundings. Once the sun had completely dropped below the horizon and night fell, he had crawled out of the lake and lay in the grass in the middle of a park to think and get his bearings. There was no one around; the lake was deathly quiet. He thought about calling Connor on his cell but decided against it. I will do as my friend requested and go back to make sure his wife is okay. He is once again on his own.

Eventually Peter walked into town and secured a room in one of the inns to seclude himself and make a plan. He pretended to be drunk after a night on the town and played the ugly American who fell into one of the canals. The proprietor of the inn shrugged him off in the rudest French way possible. Peter was pleased at his acting job.

The next morning, having dried and ironed his clothes, Peter caught a taxi, then a train to Paris, Charles de Gaulle airport. He did not risk crossing the Swiss border and the shorter distance to Geneva. He had decided he'd taken enough risks for a while.

The flight to Tel Aviv was uneventful and rather short. Peter caught up on his sleep inflight as much as possible and spent the rest of the time deciding what his actions would be once he was debriefed by the Mossad.

Upon exiting the train from Ben Gurion Airport in the center of Tel Aviv, he was immediately escorted by Israeli intelligence into a waiting car for the short drive to the Mossad headquarters.

Ahmed walked into the crowded coffee house in Tehran. The hookah pipes created a smokey glaze over the whole establishment, almost like a camouflage blanket hanging over each table. That was fine with him. He did not really want to be noticed. A male waiter took his order and he asked for an espresso. *I need to think.* After the coffee was delivered, Ahmed sat back in his chair and observed. No one was watching him; that was a good thing. He was sure he had not been followed on his route here. In addition, the noise from the men chattering and smoking was rather loud. That was good as well. He did not want any intelligence devices listening in on his imminent telephone conversation. *This is the perfection location for the conversation to come. I can completely disappear in this place. God is great!*

Ahmed had decided to make a move. He had to recover from the failure of the operation and he wanted desperately to kill his nemesis, Connor Murray. Ahmed was not one to be insulted, much less threatened. He would show the American dog who was boss. *And I will enjoy killing him with my bare hands. That is, after I play with him a little bit. Yes, I will show him how we treat traitors in an Islamic prison. He will be my bitch for a few hours. Just like I was*

155

for my father. Then I will kill him.

Once he was very confident he was secure in his location, Ahmed took out his phone and dialed a number. He was taking a great risk. Iran's intelligence contact within the Mossad was delicately placed and deeply undercover. His superiors would string him up if they knew what he was doing. Ahmed did it anyway. The consequences of failure were too great. At the least, his career would be ended. At worst, well, he did not want to think about that.

The phone rang and the call was answered on the other end. "Al-o?"

"Amir. It is me, Ahmed. I need to talk. Can you now?"

"Call me back in ten minutes." The call was ended abruptly. Ahmed waiting impatiently and ordered a hookah pipe to calm his nerves. The waiter brought the bong-like device and poured in the hot coals on the tray near the top to heat the tobacco and create the smoke. Ahmed drew on the hose pipe and the smoke was drawn through the water and into his mouth. He relaxed somewhat and looked at his watch. Two more minutes.

Suddenly his phone rang. "This is Ahmed," he responded.

"Why are you calling me like this?" Amir asked. "It is totally out of protocol!"

"Yes, I realize that. It is a, well, rather delicate situation and requires extreme measures."

"Go on, you have two minutes."

"The American, Connor Murray. I want to know if he is confirmed alive and where he is. I want to, I mean I need to, kill him, as soon as possible. When you find out the information, text me and I will call you."

"I will do as you ask. Give me twenty-four hours." The line went dead. Ahmed leaned back in his chair and smiled. Soon Mr. Murray, soon! If it is Allah's will.

Chapter Sixteen

Connor sat outside at a small cafe in Buenos Aires. The air was filled with magic even at this late in the evening. He could smell the sea wafting in from the coast as the festivities surrounding him raged as people danced all around him under the decorations and lights. The city was magical and reminded him of Barcelona with the architecture full of art, style, and history. The evening was just getting started as the clock approached midnight. But he was not here for a good time, even though he was tempted. He was here to find Anatoly. He had to remind himself of that as the gorgeous women danced the flamenco near his table in the open street.

The trip to Argentina had been rather easy. Connor had also taken the train to Paris, as had Peter the evening before, and bought a direct flight to the Argentine capital. From there, a taxi brought him into the city to an area near the sea he had visited long before during Connor's military days in the Air Force. The area near the water looked almost exactly the same although it had been over a decade since he had walked these streets.

Connor' roommate at the Air Force Academy had been an exchange student from the Argentine Air Force. He and Fabian had been like brothers and talked constantly over the years. Connor had visited the city with him ten years before during his Wall Street career and enjoyed the time of his life. This time however, he wasn't so carefree. *Those were the days. The only thing I had to worry about a decade ago were the markets. No one was trying to kill me and destroy an entire race of people.*

He had contacted Fabian earlier in the day and asked him to meet him here. Fabian was now a high ranking officer in the Argentine military and once was a hell of an A-4 pilot, although now he was mostly relegated to command duties and rarely was able to get in the cockpit. When he did fly, he was no longer proficient, so he flew with an instructor in a two seat aircraft, though he still loved being at the controls of a fighter jet.

Fabian's beloved Air Force had been in decline for years and now was only a shadow of its former self. Decades of mismanagement by a corrupt government had seen to that, with funds meant for acquisition and maintenance routinely stolen and spirited off to some far off island in the Caribbean, never to be seen again by the Argentine people. However, Fabian did the best he could with the resources he had and was a true patriot to his country, if not so much to the current government. Connor respected that.

Connor's phone rang.

"Connor, my dear friend, how are you? Are you really here in Argentina?" his friend asked on the phone. Connor had secured a cheap disposable phone once he had entered the South American country. No one knew the number to track him.

"I'm here my man, down by the sea at our old haunt. Come on down to meet me. But do me a favor, be discreet. I'm not here to play this time. I need your help. And don't tell anyone I'm here please. This is between me and you my old friend."

"Hmmm...sounds serious. I'll be there in an hour. How do you Americans say it? Hang tight. Ciao!" Fabian hung up.

Ahmed dialed the phone number again of the Iranian intelligence service's deeply hidden mole inside the Israeli Mossad. It was twenty-four hours later. This time Ahmed was in a crowded market, where no one could overhear the conversation. He kept walking through the noisy food bazaar, stopping from time to time to pretend he was checking the vegetables and seafood and kept an

MOTHERLAND

eye out for anyone that looked suspicious or who may be surveilling him.

Amir answered the phone also at a secure location in Tel Aviv. He was nervous.

"You do not know what you have asked of me my friend! This has been really dangerous. My cover is on the line here. I do not want to be blown. However, I have the information you requested. I cannot do any more on this issue. You will have to make do with this information.

"Murray is alive and escaped from an attempted hit in France. His Russian partner was killed. It was a heliborne raid. The Israelis are trying to find out who was behind it. They suspect the Americans. They are very suspicious of them. They do not trust Chahine. They are also aware of our weapons deployments and are extremely concerned. I am worried about their response. The deployments are not being taken lightly and I hear talk of a substantial Israeli pushback. You should pass that on to your superiors.

"Here is the info you requested. Murray, as I said, made it out of France alive. All I know is that he is on his way to Argentina. Supposedly, this scientist you are looking for may be there. Murray is trying to find him and find who has the bio weapon technology and who is developing it. That is all I have. Do not call me again. I will not answer. This number will no longer be valid. I have done enough. I am going to deep cover. Tell our superiors I will surface in a year. Goodbye." Amir hung up the phone.

Ahmed put the phone back in his jacket pocket. He smiled absentmindedly then wiped it off his face. He could show no emotion. *So now I know where the dog is going, to Argentina. We have assets there. I will find him and I will kill him slowly. And the best thing of all, he will lead me to the scientist and to the bio weapon. It is perfect. My career will be saved. Even more than that, I will be a hero of the Islamic Republic.*

Ahmed picked up his phone again and dialed another number. He spoke firmly to the person that answered, "Go through Murray's file once again. Find a connection to Argentina. It's there somewhere. He's on his way there. I want to know why and who he is seeing. I want this information before you leave the building today. I am on my way to the airport. Put me on the next flight to Buenos Aires."

"Why all the secrecy, Connor? What have you gotten yourself into my friend?" asked Fabian once the waiter dropped off a glass of Argentine Pinot Noir.

"What do you know about Nazis in Argentina?" Connor asked bluntly.

"Nazis? Jesus, yes, you have gotten yourself into something that stinks haven't you?"

"Yes, it is serious all right. Really, what do you know?"

"Me, I don't know much of anything about that subject. However, I have friends that would know. But you've got to give me more. What the hell is going on? This is scary stuff. The kind of stuff that can get you killed. These aren't nice people Connor. But you know that don't you?"

"Yes, I know that. But I've got to take the chance. Can you keep a secret?"

"Between us? Sure. I still haven't told anyone about that eighteen year old girl and that weekend at your Dad's condo. And that was thirty years ago. So, yes, I think I can keep a secret." Fabian smiled a wide smile but then saw that Connor was in no mood to laugh about their past glory days.

Connor told Fabian what had led to him coming to Argentina. He left out a few details but enough so that his friend could get a clear picture of what was going on. When he finished, Fabian let out a long whistle.

"Man, you've really stepped in it this time. But what are friends for? I'll do some asking around and get you a way forward. However, I don't want my family mixed up in this do you understand? My involvement in your little adventure stays between you and me. Capiche?"

"Agreed, my friend. Thank you for your help. Now, tell me about that beautiful wife of yours. How is she?"

Peter sat in a secure room in Tel Aviv, surrounded by Mossad superiors as he recounted his story of what happened with Connor in Russia, Moldova, and France. "He's on his own now. He's on his way to Argentina."

"What does he hope to accomplish?" one of the men asked.

"He wants to find out who is behind this bio weapon. He wants to bring this information to the light of day, expose them, if you will. He believes this weapon is so dangerous that the world has to be aware of its existence. And he's determined."

"Does he think it is the Russian? The Iranians? The Islamic State?"

"I don't think he has any idea. But I know he wants to find out."

"How is one man going to do this? He is on his own you know. We cannot help him in this endeavor. It's not in our national interest to be upsetting the Argentines."

"I don't think he is expecting help. He said he is on his own. I think he has learned a lot over the last few years and feels he can take care of himself."

Peter then looked at Natasha who was sitting in a chair in the corner away from the table. She appeared deeply distraught, like she hadn't slept in weeks, which she probably hadn't.

"Natasha, he is worried about you. He asked me to come look after you until he returns. I agreed to do so."

"Thank you, Peter," she responded softly.

The senior man in the room, who had yet to speak, then intervened in the conversation. "Yes, we have been in contact with Vasili and Sofiya over the years. They were helpful. They were risking their lives helping us but were completely aware of that fact. It is unfortunate she was killed. We need to find another way to connect with Vasili and stay on top of this situation. I'm more interested in who had her killed and who tried to kill you and Connor. That is what I want to know. So find out!" he said the rest of the men in the room. He stood up, and walked out. The meeting was over.

The Sultan leaned back in his Oval Office chair and gave his orders. The Iranian-backed, Shia militia, Hezbollah, was to begin to put pressure on Israel from the north in Lebanon. They had been resupplied with thousands of medium and long-range rockets that possessed increased accuracy and were very deadly to Israeli cities, airfields, and military installations. The Israeli Iron Dome could destroy many of them, but not all of them. Some would get through. In addition, Hezbollah was in possession of U.S. shoulder-launched ManPADs or man portable air defense weapons, heat-seeking, shoulder fired missiles, to threaten Israeli aircraft. These weapons had been smuggled out of the disastrous U.S. Libyan excursion and also from Syrian Sunni militias who had turned their weapons over to opposing forces after being trained by the Americans for billions of dollars. Anti-tank missiles were in abundant supply as well.

MOTHERLAND

Hezbollah now comprised a potent force against Israel's north flank. The conflict would be bloody, long, and deadly. Israel would most likely have to push into Lebanon to eradicate the threat as they had done before, tying up resources and energy. The previous conflict had been fought to a draw. Hezbollah was itching for a rematch.

In the territories of the West Bank and Gaza Strip, Hamas was to ramp up attacks on Israeli Defense Forces and civilian targets as much as possible. New access tunnels had been dug along the Gaza border and raids against Israeli settlements were to commence in earnest. There was no way Israel could find and destroy them all in time. The technology simply didn't exist. In addition, rocket fire was to explode against Israeli towns along the border and even further into the country as far north as Tel Aviv. Again, the Iron Dome would be effective but not a complete security umbrella. The goal was to empty the Iron Dome of missiles. The Chahine administration had quietly decided to stop the resupply of rockets to the system from American factories. Hamas had also been sheltering Islamic State leaders in the territories. Attacks by ISIS from Syria near the Golan, and from Egypt, would commence as well against soft targets in Israel, such as settlements and transportation systems like buses and trains.

The third Intifada, or uprising, would start as well. Terror attacks against Israeli citizens would commence throughout the country from long-planted sleeper cells bent on terrorizing the population. Stabbings, hit and runs by vehicles, shootings, hammers, whatever it took for the Palestinian terrorists to inflict horror on the Israeli population, would be used. Violence would explode against Jewish citizens from every angle, from every corner of the country. The Israeli Defense Force would be overwhelmed.

At the same time, Iranian forces would start to advance across the Fertile Crescent of Iraq now that the Shia elements in the Iraqi government had taken control of the former Sunni territory. The mobile S-400 missile systems would advance with them. In a couple months' time, Iranian forces would be mobilized across Syria and Iraq, threatening Israel from the northeast.

The United Nations and their useful idiots in the European Union would also be pressuring Israel to return to the 1967 borders, an indefensible position. Economic blackmail would continue to be used against Israeli companies. The Sultan would push the American public to follow suit. The narrative that Israel was the enemy would continue to be pushed by an oh-so-willing corrupt media.

The overall goal of the Sultan's plan was to fight a war of attrition on all fronts with Israel and slowly strangle her as America refused to re-arm the Jewish State as the United States had done so many times before in previous Israeli-Arab conflicts. The coup-de-grace would be Iranian nuclear weapons which would threaten the Holy Land. Iran had made great progress developing ballistic missile technology and miniaturizing the warheads to arm them with nuclear weapons. Israel had its own arsenal, but would be hard pressed to deliver against Iranian targets with the Russian integrated air defense system in place, targeting aircraft-dropped gravity bombs and ballistic missile delivery systems. In addition, Iran had dispersed its critical, nuclear infrastructure across large amounts of territory and hardened the sites significantly. Some Israeli nukes would get through but not enough to destroy the Islamic Republic. Israel, tiny as she was, did not have the luxury to disperse in that way.

This was the plan the Sultan ordered from the Oval Office to his minions in the Islamic world. Yes, soon, the Jewish State would cease to exist and the caliphate would resume its rightful place across the Arab and Islamic territory of Sultans before him. *I will rule with an iron fist.* It was only a matter of time.

Chapter Seventeen

Ahmed's phone rang as he exited security at the airport in Tehran on the way to Argentina. He continued walking down the ramp into the main gate area where it was less crowded before he responded. "Yes?" he answered.

"Murray had a roommate at the U.S. Air Force Academy where he started his training in the military. He was what they call an exchange student, meaning he was from another country. The country was Argentina. His name is Fabian Ramos. Commodore Ramos is now one of their brigade commanders although many of his aircraft are grounded due to maintenance and support issues. I will text you his address. He lives in Buenos Aires with his family but commutes to the airfields in the interior of the country regularly. That is all I have."

"Thank you. You have done well. Keep this request to yourself and it will be worth your time soon." Ahmed hung up the phone with a smile on his face. He checked in at the gate and soon boarded the plane.

Prime Minister Dahan sat at his desk, pouring over intelligence data of Iranian and Hezbollah troop movements. The deployments were aggressive. The logistical support being assembled was threatening. It was always the logistical issues which foretold of a war. If an analyst was smart, they could spot the preparations long before the actual conflict began. *The Iranians are moving to attack. It's as clear as the light of day. I can no longer count on the Americans. We are alone. We cannot survive alone in this sea of wolves forever. We* need a partner. *Even a partner with whom we don't agree, or with their government or their behavior. In the end, we still need a partner to survive the storm that is coming.*

The prime minister sat back in his chair and thought further. China appeared to be out of the question. They had shown no interest in Israel and were not in a position frankly to help if they had.

Dahan had been to Moscow several times already since the Russians had become involved in the Syrian civil war. Russia was now Iran and Shia Islam's ally in the Middle East, but mostly because of their recent buying power, courtesy of the billions sent to Iran by the United States. It was a marriage of convenience but Dahan sensed there was not a lot of trust between the two. *Perhaps there is an opening. Perhaps if he allied with Moscow, used them as a protector. But they would not protect us for free. They will want something. Something very dear to us, like our self-determination.*

But we are a democracy. We value the rule of law. We value freedom. Arabs here are more free than anywhere in the Middle East. If we cease to be free, we cease to exist. Dahan continued to mull over the satellite photos of Iranian missile systems once again. *Perhaps we need to make a deal in any case. Perhaps I should fly to Moscow once again. America is no longer in our corner. We need someone. Russia is the only answer.*

Dahan called his aide to make the arrangements for a trip as soon as possible to meet with the Russian president.

Vasilovich received the news of Sofia's death much harder than he thought he would. However, finding another *devochka* (girl) in the Russian Federation would not be difficult. Beautiful women were a dime a dozen. Yet, finding one of, shall we say, her talents, would be hard indeed. She had touched him in a certain way and he did not think that was possible. However her death would serve a purpose. News of the incident had reached the Kremlin and it was very easy to blame the connection to the American Murray on Sofiya. Vasili made up a good story. *She was Ukrainian anyway, not really one of us,* he thought as he boarded his private jet on his way back to Siberia, back to where he felt comfortable, away from all the stress and pageantry of Moscow.

The Kremlin had been very interested in his entire story, especially in light of the disappearance of Anatoly some years before. This did not paint Vasilovich in a kind light and he knew it. He had to get back in the good graces of the Kremlin's leaders. Therefore, he blamed it on the Iranians as well. It was their plot, through espionage, to find out more from Russia about the progress of the bio weapon and who controlled the technology. Perhaps they were the ones who kidnapped Anatoly, he told the Kremlin. All Vasili was doing was making good weapons for Russia and lots of them. He was a good, patriotic Russian. They did not question his Jewishness or ask about his relations with the Jewish State. *All the better,* he thought.

His crew was buttoning up the jet for the return trip when he heard the noise outside. Looking out the window, several large military vehicles were speeding towards his aircraft. One stopped in front to prevent the plane from moving. Large numbers of soldiers and FSB officers jumped out of the trucks. They surrounded the plane.

"Vasilovich. Come out with your hands up! You are under arrest!" they shouted in Russian through a bullhorn.

His heart sank. He briefly thought of his family back east he would never see again. "I guess I counted my blessings too soon," he said aloud. "I wanted to get back to Siberia but I think I will be going a different way from whence I came." He moved towards the door and motioned for his assistant to open it. He said goodbye to his crew for the last time and walked down the stairs. The security agents threw him to the ground, handcuffed him, and pushed him to back of one of the vehicles. It soon sped away.

Connor met Fabian the next evening, this time at a cigar bar further into the center of the city, away from the shoreline. It was a very busy place and they chose a quiet table outside, away from most of the customers and the thick smoke which penetrated the clothing of anyone inside the establishment. The black night of the Buenos Aires sky was filled with stars. They talked small talk for a bit, reminiscing old times back in their college days in Colorado.

Slowly the conversation moved to more pressing matters like the decline of the Argentine Air Force. Fabian was disturbed by the direction his government had taken. The socialists had corrupted everything, including the military. It was not a pretty picture. Argentina really had no combat capability any more to speak of. The military was a rusting hulk of corruption. Aircraft didn't fly. Tanks didn't run. Officers didn't do their duty. At least most of them. "I still try to do what I learned at the Academy, Connor, but it is difficult when everyone is just out for themselves. We have been corrupted."

"I'm afraid you're not the only one my friend. We in the United States are moving down that path as well, very quickly I might add."

"I'm sorry to hear that. Your country was once one the world looked up to. I pray that it will be one day again."

"I pray for the same thing. We have serious problems. I'm not sure they can be overcome. The socialist cancer is spreading fast. The young people know nothing. The Marxists destroyed our education system, once the finest in the world. They did it over 30 years while no one was looking."

Fabian sat quiet for a minute and took a long drag on the

cigar, the smoke curling out from his mouth slowly and disappearing into the dark, Argentine night. Finally he spoke. "Connor, I've asked around. I know where most of the old Nazis live. I have a few contacts. We may be able to find what you are looking for. However, I warn you. It will be dangerous. As I mentioned, these are not nice people. They have their own security force. Our government has left them alone for decades. They live amongst themselves, preserving their culture, their way of life, their beliefs. No one goes there without being invited. You can peep around the edges of course in the nearby tourist destinations, but no one goes into the interior, where they live without fear of the authorities. It has been this way for a long time. All the great powers have known about them. However, they have left them alone for various reasons. Mainly they want information. Your country is not immune to this. They have all visited them from time to time. I fear the person you are looking for is there, living amongst them. Probably not allowed to leave for some reason. Or maybe he doesn't want to, I don't know. Anyway, that is what we are up against. If you want, I can make some inquiries, and we can try to get access into their secret lifestyle. But, it will not be easy and it will be dangerous."

"What do you mean we? I'm doing this alone. All you have to do is point me in the right direction."

"No Connor, you cannot do this alone. You will be killed and I would like to meet this gorgeous wife you talk about some day in the future, with you along with her. I'd like the four of us, my wife included, to become good friends. I miss you and I want you both to have the life you deserve. No, my friend. I will help you. Otherwise, you will die."

"Don't lie to me Vasili, tell me the truth," the man in the dark suit ordered him. Vasili tried to look up but could barely see, his eyes were almost swollen shut. He caught a glimpse of the man and tried to say something but his mouth wouldn't work. He tried harder but his broken jaw would barely let him speak.

"I've told you everything I know," he whispered softly. His head slumped down again and he drifted in and out of consciousness. Blood drained from his mouth and nose and out of the lacerations to his scalp. His eyes were a congealing mass of bodily fluids.

This was the beginning of the process, the arrest, the interrogation. The Russians were very good at it, very good at instilling fear and getting a victim to talk. They had learned from the masters, the Soviets. Solzhenitsyn had written about it in *The Gulag Archipelago*, "*At what point, then, should one resist? When one's belt is taken away? When one is ordered to face into a corner? When one crosses the threshold of one's home? An arrest consists of a series of incidental irrelevancies, of a multitude of things that do not matter, and there seems no point in arguing about one of them individually...and yet all these incidental irrelevancies taken together implacably constitute the arrest.*"

The beating had been merciless. It had started in the back of the military truck, in the covered compartment, and hadn't let up since. He was near death. Along with the psychological torture, it was extremely effective in removing all hope from the victim while extracting critical information.

He had told them about Murray, about Sofiya, about his dealings with Israel, he had told them everything. There was nothing left, nothing left except to die. He was no longer afraid. He just wanted it to end.

They knew now that he had liaised with the Israelis. They knew now that he had not reported Murray's little adventure to the authorities. They knew he had helped Murray escape, a man who was spying on Russia. That is not a transgression that is ever forgiven. They even knew that Murray was now in Argentina and that Anatoly was likely there as well. That was all the information that Vasili had to give. The man interrogating him in the crisp suit seemed to know that as well.

"We are going to let you die, Vasili, but you have to make sure you have told us everything. Are you sure there is nothing else?"

"No, he said quietly, there is nothing."

"Very well then." The man picked up a pistol off of a nearby table and shot Vasili twice in the head.

President Chahine shook with rage as he sat in the briefing room at Camp David. *So, Murray was still alive.* His staff had just confirmed this little tidbit of information. *At least, they think he is still alive.*

NSA had picked up signal intelligence of Vasilovich, the Jewish, Russian oligarch in charge of some of their very important weapons factories, communicating with some of his team several days before. They had mentioned they believed Murray was on his way to Argentina.

Murray is still alive and on to something. I need to know what that something is. "Why is he going there?" the Sultan asked his staff.

"We are not sure Sir. It seems he is looking for something, possibly the scientist that he mentioned to the Iranian intelligence operatives before they lost control of the situation. We are attempting to find out. He has a contact in Buenos Aires, an old Academy colleague. We are monitoring this person of interest to see if something develops. We don't know the name Murray is traveling under but we have facial recognition capability in action at the airports and elsewhere. As soon as we hear something, we will notify the White House staff," said the CIA representative.

"He's going to look for the scientist. I'm sure of it. We need to be one step ahead of him. Put the CIA station in Buenos Aires on it, top priority."

"Yes, Mr. President."

"I don't want him picked up just yet. Let's see what he can find for us. It may be interesting."

"My thoughts exactly, Sir. We will let you know immediately if we find out anything interesting."

"I couldn't give a rat's ass if it's interesting to you or not. If you get anything at all, I want to know about it!" The meeting adjourned.

Chapter Eighteen

General Kursk entered the conference room at the Kremlin and shook the Iranian diplomat's hand but his face gave away his displeasure. "Minister Javadi, how nice to see you." His lips were drawn into a tight, thin line.

"And you as well General Kursk. Moscow is so pleasant this time of year, don't you think?" The Iranian noticed the coldness of the introduction.

"Why don't we cut through the pleasantries Minister, I am not in the mood."

"As you wish, General Kursk."

"I understand you wish to purchase more weapons?"

"You understand correct. The Americans have been most generous and we have more money than we know what to do with, so naturally weapons are on our shopping list. Your weapons, General. Your quality is hard to beat, especially since we neither could, nor would, buy from the Americans." The Iranian let that insult sink in for a few seconds before he resumed speaking. *Yes, let this bastard think his toys are second rate.* He would not let this barbarian Russian get the best of him today. He was not in the mood to play around either.

"I'm not sure the store is still open, Minister."

Now, instantly, Javadi was worried. He tried to remain calm but the tension in his face gave away his discomfort. The Russian saw this and smiled a sly smile. "It has been brought to our attention that there was an operation conducted by your intelligence services against one of our weapons labs in Siberia. Do you know anything about this little incident, General?"

The Iranian officer was taken aback. *No, I do not know about this. But I should. Or is this goat just playing with me? What could be the point of this?* "I'm sorry, I am not familiar with what you are talking about," Javadi said rather sheepishly, his bravado suddenly long gone. "But now that you have informed me of your concerns, I will of course research the matter and provide an answer to your question."

"I will pretend for a few minutes that you indeed do not know what I am talking about. I will humor you. A few days ago, an American spy, a man we have been after for several years, who is now living in and working for Israel, made an attempt at infiltrating one of our research sites in Siberia. We were informed by an unnamed individual, who was in no position to lie to us, that the American was sent by your country, under, shall we say, duress? He failed to gain any knowledge that was material but just the fact that you are operating on Russian soil without our knowledge, while we help you to rearm, is frankly very troubling."

"I have no knowledge of such an operation, General. That is not my area of expertise. I am not an intelligence officer. I am a diplomat. However, Iran values the relationship we have with the Russian Federation. Sometimes, as you may know, certain elements within a government can operate outside the norms of civilized behavior. If what you say is true, and I have no reason to believe you would fabricate such a tale, I am sure that is what has happened in this circumstance. I assure you that we will deal with this rogue element and report back to you in due time with the results of our investigation and the actions taken. Will that suffice?"

"Yes, Minister Javadi. That will suffice. Shall we table discussions about any weapons purchase until this little matter is taken care of?"

"Yes, fine. I will contact you in a few days to set up another meeting. Good day, General." The Iranian left the conference room, shaken. He did not dare call anyone at the embassy on an unsecured

MOTHERLAND

line from the limousine. He knew too well the Russian penchant for signals intelligence and their prowess in capturing just about everything in Moscow that floated on the airwaves. That meant he had to sit in the back of the vehicle for thirty minutes during the drive back to the Iranian facility in Moscow before he could scream at the intelligence officer at the embassy. *These idiots, they have jeopardized our weapons modernization program. I will have them shot myself!* He no longer noticed the warm, bright Moscow day as the children frolicked in the parks and along the Moscow River as was his usual past time. Minister Javadi was too occupied for that on this troubling day.

    The Prime Minister of Israel arrived at the Kremlin as the dark sedan drove across the bridge and through the gates of the ancient fortress. The red brick walls built in the 15th century by Italian renaissance architect Petrus Antonius Solarius, engulfed the car like a giant whale as the vehicle passed through the tunnel that led inside. Red Square with St. Basil's Basilica loomed opposite the entrance that lead to the bowels of the Russian government. Many believe that Red Square was named during the Soviet days and refers to communism, but the truth is, the square and the Kremlin's red wall were named and built centuries before by the tsars of generations past. Initially a fort on the Moscow river (kremlin is Russian for citadel), the grand walls now enclosed the secrets of the new Russian empire now blooming like a perennial flower.

    The prime minister once again marveled at the cathedrals and other historic sites inside the Kremlin's walls, with artifacts dating back to Ivan the Terrible and beyond. The infamous tsar was buried next to his son, the son he killed with his own hands. After the death of his young, nubile wife, Ivan went completely insane, hence the moniker, the Terrible.

The golden domes of the Orthodox Church decorated the horizon. He'd been here before to meet the Russian president but the prime minister always respected history, no matter where it was located and preserved.

The car stopped in front of the president's official residence and he was escorted into the building and to an ornate conference room. The double-headed golden eagles of the Russian throne dominated the walls. The president showed up promptly a few minutes later. The immediate response was a show of respect to Israel and the Russian hope of pulling the Jewish State further into its orbit.

After the pleasantries, the real conversation started.

"Mr. Prime Minister, I am glad you came for another visit, but why don't we cut to the chase and you tell me what you want from Russia?"

"Thank you Mr. President. I will get to the point, as they say." The prime minister paused for effect. "We have a problem. I'm going to be very honest. We can no longer trust the Americans to stand by Israel. They have been pushing for agreements that they fully realize will destroy our ability to defend ourselves. I am sure you are very knowledgeable of this and I am not telling you anything surprising. They, as you well know, have aided Iran in the development of their nuclear capability, as has Russia. They have provided hundreds of billions of dollars in funding which promptly flowed into the Russian treasury through weapons purchases. Obviously you are well aware of these facts as you have benefited. However, now Israel finds itself at a crossroads. We do not have many friends. We have many enemies. We do not want Russia as one of those enemies."

"So what do you propose?"

"I would ask that you put pressure on Iran to stop its march towards war with my country and to stop pushing for its destruction. I propose Russia and Israel move closer together in a geopolitical

MOTHERLAND

sense for peace in the Middle East. Russia is a great power and we want to work with you in our neighborhood."

"And what does Russia get in return?" the Russian president asked.

Connor and Fabian walked out to the aircraft, opened the doors, and began strapping themselves in. The plane was a Canadian built, de Havilland DHC-3 Otter, a famous aircraft built for short takeoff and landings in the bush. Otters were used extensively in Alaska, Canada, and other mountainous terrains, including Argentina, and were known for their rugged, workhorse, reputation. Although the Argentine Air Force had eight of the newer turbo-prop, dual engine, DHC-6-200 Twin Otter, Fabian figured he would know how to fly this older version as he was current in the twin. *I just need to make sure I don't miss any different items on the checklist*, he thought to himself. *Classic way to kill yourself with overconfidence.*

"I remember you and I jumping out of one of these things back in the day at the Academy my friend!" Connor said to Fabian as he saw the aircraft they were going to use. "Brings back memories, doesn't it?"

"Yes, my American gaucho. I thought you would enjoy this!"

The large piston engine growled to life, sounding like a Harley Davidson, and the two men taxied out to the main runway at a small airfield outside of Buenos Aires.

Fabian had secured two weeks of leave in order to help Connor with his quest. He was glad to help. "I feel alive again! I'm not chained to a desk! I can get out and fly with no restrictions! No maintenance issues, and to top it all off, I get to fly with a good friend for a few days!"

"The feeling is mutual, Fabian. I will enjoy being out in the bush with you as well."

"We will fly south to Bariloche. I am not filing a flight plan. No one will know we are coming. No one knows I've borrowed my good friend's aircraft. There will be no tickets, no record of our trip, no one to wait on us upon arrival. The downside is this plane only cruises at about 160 knots. So, it's going to be about an eight hour flight. We will stop to refuel and eat of course. We have the day together my friend!"

"What does your wife and family think about you taking off into the mountains with an old flying buddy?"

"She was overjoyed! She can hang out with her girlfriends in the city for a while. They will have a blast."

"She is a good woman, Fabian. I'm envious of your calm, cool life here in paradise."

"And I am envious of your James Bond lifestyle Connor! Maybe we can both enjoy each other for a few days?"

"Agreed. However, I get to do most of the flying," Connor said with a grin.

Ahmed arrived from the airport in Buenos Aires to the center of town via a rented car, rented in an assumed name of course. He had already contacted his intelligence counterpart at the Iranian embassy and was expecting him to be waiting for 'the package' soon at a safe house already prearranged in the Argentine countryside.

Ahmed enjoyed tasks like this. He was always up for the 'wet work.' Although this task initially would not go that far, he expected he would get to enjoy his passion several times during this little operation of his. Ahmed was happier on his own, he realized. *I don't need any supervision. I can make these things happen by myself, off the grid, operating in the shadows. I alone have the will and the nerve to do what needs to be done in these types of situations.*

He parked the car several dozen meters down the street from the target, a brownstone row house in a tony neighborhood of the old city. Then he waited. He was used to waiting. He had done it for most of his life. Waiting for permission. *Waiting for a target. Waiting for a promotion. Waiting for the fucking Mullahs to notice my hard work for Islam. No more. I will work on my own from now on. I will be a contractor, someone the Mullahs can call if they need me.* Ahmed was already thinking of ways he could steal money from Connor and Fabian. His idea was brilliant. He would kidnap his wife for ransom. Then he would force the Argentine to turn over Murray and the location of the scientist. He would also demand all the Argentine man's wealth and then some. The man and his family would pay. He was from a wealthy, Argentinian clan that went back generations. All the higher ranking military officers, like Fabian, had money. Soon it would be Ahmed's money. Once he had secured the scientist and information on the bio weapon, fattened up his own offshore bank accounts in Singapore, and won the praise of his current superiors, he would kill them all, Murray, Fabian, the woman, all of them of course. He would leave no evidence.

Ahmed perked up in his vehicle as he saw a car approaching from behind. The sedan pulled in front of the brownstone and parked. A woman about forty years of age got out of the car and headed towards the house. *Wow, Mr. Ramos. I'm impressed. She is quite attractive. Maybe I will have even more fun than I thought on this job,* pondered Ahmed. He unlocked his door and nonchalantly followed the woman up the small flight of stairs that lead to the front entrance. She did not notice him. He checked up and down the street; there was no one around. When she turned to go back to the car to get some shopping bags, Ahmed forcefully grabbed her from behind and cupped her mouth with his hand and forced her into the house, slamming the door behind him.

Chapter Nineteen

General Kursk was in a good mood as he strolled down the ornate Kremlin hallway to meet Iranian Minister Javadi once again. It had been a good few days. As expected, the Kremlin bosses had rewarded his family handsomely for the negotiations he had conducted with Iran, which resulted in tens of billions of hard currency, U.S. Dollars to be exact, flowing into Moscow's treasury. Of course with the devalued ruble, selling these dollars for the Russian currency went a long way to plugging the budget holes in the Russian federal deficit. Oil prices were still relatively very low and the financial pressure on the central bank and the executive branch were severe. Moscow would not roll back weapons modernization programs so social services were cut to the bone. Hospitals, schools, roads, they all suffered. Therefore, strong weapons sales in dollars were an absolute priority. Kursk had done well. His bank accounts were now full, his status with the Kremlin elite was secure, or as secure as it could ever be in Russia, and his wife could do all the shopping she wanted in Europe. *I would love it if she would spend more time there so I could spend more time with Svetlana, such a goddess she is. I have never known another woman like her.*

Kursk had made it. Within the Kremlin halls of power he was now a 'big swinging dick,' as the Americans on Wall Street liked to say, a 'senior guy.' He could feel the newfound respect and a little fear from others who were trying to climb the ladder of Russian power. He could read it on their faces. He was now untouchable. He was free to do as he wished, with discretion of course. The only man who could harm him now was the tsar himself. There were purges from time to time, just to shake people from their comfort zones. However, for the time being, his position in life was secure. *I will have to be careful. I cannot become cocky, arrogant. I wonder what the future holds for me? Will I become defense minister?*

Kursk reached the conference room and let himself in. The guard outside the door waved him through as Kursk was now a household name inside the ancient fortress walls. The room was empty except for the Iranian diplomat sitting meekly at one end of the table. "General Kursk, it is so good to see you again so soon. I trust you and your family are well? I detect the hint of a smile on your face, Sir. I dare to say that is not because you were to meet me? Whatever it is, I am happy for you. Now, I'd like to get to the business we have at hand, even though it is rather unpleasant for me I must tell you."

"Minister Javadi, it is good to see you as well. Yes, you caught me. It has been a rather wonderful few days seeing a close friend, a female one at that." He smiled briefly and the Iranian returned a knowing grin. "Thank you for returning to address this matter so quickly. Obviously it is of prime importance to the Russian Federation."

"General, I am afraid I am the bearer of bad news. You were correct in your assertion that Iran did have an operative inside your territory who attempted to glean information on one of your bio weapons programs. When I mentioned gaining access to this research in our first meeting, I had no idea that a part of my government was literally on Russian soil committing espionage. We do not do that to our friends. I am authorized to tell you that one of our operatives has gone rogue. His name is Ahmed and he is in our Revolutionary Guards intelligence division. They are the elite troops in Iran and given large latitude in their activities. He and his team put together this operation obviously without the knowledge of our leadership. I am authorized to offer you our most heartfelt apology and an offering of sorts; that is if you wish to take our suggestion of how to settle this matter between our two great nations."

MOTHERLAND

"I'm listening, Minister. Tell me please what you propose."

"Ahmed, as I said, has gone rogue. This is what I can offer." Minister Javadi leaned forward over the table between them and almost whispered to the Russian general what he had been authorized to offer in exchange for continuing the weapons contracts and deliveries.

Connor and Fabian landed at the small airstrip in the middle of nowhere to refuel. They had been flying for four hours and were about halfway to their destination. Connor took the chance to walk out into the landscape beside the airfield and take in the scenery. The ground was almost uninhabited by wildlife and seemed to be practically a barren slate that covered the soil. Stubborn plant life pushed its way through the openings in the earth but insects and smaller wildlife were scarce. Looking upwards, Connor took in the mountains in the distance and noticed the terrain sloped up to them steadily. The snowcapped peaks of the Andes dramatically backstopped the Patagonian scene.

Fabian walked up behind him now that the aircraft was refueled. "The flora and fauna change rapidly as you close in on the mountains, meaning, it gets more dense, more vibrant, more full of life. Out here, it's almost a desert."

"It's beautiful. I love it!" remarked Connor.

"Yes, it is that. They say the first European explorer to reach this area, Magellan, named it Patagonia because he thought the indigenous people were giants. The name came from some monster in a story that was popular at the time. That's the rumor anyway."

"I'm enjoying spending time with you Fabian, even if it is under rather difficult circumstances. Truly good friends are a rarity in life. I cherish my friendship with you."

"And I as well. You have no idea how welcome a little adventure is for me. My life had become just plain boring and stale. This quest we are on has made me young again. Come on, let's get in the air. We still have a lot of flying to do."

"You haven't told me where exactly we are going, Commodore Ramos."

"We can go over it in the plane. There's only so much daylight in the day and I don't want to do this landing at night. As they say, I'm not as good as I once was, but I'm as good, once, as I ever was."

"Ha, I used to love night time landings. But you're right, it's a young man's game."

"Especially night time landings in the mountains!"

The two walked back to the Otter, started the engine, taxied to the end of the runway and took off into the wind. Fabian gave an advisory notice over the radio that there was an aircraft on takeoff to the south. There was no one in the area to hear it.

President Chahine sat in the situation room at the White House. His advisors were seated around the table as a uniformed officer of flag rank was standing at the opposite end from where the president was seated, awaiting instructions. The man was nervous as the information he was about to present was quite shocking. "General, please begin the briefing," he ordered.

"Mr. President. We have been given information by the Iranians that points to a weapons lab being operated in the Bariloche region of Argentina. Shockingly, we believe, again per the Iranians suggestion, that an elderly Nazi scientist, formerly a Soviet spy in Berlin during the war, is leading the effort to develop these weapons. The man, known as Anatoly Ivanov, was previously doing the same work in the Russian Federation, deep in Siberia at a similar facility.

However, he was kidnapped by forces unknown.

The President interrupted, "Didn't we get word of Mr. Murray heading to the same general area just recently?" he asked firmly.

"Yes, Sir. That information was passed on to us through another Iranian contact who received it from a mole deep in the Israeli Mossad. We cannot verify any of this information however."

"Well, it seems to be too much of a coincidence, don't you think? It seems the verification from two sources that there is *something* in Argentina adds credibility, no?"

"Yes, Mr. President. It would seem so," responded the general.

"Who do we think is managing this laboratory and forcing this scientist to work there against his will?"

"We do not have information on that Mr. President. Although, we do have theories. Some of our team believe it is the Islamic State. There are other theories but that is the one that is receiving the most attention at the moment. The Bariloche region is crawling with former Nazis who escaped via the ratlines to Argentina after the war. The Juan Peron regime actively encouraged this migration. It provided fascist Argentina with money, prestige among the anti-Semitic world at the time, and scientific know-how. This current facility has not been on our radar; that is, at least until the Iranians recently provided a possible location to us. We have known and followed other operations or facilities in the region for decades but frankly the stories coming out of Bariloche simply haven't been a priority since the early 1980s. Elderly Nazis just don't threaten the United States that much anymore. However, this story is different. Iran has been very helpful to us by providing this information unsolicited. Without it, we would not be in a position to act."

"Due to the signature achievement of my presidency, the nuclear deal with Iran, we now have a very good relationship with the Islamic Republic and their leaders. I expect more information sharing and no, this is not surprising. I expected such cooperation in due time. Go on with your briefing. Why is this bio weapon so dangerous?" *I know the answer but I want the rest of the room to hear this.*

"Sir, the information we have gleaned is disturbing. This information is highly classified under TS SCI procedures. Everyone in the room has now been cleared to be read into this program. I'm mentioning this to make sure everyone here understands the penalties for releasing this information." He stopped talking for about ten seconds to make the point.

"During WWII, the United States was cooperating with the Soviet Union to develop weapons of mass destruction to use against the Nazi regime. These weapons were quite terrible as we all have come to understand. However, some of them were more terrible than others in our opinion, the biological warfare weapons in particular. Luckily the computer power to unravel and map the DNA of the human body was not yet developed in sufficient capability to finalize the development of one certain agenda, even though the knowledge of the human body was much farther along than most people are aware of. The information is still highly classified as I have said. This scientist, Ivanov, was secreted out of Berlin to the USSR right before the end of the conflict. It has been his life's work to develop this weapon. We believe he was kidnapped to finish constructing the greatest weapon ever known to man, the ability to target one race or even one certain family or person specifically for death or illness via a genetically modified virus. The ramifications of such a weapon are sure to shock everyone in this room. In short Mr. President, Iran has given us the most probable location of this laboratory which has been in operation for several years. We have been surveilling, by satellite, the mountainous area for a facility matching the required parameters for a few days now, given Iran's information. So far the profile of one particular area, its activity and potential, matches what our expert team determined to be the necessary characteristics of such a lab.

We believe we have found it.. It is located deep in the Bariloche mountains. That is why this meeting was called Mr. President, to finalize a way forward to neutralize this threat to mankind and especially the United States." The officer stopped talking and let his words sink in around the room. There was complete silence for a few seconds.

Then the president spoke. "I would like to prepare a targeted action against this facility once we are in agreement on its purpose and have verified to a respectable probability it is what we think it is. However, I am inclined to believe what our Iranian brothers are telling us. We cannot let this capability go unchecked or fall into the wrong hands. I want options within 24 hours on how we can use direct action to put this facility out of business and capture the research for ourselves. I understand that is a difficult undertaking but that is what I want. *I will use this capability myself, one way or another, to destroy the Jewish State. We have to acquire the technology, before someone else does and uses it on us.*

"Yes, Mr. President, the general replied. The rest of the national security staff began to ask the briefer questions; however, the Sultan had made his point.

Ahmed drove calmly to the safe house. He really did not want some inquisitive traffic policeman opening his trunk and finding the Argentine officer's wife. The Iranian operative did not want to spoil any of the fun he dreamed that he would be having over the next few hours. The woman had put up quite a struggle. He even had scratches on his face and arms. He definitely didn't want a policeman seeing those. So Ahmed drove ever so carefully, obeying all the traffic laws. He had been taught years before that police agencies loved to use traffic violations to catch suspected criminals. Therefore, it was imperative to deny them this option to apprehend you.

She had been quiet the entire drive. Ahmed hoped she was not injured. He had been quite rough with her. Either way, it didn't matter. He had already extracted the family's financial information. This was his part of the deal. He would get the Mullah's their scientist but he would get the money. That was the way it was going to work from now on. As soon as he dropped off this woman at the safe house for 'safekeeping' for a few days, he would start his search for Murray and the weapons laboratory. On the way, he would start the process to transfer the money to his offshore accounts with the account credentials given. If he needed to, he would go back for the woman to have her do it over the phone for him, with a gun to her head of course.

Ahmed finally spotted the home in a sparsely populated neighborhood twenty kilometers outside the center of the city. He pulled into a garage which immediately began to close behind him. He knew the drill. He had to authenticate himself before being allowed entry into the facility. Ahmed went through the motions with the biometric apparatus and the outside door was electronically opened. He stepped inside and was visually identified a second time by personal in the house. He was allowed entrance through the final door and stepped into the home.

"The woman is in the trunk. Bring her in and make sure she is secured somewhere safely. I don't want her getting away or making any noise.'

"Yes, Sir," the agent in charge replied as he went out to the garage to do as instructed. "Oh," the agent added. There is someone in the main room waiting on you." The agent turned and went through the exit to retrieve the woman. Ahmed stepped further into the facility.

As he passed through the threshold to what used to be the living room of the house, but now housed a meeting area for Iranian

MOTHERLAND

intelligence, Ahmed as grabbed from behind and thrown to the floor. A bag was placed over his head while his hands were cuffed behind him. He was dragged to his feet and thrown into and tied to a chair. His mouth was gagged. Once he was secured, the bag was ripped off his head. What he saw surprised him.

"Hello, Ahmed," said a man with a Russian accent and dressed in the uniform of a Russian soldier. The man studied Ahmed's face and then continued, "I guess you didn't expect to see me now did you?"

Ahmed tried to talk but the gag wouldn't let him. "You don't need to talk. You see, I don't really care what you have to say. The truth is Ahmed, your bosses now consider you to have gone rogue. They have turned you over to us, I mean to Russia that is."

Ahmed looked around and tried to find a familiar face. There was none. The station keeper came back in the house with the woman but he ignored Ahmed. He took off her bindings and allowed her to use the restroom. The window was frozen shut of course. She could go nowhere. Ahmed turned his gaze back to the Russian, trying to figure out what he wanted. *So, my gig is up,* Ahmed thought. *I wonder what happens now.* He furiously tried to free himself from the restraints, but it was no use. *Why has Allah done this to me? What does he want from me? Is this my destiny?*

The Russian began speaking again. "You see Ahmed, you are a spy. You are also, unfortunately, a spy who ran an operation on Russian soil. That is not a very smart thing for you to have done Ahmed. Russia doesn't like that, doesn't like that at all. Your government wants to buy weapons from us very badly. You almost destroyed that opportunity. They are not happy at all either. It seems your little team did this and some other things without your leader's permission. So, they told us that we could do what we wanted with you. So, you see, we don't want any information from you. You don't know anything that your superiors have not already told us. At this point, we only want to videotape you. Is that alright with you, Ahmed?"

Ahmed shook his head in the affirmative. *Maybe I will get out of this in one piece after all. Maybe I will be able to enjoy those stolen millions after all as well.*

"Well that is very kind of you, Ahmed," the Russian said. "We thank you for giving your permission." He motioned to another Russian who was in the room and they began setting up a video camera to film the Iranian operative. He actually relaxed a little. *They must want to show they can capture an Iranian*, he thought to himself. *No big deal, we do it all the time. They will not hurt me it seems, only film me.*

"Oh, Ahmed, I forgot to tell you one thing. Yes, we are going to film you, but unfortunately for you, we want to make an example out of you. So, we are going to hurt you very badly before we kill you. First I am going to gouge out your eyes. Then I am going to cut off your nose and ears. Then I am going to cut off some other parts of your body and stuff them in your mouth while you are still alive. Then we are going to show this video to the world so no one will dare run an operation on Russian soil again."

Ahmed began to shake in his chair with fright as he struggled to free himself as the Russian moved forward with a switchblade. Ahmed's eyes darted between the Russian's knife and the bonds holding his wrists and legs tightly to the chair. Ahmed remembered growing up, when he had been tied to the chair before, when his father had beat him. He had tried to get free then as well but always realized it was hopeless in the end. This time he knew there would be no escape.

The Russian bent down to pull tight the zip ties which held Ahmed's limbs to the wooden extensions of the chair. The man then put his arm in a vice grip around Ahmed's head, so it wouldn't move as he worked.

The cameras began filming.

Chapter Twenty

Natasha and Peter sat around the table once again in the conference room in Tel Aviv. There were others in the room, high ranking officers of the Mossad and several others who were of lesser importance.

The topic was Murray.

"He is in danger," said Natasha. "Besides the fact he is my husband, he needs our support!"

"We have more important things to think about Natasha. You must understand. The survival of the state of Israel is more important than one man," said one of the higher ranking men at the table. "We don't have the luxury to allow emotion into this decision making process."

"I understand that," said Peter. "However, are there not very important intelligence targets surrounding his presence in Argentina? This bio weapon has to concern you all. If there was ever a weapon that could destroy the Jewish State, this is it!"

"Yes, it concerns us," said the man. "However, it is not the priority at the moment. We must address the most existential threats first." He turned to the briefer standing by the view screen and suggested he continue.

"Hezbollah is massing in southern Syria and Lebanon." He turned on the screen and maps showing troop concentrations started to populate the presentation. "We know their capabilities in Lebanon since we faced it in the last conflict. However, this time they will be much stronger with hardened, bloodied fighters from the Syrian civil war. They are now also a much more mobile force with tanks and other armor available to them, either captured by the rebels, or supplied by the Russians.

"Hezbollah has also built up its base in Qusair, a Syrian town near the Lebanese border. Here they are stockpiling heavy weapons such as over 60 Russian-built T-72 tanks and Shahabs and Fateh-110 ballistic missiles. Qusair is now essentially an Iranian military base inside Syria and continues to be heavily fortified and militarized by the Mullahs.

"However, our most pressing concern at the moment is the continued militarization within the Syrian parts of the Golan Heights. The old capital of the region, Quneitra, seems to be the focal point for artillery and missile units. We see an attempt to link up the Hezbollah fighters in Lebanon with the Golan units, creating a northern front in an attack against Israel that stretches from the Mediterranean to the Syrian desert. As you know, we killed Iranian Revolutionary Guard officers and other technicians in the area during an airstrike a few years ago. Since then, however, the Iranian influence has only grown. In short, we face a massive, coordinated attack from Iran, Iranian backed militias such as Hezbollah, and linked Hamas militants in the territories. It is a threat we have not seen since the Israeli, Arab wars of the 20th century.

"Israel has faced these threats before and has come out on top with the help of the United States, why do you think the outcome will be different this time?" asked Peter.

The briefer looked at the older man for guidance. The older officer hesitated.

"What is it?" asked Natasha.

"Tell them," said Reshma Nadir, an Arab Mossad agent who had uncovered the truth about the Sultan earlier in the year. She knew Connor, Peter, and Natasha well as she was in charge of the small tactics unit in Brazil which saved them from certain death at the hands of the Russians the previous summer. "They deserve to know. They have been active in this scenario for some time. It is the right thing to do. They can be trusted." The old man, obviously the officer in charge, nodded his head in the affirmative.

MOTHERLAND

The briefer, having received clearance, continued. "After much laborious, detective work, agent Nadir uncovered the real identity of the Sultan, a man we have been trying to unearth for almost a decade. She accomplished this feat by tying together intercepted communications from overseas operatives and running them through a very sophisticated software tool that Technion, our MIT, had developed. The software has given us a very high probability of the identity of the Sultan.

"He has been coordinating the attacks against Israel from all parts of the Islamic world for years. He has been very successful in weakening the support for Israel within the United States and Europe. It is for this reason that we do not believe we can trust or count on America for support and rearmament during the next conflict. Israel is on her own. That is why this threat to the north is so serious."

"But how does he wield so much power within the U.S. if he is in the Middle East?" asked Peter. The briefer again looked at his chief who nodded in the affirmative.

"Because the Sultan, the man who is trying to destroy Israel, the man who engineered two tactical nuclear weapons into the country last year which were thankfully detected and destroyed by the Shin Bet, the man who has organized and spearheaded this latest threat our country, the man who could be behind the bio weapon, the man who allowed Iran to gain a nuclear capability, the man trying to pressure Israel back to the indefensible 1967 borders, well, I could go on and on. This man is none other than the president of the United States, President Chahine."

Peter and Natasha were thunderstruck. Reshma looked at them and slowly nodded her head in confirmation. Peter sat back in his chair and let out a long whistle. "Where do we go from here?" he asked.

"And what about my husband?" asked Natasha.

"Let them go," said Reshma. "Perhaps they can be helpful in

Argentina as our hands are full here." The older man nodded his head once and left the room. Once again, the meeting was adjourned.

Connor pulled back on the yoke of the Otter and the aircraft gained altitude to cross a ridge that was in their flight path. The two men were enjoying flying at rather low altitude as they were literally completely alone in this part of the country. An occasional road, powerline, etc. was seen but no sign of large-scale civilization. It was just the way both of them wanted it.

The Otter is performing magnificently, thought Connor. *I haven't had this much fun in a long time. What a fabulous, powerful aircraft.* The Andes foothills were now in their crosshairs and Connor could feel the air start to thin as they climbed higher and higher. *This is complete freedom and I love it. I'd forgotten how much I love it.*

As they crested the ridge and powerfully careened down the opposite valley, Connor noticed a cell tower to his left along the ridge, strategically placed to further communication to the small village down below to their twelve o'clock low. At the same moment he noticed the tower, he felt his phone buzz in his pocket as the device synced to the global network. "You have the controls," he said to Fabian.

"I have the controls," Fabian responded in a military manner.

Connor pulled out his iPhone and noticed a message in his long dormant high yield account that he only used for communications with Peter. He opened the page and the message popped up on the screen from his dear friend.

I'm in Tel Aviv. Your mate is fine. Be careful. Sultan is POTUS.

MOTHERLAND

Connor felt like a brick had hit him in the head. *The president of the United States is the Sultan? This is the man who caused me so much trouble last year and almost had me killed? Is he the man behind this little adventure I have been on?* Connor continued to try and make sense of the situation. He had no reason to doubt Peter's assertion but this was hard to believe. Connor's entire world was now upside down. Everything he had been taught to believe in, was it wrong? *Jesus, where do I go now? Who do I trust?* Connor sat there in the cockpit, thunderstruck. *I trust my friends, that is who. And I have to trust that this bastard will be removed from power and the America I knew will one day be reborn. Until then, I trust my friends, and my friends only.*

Fabian noticed the look on Connor's face as he stared at his phone and said, "Well, whatever it is, you might as well tell me about it, since we are in this thing together, you know."

"Yes, my friend, I will fill you in. In the meantime, we need to talk about where we are going don't we? The air is getting thinner and time is growing short."

Anatoly looked out the window at the deep, blue sky of the Andes mountains. Then he scanned the craggy peaks of the summits which were dotted with patches of white snow. It was a beautiful scene, he had to admit. He also had to admit to himself that he loved it here, where he could be with like-minded people, Germans, lots of them. Even Nazis, he did not care. But he was here to develop the bio weapon for the Motherland. Anything else did not matter. However, God was kind to him. He had lived to see the day when his life's work would be fulfilled. They had finally been successful with recent tests. The previous trials, unfortunately, had casualties, but that could not be avoided. *There were always sacrifices to be made to further the cause of the Motherland.* The final architecture of the weapon, however, was perfect.

The leaves of Alpine trees were turning. Pungent golds, yellows, and orange filled the ravines in a collage of bright art from nature. *It is fitting. It is poignant that I will die in Winter, when the leaves have turned to nothing, when the snow comes.* Anatoly knew he would not live another year. Something in his body had told him that. He could feel his internal processes shutting down. He could accept that now. His time on this earth was over. *But I have lived to see my dream come true! The Motherland will now be saved! My people will be secure, their future bright and filled with peace and happiness! I can go in peace and with contentment.*

There were only a few more tests and the bio weapon would be operational. The only task would be to acquire DNA material from the target and then a bespoke weapon could be created within months. It would change the nature of warfare. It would alter the course of human history. The enemies of the Motherland would be vanquished. *It is God's will. Let it be done.*

Fabian gave Connor back the controls and they continued flying up into the Andes mountains. "Connor, we are going to the Bariloche area. It is a region of the country where many of the Nazi leaders and collaborators fled after the war, during the late forties and early fifties. Your own government helped many of them escape. The Americans did not feel they would get a fair trial in the Soviet Union. They also wanted to understand the science the Nazis were working on as much of it was not fully understood at the time. The Nazis were much further along in many areas than the world thought and it is frightening how close they came to developing their own weapons of mass destruction. The world would be a much different place than it is today.

"The built a society up in the mountains to continue their beliefs and traditions. It's like going back to Berlin in 1942. The Juan Peron regime encouraged it, help them flourish. There are Nazi symbols everywhere. There were many secret enclaves built to support the Nazi leadership all over the Argentine mountains and jungles. Some parts of the society are known to the world, such as Israel, the U.S. and so on. Other parts are not. That is where we are going. A part that very few people know about. I can get you in there because of some contacts I have inside the government which allows this part of their society to exist. Not very many people know about this facility. I believe your scientist is there. A little bird told me that might be true. I really don't know. However, I know it will be the best place to start to look for him."

"Well, this should be interesting," replied Connor. "Do you know any of these people?"

"No, we only have permission to land at a small, secluded airstrip up in the mountains."

"You can make the landing? How long is the strip?"

"Not long enough."

"Great. I guess I have something to look forward to then."

"Yes, you do I'm afraid. The strip is right off the shelf of an ancient glacier, several kilometers west from Bariloche. You may remember from your Alaska flying days, the glacier creates its own weather patterns. The change in temperatures play havoc with the gusts of wind flowing off the ice. It's kind of like what Forrest Gump's mother said, you never know what you're gonna get."

"My kind of landing."

"We have to keep the power up coming over the ice formation, in case we have to power our way out of a downdraft, but once we clear it, we have to cut power and slow to stall speed to have any chance of making the landing. Then we have to pray."

"Have you ever put a plane down here?"

"Yes, I ferried a military commander here years ago. I hear nothing has changed. I have to admit, it's a sporty landing my friend, even for an ace pilot like myself."

"Well, you were never one for bravado." Connor looked at his friend and smiled. "We'll get her down together."

Chapter Twenty-One

The two flights of MV-22s took off from the U.S. Navy ship in the Atlantic Ocean in the dead of night. The rather short flight inland and through the valleys and ravines of the Andes foothills masked their radar signature perfectly. The line of giant aircraft hurtled through the air at close to two hundred knots airspeed, creating an enormous sound that shook the valleys as they sped over the treetops. No one in the area had the need to worry about an insertion of ranger and special operations troops so only air traffic control radars were in operation in Chile and Argentina. The USAF and Marine aircraft had no problem evading detection, even though they were a rather large target.

The MV-22 was a hybrid between a helicopter and a fixed wing aircraft. The engine nacelles could be transitioned upwards to act as a helicopter rotor in a hover and then brought forward to cruise at higher fixed-wind speeds. The unique design had given the military, and especially special operations aviation, the ability to insert and extract troops quickly into and from distant, remote areas.

There was no landing zone at the target large enough to allow for touch down of the multiple large machines. Therefore, the ground force was to be inserted four kilometers away in a large pasture meant only for the local sheep to graze. There were no human eyes any anywhere to be found according to satellite and signal reconnaissance. As the target approached, the MV-22s slowed their airspeed and spread out to land in prearranged order. The ramps lowered and the troops ran out. The insertion was done quickly and the MV-22s egressed back out to the ship for refueling and remained on standby with engines running while they waited for the call to return and pick up the strike force.

Two hundred rangers and one Delta Force unit were inserted

at midnight and began the trek to the target, up a long and winding mountain path. These were troops especially trained in mountain warfare. The Rangers were there to back up the special operators as they hit the target and to secure the perimeter. The plan was for the entire force to egress back down the mountain to the waiting MV-22s several hours later. All electronic and signal communications were jammed by Navy electronic warfare aircraft in the area. No one in Argentina would know the hit even happened until it was too late. The operation was being watched and monitored directly by Joint Special Operations Command (JSCOC) at Fort Bragg and by the White House itself in the Situation Room.

As the large ground force neared the target, the Rangers spread out and established an impenetrable perimeter. The target with the hoped-for 'precious cargo' was directly ahead. Delta Force prepared to infiltrate and remove Anatoly and the research into the weapon. As verified by satellite photos which had been pored over for days, the compound consisted of one large building, thought to be a laboratory, and several smaller dwellings which looked to be sleeping quarters and a cantina. No recent human activity was seen as the inhabitants were thought to be asleep as expected.

The Delta operators moved in for the hit, hoping to not have to use deadly force. Two of their party were specialized scientists trained in the use and recovery of biological warfare agents. Overhead, satellites monitored the situation real time and transmitted troops movements and video to the command chain. Strike aircraft were orbiting offshore in case they were needed for fire support which was not expected to be called for. The Rangers carried enough firepower to deal with any possible situation that could arise. The Argentine and Chilean troops were located far from this area. No security force at the location had been spotted for days. It looked as if the operators felt their remote location was secure enough against any unexpected, foreign threats to the facility.

MOTHERLAND

Delta moved in for the hit.

The Russian officer walked into the room where the woman was being held. He saw her eyes widen with fright as she looked at him. Her gag prevented any screams coming from her mouth. He wondered why she gave him such a response and then he looked down at his shirt which had the Iranians blood all over it. *He had spurted a good bit when we cut off his nose,* the Russian thought. *I forgot about that. I rather enjoyed the exercise however,* he admitted to himself. *It's good to keep active in the wet arts.* It was the thrill the Russian enjoyed. The look in the eyes of his victim—the terror, utter terror. *Maybe I enjoyed it too much,* he thought.

"Don't worry," he said to the woman in Spanish. "We are not going to hurt you. However, we cannot let you go just yet. This room is impossible to escape from. The walls, and the door are hardened. There are no windows. There is a camera in the corner of the ceiling. We can see everything. So, I am going to untie you and take off your gag. However, as I said, you cannot leave yet. Your husband is ok. This Iranian thug who took you was going to kill you and your husband for your money. We prevented that. But, there are other issues at play here so I can't have you running to the police, not just yet."

He took off her cuffs and the gag. "So, make yourself as comfortable as possible. He pointed to the bed. There are blankets also in the closet, along with a pillow if you would like to rest. You will be escorted to the bathroom every two hours."

"I would like to speak to my husband," she said.

"That will not be possible at the moment. However, soon, we are going to take you to him. As I think you know, he is not in Buenos Aires at the moment. As soon as we find out exactly where he is, we will take you there. Thank you for your patience. Oh, and by the way," he said as he pointed to his bloody uniform, "The Iranian will not be bothering you anymore. Take care." The Russian closed the door and locked the room.

Connor held the portable GPS navigation instrument in his hand and guided Fabian in to the landing strip. He hated GPS. *In the old days, it was just finger on the map. You either made it or you didn't. None of this electronic video game stuff. That's the way it should be.* Connor's old habits died hard. In the other hand he held a topographical map that Fabian had secured for the site, his finger following the path of the Otter. Light was falling and they would get only one, maybe two chances at landing, then they would have to go to an alternate for the night. That was not a prospect that either one of them relished, flying through the mountains without being able to see. So, it was now or never in both of their minds.

My flight instructor always said, what if the golden bee bee hits you right through your little class cockpit, what are you going to do then? You need to have a map. Connor literally traced their progress up the ravine on the paper and soon the glacier opened up in front of them. It was a massive sight. They flew about three hundred feet over the ice and the giant caverns opened up underneath them inside the slowly moving fortress of frozen water. It had been like this for the millennia.

Unexpectedly, a downdraft caught the Otter as the wind shear from the temperature changes on the glacier played havoc with their flight path. Fabian gunned the throttle and the piston engine groaned against the strong winds. As quickly as the downdraft came, it suddenly disappeared and the aircraft shot up in the air with all the power that Fabian had applied. He chopped the throttle to maintain the glide path to the airstrip which Connor suddenly saw opening up to them straight ahead. *It's a very short landing distance and actually sloped upwards. That should help bleed off our ground speed when the time comes,* he thought.

Fabian looked for a wind sock and there was none. "Can you tell which way the wind is blowing?" he asked Connor.

Connor looked outside the window and saw a small pond in one of the ice caverns of the glacier. The cool water was rippled to one side which pointed out the direction of the wind. Noticing that ripple was a technique he learned in flight school. One could also look at the direction of the leaves blowing in the wind. If you saw the underside, you had a tail wind. Smoke from a fire was also a dead giveaway.

"We have a slight crosswind to starboard, to the east. You're doing great. The strip looks like it has an upward slope so that should help bleed off groundspeed once we touch down.

Fabian fought the Otter over the glacier. As they neared the opposite side of the ice flow, he began to prepare for landing, running the pre-landing checklist. Connor assisted. Once the aircraft left the icy flow underneath them, Fabian reduced power and pulled up the nose of the plane in order to bleed off airspeed as quickly as possible. The stall warning horn began to go off in both of their ears. Any further reduction in speed would cause the lift on the wings to stall and the plane would sink like a rock; just stop flying. Fabian expertly guided the plane down, like riding a bubble, always on the edge of losing lift, barely maintaining a flight path, and when they were about five feet above the ground and very slow, he literally stalled the plane and it sank down, landing hard at the beginning of the airstrip. He cut power completely. There would be no go-around. There was not enough room. The Otter violently slammed into the ground and the over engineered bush landing gear performed perfectly. Soon the plane came to a stop near the opposite end of the runway. Both

Connor and Fabian slumped back in their seats in instantaneous relief of built up stress. As they turned off the engine and got out to chock the Otter, the sun sank below the horizon.

Fabian and Connor secured the aircraft and then began walking back to the small hangar that was located in the center of the strip to the east. "So what do we do now Commander? We're here, what next?" asked Connor.

"I'm not really sure. However, I'm positive the welcoming party will arrive shortly. As I told you, I've been here once but didn't get out of the plane. It was just a drop off. Let's see what happens."

They didn't have to wait long. As they neared the center of the strip, two military-looking vehicles sped in from the north along a small dirt road. They quickly encircled the two men and about a dozen armed men jumped out of the trucks. They were in civilian clothes but had some type of armband with a Nazi symbol emblazoned on their upper arms.

"Halt!" one of the men, obviously the leader, commanded in German. The men seemed agitated, nervous, possibly trigger-happy. Connor and Fabian did as they were told.

Fabian replied back in the same language. "We are here as a guest of the mayor. There is no need for violence. We are expected. I have pre-arranged the meeting through specific channels in the government. Please take us to him."

"Get in the truck," the man responded.

The vehicles made their way up the mountainside on the

MOTHERLAND

narrow, dirt road for approximately thirty minutes. Connor and Fabian were in the back of one of the trucks, guards watching them with automatic weapons. Connor studied the men. They were young and strong and all had blonde hair, very Aryan. Connor looked closer at the band around their upper arms. It seemed to be related to the Nazi regime but different in some ways, a variant but distinctly fascist. *Nice,* he thought. *Good thing I'm not a Jew, or a gypsy or anything like that.* Soon they began to slow and Connor strained to see their surroundings in the dimming light of day. It seemed they had been brought to some type of village or town, except the structures were hewn into the mountainside. They were of a certain German design on the outside, stone and wooden classic German architecture. However, as he looked closer, he noticed they were designed to not be seen from above. *They're camouflaged! Brilliantly as a matter of fact!* Fabian was noticing the same thing Connor could tell. They made eye contact.

    The vehicles entered some type of underground storage area which would never be picked up by satellite. They parked and were ordered out of the truck. As Connor and Fabian complied, an older man approached from a door that led to an area dug out of the mountain, some type of facility that looked like a German beer hall. "Hello, my friends. Welcome! My name is Herman Fischer. I am the mayor of this town. My surname comes from the outskirts of Berlin. My ancestors were fisherman, hence the name Fischer. We do not do much fishing here but sometimes we make it to the mountain lakes where there is some fantastic trout." He seemed to be waiting for a reaction from his guests as he ascertained he was a comedian and his words should have elicited humor. Not getting the reaction he anticipated, he continued speaking after a few awkward moments. "Please follow me. I will show you where to make yourselves comfortable. And as I initially said, welcome! We mean that. Follow me please."

General Kursk shook the Iranian minister's hand once again as they sat in the conference room of the Kremlin. The Moscow weather had started to turn and the Iranian was dressed more warmly than before with a sweater under his sport coat. "I am enjoying the Russian autumn General Kursk. Such a lovely time of year in your city. I hope you will accept my compliment and I hope we can move forward with our weapons purchases now that our little episode has been dealt with. I had a chance to see the little film your intelligence services made. It was very convincing I might add," he said with a forced smile.

"Thank you, Minister Javadi, it was *meant* to be. However, we have one more little item to discuss before we move forward with selling you the fighter jets and other weapons you desire. The Russian government has one small request."

"Anything you ask for General, we will do our best to comply with the request of a friend." His faux fondness for the Russian was palpable.

"We would like you to cease your attacks on the state of Israel."

The blood drained out of the Iranians face. "But General, what does our response to the Jewish pig's aggression have to do with Russia? I beg to ask!"

"We know full well you are considering a full-fledged, multi-pronged attack on Israel, soon, which may also include the use of nuclear weapons. I am here to tell you that action is no longer possible for Iran to take. Israel is a friend of Russia from now on. If you plan to use the weapons we sell you against her, we will destroy them. And certainly, we will no longer sell them to you. There are a lot of Russians in Israel. We mean to protect them as we do Russians around the world. Do I make myself clear?"

"I do not understand why the stance of your country has changed with regard to the Jews. You have not shown any qualms about us moving against them before. Let's just be honest with each other General."

"That may be true but some things have changed. We will sell you weapons for defense only. However, Israel is not to be touched."

The Iranian diplomat slammed his fists down on the table. "I will report to my superiors and give you my answer in due time, General. Good day!" Minister Javadi quickly grabbed his unopened briefcase and stormed out of the room.

The Russian sat back in his chair once the Iranian had left. *I really don't like that Persian prick. But, I am happy the meeting adjourned early!* Kursk picked up his phone and called his driver. "I want the car ready to go the special flat in ten minutes." *It was time to see Svetlana.* It had been too long.

Sitting in the back of the limousine on the way to the Iranian embassy in Moscow, Minister Javadi was fuming. *The Israeli dogs got to the Russians somehow. These Russian barbarians have made the Islamic Republic look foolish for cooperating with them. How do I tell this to my superiors? There will be Hell to pay. It was my idea to give them Ahmed in return for assurances the weapons sales would go through. My time on this earth may now be limited. It is in Allah's hands now.*

Chapter Twenty-Two

The Delta Force operators closed in silently on the facility. The Ranger perimeter was set and no other threats would be allowed to enter until the precious cargo (PC) was secured. This would be the scientist and any data, materials that could be secured on the weapons program. Once in place, the soldiers waited until the order was given, then upon receipt of the command they stormed each of the buildings in the entire facility at once. No shots were fired.

Short bursts of communication came over the secure, headset, radio net. "Building one secure."

"Two secure."

"Three secure."

"Four secure."

In fact, they all came out empty-handed. There was nothing. No one was inside. There was no laboratory. There was some evidence people had been residing there recently but no evidence of any kind of research going on. The on-scene commander relayed this information up the chain of command and waited on instructions. He was professional, with no hint of emotion or disappointment in his voice as the satellites carried his communications to Washington and beyond.

"Rodeo 56, this is Snake 32. We have negative PC over. Target is empty."

Upon receiving the order to withdraw, the entire force made their way back down the mountain to the extraction site. Soon they were airlifted back to the U.S. Navy ships waiting offshore. As it happens many times during special operations attempts with faulty intelligence, they had hit a dry hole.

The Sultan was enraged, to say the least. "Those damn Persian animals! They betrayed me! That will be the last time!" He tried to calm himself, but to no avail, he was shaking alone in the chair behind the Resolute Desk. "They will pay for this! Obviously, they have given me the wrong location of the lab facility. No doubt on purpose. They have made me look like a damn fool in the eyes of the world, my staff, and the Jewish pigs!"

The Sultan angrily buzzed his aide from the Oval Office. "Get me the Iranian leader on the phone immediately!" ordered the president. He then sat back again in his chair, trying to soothe his anger. But, it was no use.

How did this happen? Who are they in bed with? What am I not seeing? Something is going on which is out of my control. I am not used to this. The Sultan again tried to force himself to calm down. *It is in Allah's hands now.* He got out of the chair, walked to the other side of the Oval Office, retrieved his prayer rug and spread it on the floor. He turned to Mecca and knelt to pray.

Connor and Fabian were led through the door into the large room that had been carved into the mountain over time. They were aghast at what they saw. There were Nazi emblems everywhere along the walls and a giant Nazi swastika and eagle hanging from the ceiling opposite the entrance. The room was some kind of auditorium but had been rearranged to leave a large round table in the center of the space. There were several men sitting around the table facing their new guests. Some of them were quite elderly. None of them looked like someone you would want to meet in a dark alley.

Their 'hosts' seem to notice the uneasiness with which their guests took in the symbology. The mayor spoke. "Yes, gentlemen. The Reich lives. We like to think of it as the beginning of the 4th Reich. But do not worry. No harm will come to you. Your visit has been prearranged by some people you will meet shortly. However, first, let me introduce you to someone Mr. Murray for whom you have been looking for quite some time. Mr. Murray, I give you Anatoly Ivanov, our lead scientist."

Connor looked towards the table where the mayor was pointing and an elderly man, with a wisp of snow white hair remaining, stood from the table. He was very frail and looked to be a hundred years old, which he probably was or close to. However, he was in remarkably good health, for being one hundred that is. "Mr. Murray, he said in heavily accented English. It is good to meet you. I am here to answer any questions you wish to ask of me. I have nothing to hide."

Connor was taken aback. "I don't understand. What is all this? Someone please enlighten us as to what is going on here."

There was a noise on the other side of the room and another door opened to the area. The mayor looked in that direction and nodded. "Perhaps she can explain."

Reshma Nadir walked in the room. Connor was stunned. "What the Hell? Reshma, what are you doing here?" Connor looked at Fabian in disbelief. "She's an Israeli agent, one I trust and have worked with quite often over the last year. She saved my life once." He turned back to Reshma. "Reshma, you'd better tell me what is going on right now. Are you betraying your country?"

"No she is not, Connor." From behind Reshma entered another figure, a slender, very attractive woman.

"Natasha!" Connor ran to her and embraced his wife.

Prime Minister Dahan entered the briefing room. The stress of the last few months was taking its toll. He was tired. It seemed as though he could not catch up with his rest. *I am always tired it seems. Maybe I should see a doctor.* He took his usual place in the briefing hall and signaled to the young enlisted man to start giving the presentation.

"Good morning, Prime Minister. I have some good news today. We have confirmation that the Iranian forces in the Golan have pulled back further into Syria, taking their ballistic missiles with them. Hezbollah has also removed heavy weapons from near the front in Lebanon. We are also seeing their air defense network shrink back towards their border with Iraq. Prime Minister, something in the calculation with the Iranians has changed. We just don't really know what it is yet. We are working on that."

"Thank you for the information Sergeant. Please let me know when you have an update." He then turned to the IDF commander who was in the room as well. "Keep our forces on high alert until you deem their withdrawal and reduction of tensions sufficient to relax our defense posture. Notify me at that time," he commanded.

"Yes, Sir," the commander replied.

The prime minister got up from his chair and walked from the room. *I know what has changed in the Iranian calculation. Yes, I know very well.*

"Natasha, what are you doing here? I don't understand what is going on! Reshma, help me! What the fuck is going on?" Connor continued to hold on to Natasha, as if she might disappear at any minute.

"There are some more people here, who can explain things to you, Connor. I am sorry information was withheld from you."

At that moment, another woman emerged from the door. It was Fabian's wife. She ran to him in tears. Surprised as well, he embraced her and stroked her hair. "What the Hell? It's going to be okay, my love. Calm down, I am here." He too looked around, "Yes, somebody around here better start fucking talking right now!"

"I will start talking if you calm down, Mr. Ramos," said a man who emerged from the doorway with another gentlemen, dressed in the uniform of a Russian officer. "My name is Levi. I am the number three man in the Mossad, the Israeli intelligence service. Bear with me and I will tell you what is going on."

Connor and Fabian nodded they were both anxious to let him continue. Fabian's wife was still weeping. Natasha clung to Connor and he held her tight.

"First, Fabian's wife was abducted by an Iranian rogue agent. The agent was killed. Our Russian friend here saved her and brought her to us. The Iranian agent was going to rob Fabian of his wealth and also use his wife to find Anatoly via Connor. Once that was done, he was going to kill both of them and attempt to take Anatoly to Iran. Ahmed will not bother anyone anymore. You can be assured of that Fabian."

"I can confirm that," the Russian officer added, with a smile. "He is of no concern to anyone, ever again."

Levi continued. "Second of all, I believe you now know the Sultan, or the American president, was conspiring with the Iranians to destroy the state of Israel. We have interrupted that plot. This was going to be done by amassing troops into Syria and Lebanon and threatening the use of nuclear weapons by Iran. To prevent this outcome, and in light of efforts by the American administration to assist in destroying the Jewish State, Prime Minister Dahan flew to Moscow to negotiate with the Russian president. A deal was made and the Iranians have been told to back off, for the time being anyway. We have breathed a collective sigh of relieve in Tel Aviv and Jerusalem."

"What did Israel trade to Russia for this security protection?" asked Fabian.

"I will get to that shortly," said Levi. "Next, this facility. Israel has known for decades of this facility, the culture, the society, and the laboratories. The first two we could ignore, the laboratories filled with Nazi scientists we obviously could not. So, years ago, we made a deal. As you know, the Jewish Special Forces have killed many a Nazi across the planet since the end of the Great War. We offered these people a deal, the scientific research, for their lives. It was an offer they could not refuse. They did weapons research for us, in turn, we left them alone."

"Then why is Anatoly here?" asked Connor.

"He is here because he was needed. His expertise is second to none. He was needed to complete the bio weapon development. So we kidnapped him from Siberia about five years ago and brought him here."

"You, are developing the bio weapon? But, why?" asked Connor again incredulously.

"Yes, it is us."

"But I thought it was for the Motherland, for Russia?" said Connor.

"It will be," added the Russian officer. "You may count on that. In a very short period of time. The Rodina will be secure.

"Connor," said Levi. "There is another Motherland. The Motherland of the Jews."

"So you traded Anatoly and the bio weapon technology with Russia for the security of Israel," Connor commented bluntly.

"Yes, our Motherland will be secure also. The Motherland that has lasted five thousand years. The Motherland of my people."

"But you will allow Russia to have the upper hand in its new Cold War with the West."

MOTHERLAND

"That is not my problem, Connor. Your country is the one who has destroyed our relationship, an alliance that has lasted since the end of the Great War. We are the only democracy in the Middle East. Arabs are more free in Israel than in any other country in the region. But your president chose to arm the Iranians. He chose to send them hundreds of billions of dollars to buy weapons. He chose to allow them to acquire an atomic bomb. Not us, Connor, not us. We are simply trying to survive. Your president is right now trying to force Israel to return to the 1967 borders which he knows are completely indefensible. Israel will promptly be destroyed if this happens. We can no longer count on America. In fact, she is against us. We needed a protector and we may have found it in Russia. We will see over time. But for now, Israel is secure."

"That is a lot to comprehend at the moment. A lot to digest" added Connor.

"Yes, I am sure it is. But remember this. There has never been a Palestine nor Palestinians. Ever. The Ottomans controlled the area for centuries, until 1919 when they lost WWI. They were Muslims but they thought the Arabs inferior. Jerusalem was an backwater city, with no significance to the Ottomans or Muslims. There was a Jewish plurality despite the Roman destruction of the city and exile of Jews. Only after Jews began to resettle a largely barren land did Arabs immigrants come from Egypt, Syria, Iraq and other Arab states in search of work, created in large part by the Jewish immigrants. After WWI, the UN created the Palestine Mandate that included what now is Jordan. Britain had promised the entire land for Jews via the Balfour Declaration. After the war they changed their minds and carved 2/3 to give to their Arab ally King Abdullah. As more Jews and Arabs moved to the land, the Arabs began to resist. In 1929 they massacred 67 in Hebron. Eventually, the UN decided to partition the remaining land between Jews and Arabs. The mandate ended on 15 May 1948 and Britain left. On that day Israel declared

217

independence on their portion of the land. The Arabs responded by attacking. The five attacking Arab armies outnumbered Israel yet Israel won. Remember at this points the Jews were known as Palestinians. The Palestinians refused saying they were Arabs instead. They lost the war and many fled to become refugees. Israel told most to stay but the Arab armies attacking Israel told them to leave because they would get in the way. They said they would run out all the Jews and they could come back and take their possessions. Jordan occupied the West Bank giving no rights to Palestinian Arabs. Only when Jordan, Egypt, Syria and Iraq attacked in 1967 did Israel take all of the West Bank and Jerusalem. The Arab refugees now calling themselves Palestinians to this day refuse to recognize the right of Jews to live in Israel. If they had their way they would push the Jews into the sea. Israel offered them a region to call Palestine in the West Bank and Gaza. They have chosen terrorism instead. There never was an Arab or Muslim Palestine EVER in history. There never was a Palestinian people. EVER. Jews have lived there literally for thousands of years continuously even after the Babylon exile and after the Roman exile. There was always a Jewish plurality in the city. The bottom line is that Jerusalem is absolutely the center of Judaism. Christianity sees it as important but not critical. Muslims could not have given a crap because the Dome of the Rock was not important until threatened by Jewish reclamation of the land. That is the simple truth my friend."

    The Russian officer spoke. "Anatoly will come back to Russia with us today. We have the bio weapon technology as well. He will never leave Russia again. If Israel lives up to its part of our agreement, we will live up to ours and Israel will be secure."

    The scientist spoke. "My new friend, Connor. You see I am Jewish. It has been my life's work to protect the homeland of my people, our Motherland. I have fulfilled my promise to God. I will continue to do my work in Russia, in full knowledge that the Jewish Motherland is secure. I can think of no other purpose for my life, or what little is left of it. I can die in peace. Israel did not kidnap me. I came here of my own free will when they offered. It was the best decision I have ever made. I will miss this place but soon I will be with Jehovah."

Irving and Anatoly sat on the veranda of the castle overlooking Lake Annecy. The Russians had been kind enough to let Anatoly see his friend one last time before going back to Russia for good. The both smoked a thick cigar.

"Irving, my friend. We will once again smoke a thick cigar, overlooking our cattle, surrounded by mountains, and the beautiful young girls will dance for us, just like they did in Berlin all those years ago."

"I look forward to that day, Anatoly. It is so good to see you one last time. I can now go in peace."

"The lake is so peaceful at this time of the evening."

"Yes, it is, Anatoly. Yes, it is."

Connor walked out into the early morning desert sun of the Negev. He carried his M-16 as usual, slung over his shoulder. He waved to the IDF soldiers guarding his complex with determination. The border to the Gaza Strip was as close as always.

Lightning never strikes in the same place twice, he thought. He looked over at his hydroponic greenhouse, the tomatoes were falling down from the baskets still like the Gardens of Babylon. He felt at peace, a possible peace that could last, at least that was how he felt. *Maybe it will last. Maybe I can live in peace like Anatoly, with the knowledge my family is secure. But, unfortunately, I guess not. There is too much hatred so close by.* He stared again at the border to Gaza, wondering if the rockets would fly again any time soon.

Natasha came up behind him and put her warm, soft arms around his waist. Her breasts pushed into his back and aroused him. "It's nice to see you here again, my Love. This is where you belong."

"Yes, it is nice. It is nice to be home. And, this does seem like home."

"Connor, I was wondering."

"Yes, my love?"

"Would you like to have a child?"

Connor laughed. "I would like to try!"

Epilogue

President Chahine walked into the room at the United Nations. The Middle Eastern cabal was assembled. The leaders of all the Arab states as well as the Iranians were at the table. The Prime Minister of Israel was also there. *He looks as smug as usual,* thought the president. The Sultan walked up to the long negotiating table and took his place beside his aide. He placed the language translator over his ears and leaned back in his chair to take in his surroundings.

The incident of the Argentine weapons lab was almost forgotten. The Iranians had apologized profusely in private and assured the president they had just made an innocent mistake with the location of the weapons lab. The president, eager to confirm that his geopolitical chessboard moves had been as successful as he thought, was eager to accept the Iranian explanation. He had not been deceived, it had simply been a mistake, his narcissistic inner-self told himself.

The conference had been called to attempt to once again solve the Israeli, Palestinian conflict in the Middle East. The deal hinged on Israel accepting land for peace. They would give back the territories of the West Bank, Gaza, and the Golan Heights in exchange for international guarantees for Israel's security. Of course, no one expected this appeasement would really bring peace. What it would bring was a weaker Israel, one that would have a much harder time defending itself. It would bring a reign of terror like none the Israeli's had ever imagined. Jewish blood would flow in the streets of Jerusalem. The destruction of the Jewish State was the preferred international outcome.

The Muslim and Islamic leaders one by one went around the table as the conference started. They all swore their desire for peace and to not be the first to attack Israel. However, none of them declared their support for the Jewish State's right to exist.

The Israeli Prime Minister took all of this in. He watched the faces of the Islamic leaders and tried to figure out how they could lie so brazenly to the world. He wondered why their hearts were so filled with hate. *They could have real peace with Israel if they would just accept it, he thought to himself. As Golda Meyer once said, "We will have peace when the Arabs love their children as much as we try not to kill them."*

The American president rose to speak as his time came in the rotation. He gave an oratory of lofty goals and dreams, but again, everyone knew these were just platitudes and would never come true.

The leader of the United Nations congratulated the American president, who was set to leave the office of the president in a few months, for his appointment to take his place at the U.N. as Secretary General. "I will be glad to relinquish my post to such an accomplished and distinguished diplomat, Mr. President," he gushed. The American president beamed in the adulation. The United Nations charter had been amended to allow this. The globalists saw to that.

Soon, it came time for a break and the entire gathering rose to depart for a few minutes.

Upon returning, all of the seats were again occupied, except for the Supreme Leader of Iran. His seat was empty.

The Prime Minister of Israel leaned over to the seat next to him and asked the United Nations representative why the Iranian had not returned.

The U.N. official responded, "The Supreme Leader did not feel well. He has taken quite ill this afternoon. He will be represented shortly by another official from Iran.

The Israeli Prime Minister sat back in his chair and smiled.

###

About the Author

L. Todd Wood is a graduate of the U.S. Air Force Academy. He has been an aeronautical engineer and an Air Force helicopter pilot. In the Air Force, he flew for the 20th Special Operations Squadron, which started Desert Storm. He was also active in classified counterterrorism missions globally supporting SEAL Team 6 and Delta Force. For eighteen years, he was an international bond trader with expertise in Emerging Markets. He has conducted business in over forty countries. Todd has a keen understanding of politics and international finance. He is a national security columnist for The Washington Times, and has contributed to Fox Business News, The Moscow Times, NY Post, Newsmax TV, Breitbart, Zero Hedge, and others.

Other Works by L Todd Wood

CURRENCY

SUGAR

DELTA

LOST BASTARDS

Dreams of the Negev, A Short Story

The Last Train, A Shorty Story

Please post a review on Amazon if you enjoyed the book!

Find out about new releases by L. Todd Wood by signing up for his monthly newsletter found on LToddWood.com

Connect with Me Online

Twitter @LToddWood

LinkedIn (L Todd Wood)

Facebook (L Todd Wood, Novelist, Correspondent, Pilot, Bond Trader)

Pinterest (L Todd Wood Author Page)

Google+ (L Todd Wood Author)

LToddWood.com

CURRENCY

by

L. Todd Wood

Prologue

Weehawken, New Jersey
July 11, 1804

The smartly dressed older man came first, sitting erect and still as death in the rear of the long oar boat as it silently rowed across the wide river. The moon cast an eerie glow across the fast-moving, silky, black current.

He was balding, middle-aged and had dark features. However, he was in a much darker mood, a murderous mood in fact. He was the kind of man that never forgot anything; especially, the stain on his honor. His eyes bored holes in the back of the man sitting in front of him and he did not notice his surroundings as his mind was lost in thought. He was there to right a wrong he had suffered.

To this end he was joined by two other men seated near him, as well as two additional young rowers and his dueling second at the head of the craft, a total of five. The only sound was the water lapping like a running brook as the oars slipped in and out of the calm silvery surface. Slowly the boat crossed the dark current. Preoccupied, the passenger did not hear. He was focused only on the task ahead of him.

They beached the long oar boat upon the bank and he and the three men quickly scurried into the woods as the rowers stayed behind. Immediately the four gentlemen began to clear the brush along the ledge facing the water. The birds awoke but no one heard. Their singing cast an odd joyful sound, contrasting eerily with the morbid events unfolding beneath them.

A man younger by a year arrived a half hour later in a similar craft with a smaller entourage. He was a person of importance and seemed rather arrogant. In fact, he had a brilliant mind. Unfortunately he had a habit of taunting others with his brilliance that brought him to where he was at this hour. His pompous mood seemed out of touch with the somber circumstances.

One of his party was a well-respected physician. His second, sitting in the bow, carried an ornate box the size of a breadbasket. Inside were two Wogdon dueling pistols, the finest in the world at the time. The pair of weapons had already claimed the lives of a handful of men. One of these killed had been the younger man's son.

The first party made themselves known and the group just arrived made their way up the embankment to join them. Salutations were exchanged.

The seconds set marks on the ground for the two men ten paces from each other. The younger man, since challenged, had the option of choosing his spot and had already selected to be facing the river. The two antagonists loaded their pistols in front of the witnesses, which was the custom, and the seconds walked into the woods and turned their backs. This way they would not be party to the scene and could not be charged with a crime as dueling was now illegal. The honorable gentleman was becoming a rare breed. Times were changing.

The blonde man's second began counting down. Unknown to his charge's opponent, the pistols had a secret hair trigger firing mechanism; just a slight application of pressure would ignite the powder. This was a slight of hand to say the least.

A loud crack rang out. A few seconds later, another. Then a cry of pain. Whether the younger man accidentally fired due to the hair trigger or intentionally wasted his shot, we will never know. Historians have debated this point ever since. His shot missed his adversary and ricocheted into the surrounding trees.

The return fire from his opponent however was deadly. The ball pierced his abdomen and did mortal damage to his internal organs before lodging in his spine. He collapsed to the ground.

The acrid smell of gunpowder still hung in the air as the dark haired man walked up to him writhing on the ground. He was confident in his errand as he stood over him and methodically reloaded his pistol.

"Where is it?" he asked as he calmly packed the powder down the barrel.

The seconds stepped forward out of the brush but the older man waived them off with his pistol. The New Jersey woods were strangely quiet; the New York lights across the river twinkled in the background, soon to be obscured by the rising sun. Its rays would soon shine a bright light on the deadly events happening below.

"Where is it?" he said again sternly but softly, pointing his reloaded pistol at the man's head as he tried to lift it off the ground and speak. The long highly polished brass barrel reflected the early morning sun.

Blood poured from an open wound in the gut. Although mortally wounded and lying in the dirt, he held his hand over the opening to try and stop the flow.

"Go to Hell!" he gurgled as his mouth filled with blood.

"I probably will but I think you will beat me there," the darker gentleman chuckled and knelt down beside him. He started going through his bleeding man's pockets. "I have heard you always carry it with you." Aaron Burr knew he didn't have much time before the surgeon and seconds gathered and pulled him off. Inside the man's blood soaked coat, he found it.

"Ahh!" he gloated smugly. He quickly hid the pouch inside own vest and stood.

"You will never find what you are looking for!" the wounded gentleman said in a whispering laugh. His strength was ebbing. He was going to die.

"We'll see," replied Burr.

"He's all yours!" he called to the second and the wounded man's supporter rushed forward and tended to Alexander Hamilton.

Chapter One

June 10, 2017

Bahamas

The seawater thundered over the stern as the old fishing boat attempted to cut through the eight-foot waves, soaking everyone on board to their core. Connor Murray felt the impact in his kidneys as he held on to the ladder for dear life. The tuna tower swayed above him. His arm muscle burned as he prevented himself being tossed into the sea from the violent movement. Saltwater stung his nose. The new motor growled like a wounded bear as it strained against the onslaught.

How long can this go on? he thought.

Connor had puked twice and didn't relish a third attempt, but the nausea in his gut and throbbing in his head told him it was inevitable. The other two weekend warrior fishermen with him on the stern were leaning over the side as he contemplated his situation. He heard them groan as they tried to empty their stomachs, but there was nothing left inside them. He was miserable.

The day had started easy enough in the predawn hours as they boarded the boat at the end of New Providence Island east of Nassau.

The water was calm this early in the morning. This part of the island was protected by natural reefs. The rapid change in depth as the ocean floor rose to the island caused the ocean and the island currents to crash into each other and protected the east end from the ocean's wrath.

He had been planning this trip for weeks with his good friend. Alex, his Bahamian business colleague, had just finished overhauling an old, thirty-two-foot pilothouse cruiser, a labor of love for two years. The boat had been refurbished from bow to stern; many a weekend night they had spent drinking beer on the deck after a day's work on the "yacht, "as Alex's wife called it. Conner chuckled to himself. She was a little bit of a "wannabe."

The boat was not pretty, but she was strong. Alex had seen to that. He took very good care of her. When someone tears down and rebuilds something that intricate, it becomes part of them. The boat had become his passion. His wife didn't seem to mind; she had her yacht.

Connor had met his friend years ago when Alex was the head trader at a large hedge fund located in the tony Lyford Cay area on the west end of the island. Alex mingled with the movie stars. After trading together for several years and socializing on every trip Connor took to Nassau, they became friends and trusted one another completely. They took care of one another as they both moved firms several times over the years. Their careers flourished and their wealth grew.

This trip was a much needed change of scenery away from the Bloomberg terminal for both of them. The constant movement of the ocean was a welcome relief from the volatility of the markets. Stress relief was critical in their business. A day or two in different surroundings did wonders for one's trading acumen. "The three-day weekend was invented for Wall Street," Alex would often say.

The sun was rising as they cruised past old Fort Montague close to East Point. He could make out the row of old, British twenty-four-pound cannons lining the top barricade. The fort had held up remarkably well through the centuries, considering it was constantly exposed to the elements. The history here ran deep. Connor loved it. The islands were in his blood now. The open ocean waited for them ahead.

Today the only possible negative was the sea, as there was not a cloud in the sky. Their luck was not good.

The trip out of the channel was hellish as they crossed the churning waves. The barrier reefs produced a literal wall of water the boat had to climb, as the underwater structures halted the ocean's momentum. It was no better on the other side, but Connor knew Alex would not turn back. He had promised everyone on board some fish and this was her maiden voyage. They all quickly decided it was too rough to make the two-hour trek to Exuma, which they had planned. Instead they would stay off Paradise Island. Connor was quietly grateful.

Later in the day, after they had landed three dolphin—a bull and two females—all mercifully decided that it was too rough to continue. Now they were making their way back to protected waters, but it wasn't easy. The waves beat the side of the boat and refused to provide a respite to the passengers and crew. The fishermen were still hugging the rail in case they had to empty their stomachs again.

Thinking he would feel better higher, Connor climbed up the ladder and leaned into the back support next to Alex. He could see a line of boats making their way into the harbor to escape the violent sea.

The tower swayed violently as Alex strained to control the craft as she muddled her way up and over the crest of the waves.

"Must have taken on some water," Alex growled. "I can feel it sloshing back and forth down below. It's hard to control this pig."

Connor wasn't listening. "Tell me the latest on our discovery," he said.

April 23, 1696

Captain William Kidd turned one last time and looked over his shoulder at the Plymouth landmass disappearing in the background. The city that produced the Pilgrims had long since lost its dominance as a critical port for the Crown. The coastal lights faded in the mist.

Kidd would not miss England. He would, however, miss his beautiful wife of five years, Sarah, and their daughter in the English colony of New York, recently acquired from the Dutch, which called her New Amsterdam. The city was on its way to becoming a cultural and economic center of North America.

Sarah was one of the wealthiest women in the New World, primarily due to her inheritance from her first husband. She had been already twice widowed and was only in her early twenties.

He had left them several months ago to fulfill his dreams. He would not see them again for three years. Such was the life of a sailor.

This voyage has started very badly, he thought to himself. Maybe it was a sailor's intuition, but he had an uneasy feeling in the pit of his stomach.

He turned his attention back to the Adventure Galley. He had overseen her construction himself in London. She was built in record time, so there would be leaks and other imperfections to deal with but she would do the job. Kidd had sold his former ship, Antigua, in order to raise funds. The King was lusting for pirate blood and treasure. He made no secret of his haste for Kidd's voyage. The new ship would have to do.

She was a strong, thirty-four-gun privateer and would be formidable when he engaged pirates. Her design was elegant at 284 tons. Her oars would be an important capability when maneuvering against an enemy. His crew, however, was another story.

He had tried to leave England several weeks earlier with an altogether different group of men. His mission was financially speculative. The men would be paid the prize booty they could seize from legitimate pirate or French ships. Therefore he wanted men of good character who were excellent seaman. Having personally chosen each of the 150 men, he took pride in his selections.

In a hurry to depart London, he had chosen not to salute several Royal Navy vessels leaving the mouth of the Thames. It had been a mistake. This was a long-standing tradition and a direct affront to the English Navy and the King. His men had even taunted the English yachts as they passed, showing their backsides. Hence the Adventure Galley was boarded, and thirty-five of her best seamen were pressed into the Royal Navy. It was another several weeks before he could get Admiral Russell to return sailors to him to fill his crew. He received back landsmen and troublemakers rather than the original able-bodied seamen.

He was now on his way to New York to fill out his crew with another eighty good men. Then he could chase pirates.

"My crew will not like to be sailing under an unlucky captain," he said aloud. Perhaps it was nothing to be worried about. "Maybe we have gotten the bad luck out of the way at the start."

He turned around and faced the bow.

The open sea helped calm his nerves.

Captain Kidd was very glad to be leaving England in command of his own powerful ship. The crew could be dealt with over time. He was a restless man.

He had desperately wanted a commission from the King to command a Royal Navy vessel and had sailed to London from New York in late 1695 in search of this honor. He loved the sea and had been a respectable member of New York society for several years. He had used his considerable maritime skills as a merchant seaman to build his wealth. Kidd was in love with his beautiful Sarah and their young daughter of the same name, whom he adored. But, his first love was the sea. He wanted adventure.

He had sailed to London with a recommendation letter to request an audience with the King in his quest to become a Royal Navy Captain. While there, he became involved in a scheme to help the monarch with his pirate problem while making money for himself and others. Several financial benefactors backed him in building a ship and outfitting it to sail against any pirate he could find, with the booty paying the mission's expenses. The profits would be split among Kidd and the powerful English gentlemen. These included the Earl of Bellomont and other aristocrats. He never met the King, but he did receive a written commission to perform this duty. The King was to receive ten percent of the take.

This was a dangerous gamble, and Kidd knew he was sailing in treacherous territory. He was already at odds with the Royal Navy, who presumed it was their duty to deal with the piracy issue. It was an unlucky start indeed.

He had no friends at sea, and he suspected as much as he crossed into the Atlantic. The rewards, however, could be great and in his mind worth the risk.

Looking out over the vast ocean, he felt at peace for the first time in many years. His wife and daughter were the furthest subjects from his mind. He was with his love at last.

Chapter Two

March 8, 1806

The West Virginia snow was falling heavily and had accumulated a blanket over the lawn of the mansion two feet deep. The trees sprang from the soft surface and reached to the snow clouds above with white-covered arms. The silence was deafening in the late evening. Aaron Burr stood in the study, looking out over the magnificent gardens, which were now covered in a winter coat. The moonlight reflected off the new fallen snow. It seemed as though they were completely alone in the Virginia woods, but he knew the staff and guards were posted elsewhere. The clock struck eleven.

He had just finished a wonderful meal with his hosts, the Blennerhassets, in their formal dining room in the main section of the sprawling home, the grandest structure in all of America away from the East Coast. The recent stroll under the covered walkway to the study was short but exceedingly cold. He was thankful the servants had started the fireplace hours ago, so the room was comfortably warm. The only sounds were the crackling of the embers behind him. He listened to the popping and hissing and was comforted by long-forgotten memories of the same. He momentarily was brought back to his childhood, being cuddled by his mother next to the fire. It was a pleasant memory.

The owner of the study was obviously an educated man. Musical instruments occupied the corners of the room. The walls were covered with books from floor to ceiling. What was most interesting, however, was a complete chemical laboratory opposite where he was standing, one of two in the entire American West. Blennerhasset was a man of many talents.

Burr was excited. His plan, which until recently had been just that, a plan, was now a distinct possibility.

After Hamilton's death, he was indicted for murder in New York and New Jersey. Although he was eventually acquitted, his career as a politician was over. Yet he still craved two things, money and power.

The only place he surmised he could acquire both was out west. When he actually thought up this grand design was unknown even to him; it had been percolating in his mind for as long as he could remember. He was a very ambitious man. He had been vice president of the United States for goodness sake. Close but yet so far.

Burr had been spurned many times before. He harbored grievances. It started with General Washington, who refused to acknowledge his bravery in the Revolutionary War. Then other dreams had been taken from him.

So his thoughts had turned west.

The Spanish lands in North America were very poorly managed; everyone knew that. What he desired was no less than conquering these lands during the upcoming war between the United States and Spain. Then he would install himself as king.

He had leased forty-thousand acres from the Spanish government in the Bastrop lands of Texas along the Ouachita River in what is now Louisiana. There he had a force of eighty men encamped, the start of an army.

I will rule benevolently, he thought.

To this end he had been contacting prominent people who he thought could help with his quest. Harman Blennerhassett was one of those individuals. Burr had appealed to his vanity and his greed. It had worked.

He was a wealthy immigrant from Ireland who controlled a large island in the Ohio River. His home was the most magnificent structure Burr had ever set foot inside. The seven-thousand-square-foot mansion contained oil paintings from Europe, silver door hardware, exquisite oriental rugs, and alabaster chandeliers with silver chains. His estate consisted of the entire landmass of the large island surrounded by the river.

Burr surmised his host wanted more money and a little glory. He was right. Tonight's dinner had sealed the bond between them and access to the resources Blennerhassett could offer.

Of course, Burr had brought his daughter Theodosia to Ohio with him. She was an asset when it came to impressing moneyed interests.

He had raised her as a prodigy with strict mental discipline. Fluent in Latin, Greek, and several other languages, she could intelligently converse with anyone. She was also skilled in the arts of dancing and music. Burr had seen to her education personally since his wife had died years ago. He loved "Theo" desperately.

She was also married to Governor Alston of South Carolina. After the birth of their son in 1802, her health became frail. Burr hoped this trip would help restore her strength. After dinner this evening, she had retired early, which allowed him to speak freely to Blennerhassett.

His host's money would help, of course, in the early days of his scheme; Burr had no resources of his own to tap. The island grounds would also be a convenient training ground for the invasion force Burr was planning. In the long run, he would need serious money, money to fund an empire.

Burr smiled. Thanks to Alexander Hamilton, I will have this. A noise startled him and he was brought back to reality. Someone was walking through the covered walkway from the main house to the study. He heard the door open and saw his host walk in with a smile on his face.

"You have quite excited my wife, Colonel. It is a feat even I have not been able to accomplish in quite some time. My congratulations!"

"It is good to have such believers in my capabilities, Harman. Let me congratulate you again on these splendid surroundings."

"And your daughter, Sir, she is an exquisite creature!"

"Thank you, my new friend," Burr replied.

Blennerhassett was uncorking a very nice bottle of Bordeaux his servant had retrieved from the cellar beneath the study.

"I drink to the surroundings to come! I must endeavor to learn Spanish," he quipped.

"Indeed," replied Burr as he raised his glass.

June 10, 2017

Bahamas

Evening

Connor parked the rental car late in the evening and walked the short distance to the British Colonial Hilton in Nassau, where he typically stayed. Nassau was very hot this summer night, and he worked up a sweat as he reached the hotel. The traffic was still heavy on Bay Street as the tourist revelers hit the bars and mingled with the locals. The scene reminded him of wolves attacking the shepherd's sheep. Many a pocket was picked as dusk descended on the pirate town.

The Hilton was built on the site of an original British fort torn down at the end of the nineteenth century. A hotel designed by Henry Flagler, who built the Breakers in Palm Beach, had replaced another military structure that burned in the 1920s. The Bahamian government then rebuilt the site, and it was taken over by Hilton in the 1990s. Hilton had preserved the colonial essence that history called for. It was a great base of operations for Connor, as it sat in the middle of his clients in Nassau, and he enjoyed working from the hotel.

The monstrous hulks of three cruise ships parked on the sea side of the building dominated the harbor and lit up the evening sky. The government had just dredged the channel to accommodate this new line of massive vessels. Their stacked decks illuminated the entire Bay Street area like a glowing sun.   Even with a bad economy, the pleasure cruise business was humming.

Connor had long grown used to the ships in the background, and the sight no longer startled him. He was tired from the day's trip as he arrived at the hotel, but his mind was racing.

The doorman opened the glass door, and the welcome blast of the air conditioning hit him full force in the face. The great mural of the town's past dominated the far wall above the massive stairway to the second floor.

The history of the Bahamas and the Caribbean always fascinated Connor. Although the Bahamas was not technically the Caribbean, he lumped them together all the same.

Most Americans had no idea of the battles that had been fought here for control of the world by the colonial powers right off their doorstep. Slavery, sugar, silver, and gold were all reasons the Spanish, French, Dutch, and English came to blows over several centuries in the West Indies and Caribbean Sea. Although Nassau was never invaded, there were many forts built to protect the port from foreign powers or, more often than not, pirates.

With the immense gold and silver harvests the Spanish mined from the Spanish Main came intense interest from competing powers and other groups intent on relieving them of their precious metal burden as it was transported back to the European continent. The Caribbean islands and the Bahamas, with its vast network of isolated cays, was well suited for pirates and privateers who were determined to pillage Spanish assets as they sailed north to Madrid.

When they were not attacking foreign ships, pirates would set up encampments on the cays and gorge themselves on their newly acquired plunder. These dry spells could last for months, until another hapless victim sailed by. They loved to roast the meat of local wild pigs in thin strips to survive. This food was called "bouchon" after the French word for roasted meat. This was the origin of today's bacon. Also, since they subsisted on this ration, the pirates earned the name "buccaneers."

Locations in Jamaica and Cuba specifically became famous for their pirate cities where the thieves could congregate between exploits and spend their ill-begotten wealth. Port Royal and Tortuga were notorious examples. Nassau was also one of those places. It was one of the last pirate refuges before the European navies were able to all but snuff out the pirate vocation in the early eighteenth century.

Men such as Edward Teach, or Blackbeard, and Captain Henry Morgan became famous during this golden age of piracy. Teach was killed by English troops, while Morgan famously died in his bed of old age and a very rich man. He considered himself a privateer, but his actions drifted into the realm of piracy over time.

As the Spanish empire waned and their mining operations slowed, the region became famous for another commodity—sugar. The agreeable climate along with a plethora of imported African slaves made the Caribbean the perfect area to grow the cane to sweeten the cups of the numerous coffee houses across Europe. The indigenous Indian population had been decimated by disease upon arrival of the white man and could no longer be counted on in sufficient numbers by the slave masters.

The difference between a pirate and a privateer was slight. Pirating was illegal worldwide and a scourge on trade across the globe. However, a privateer was basically a pirate sanctioned by a government. If, say, England was at war with France, the two governments would sanction and fund captains to capture and pillage ships of the opposing power. The end result was the same. People were killed or imprisoned and ships and cargo plundered.

Connor walked across the expansive, marbled lobby and strolled into the bar facing the harbor. He had showered and changed at Alex's place after the miserable fishing expedition. He now just wanted a drink and a quiet place to think. A dark, empty corner worked just fine.

Alex had informed him of some exciting developments, and now they had to plan the next steps, which would not be easy, considering the typical government interference with situations like this one. The one thing he was quite sure of was that he didn't place any faith in the Bahamian government's fairness or process of confidentiality.

He pulled a notebook from his briefcase and began to make plans for the next few days. He tried to keep his mind busy, but again, as always, the sorrow began to creep in. It was always in late night bars that it tended to happen, when the day was winding down. That's when he thought of her and how much he missed her. They had sat in this very bar together. He shockingly realized that probably on this very sofa he had held her. She had traveled with him frequently in the past as he visited clients. The Bahamas had been a favored destination for both of them. He tried to force the thought away and concentrate on his work.

She had died on 9/11. He still had the message on his phone. He played it from time to time.

Connor ran an emerging market trading desk for a large investment bank and was based out of New York City. Although he oversaw many traders and salesmen, his main job was building solid relationships with clients, so he traveled a great deal. Many of these clients were based in the Caribbean, where he had focused his career for the last twenty years. On September 11, 2001, he was in Jamaica. He had returned to his hotel later that evening after a fishing trip with a group of bankers, oblivious to the carnage being perpetrated on New York. He had immediately tried to call her, but there was no answer. Then he saw a message on his mobile phone.

"Connor, something's happening! There is smoke all over the place. I'm scared but I love you so much!"

He never saw her or spoke to his wife again. Much later, he spoke to the police about what had happened to her. It seems most of the people on that floor were unable to get down the stairs blocked by wreckage. She probably jumped, as the fire was intense. He shivered again. The emotional pain was still raw.

He realized again that a tear was rolling down his face. "It's been a long time," he said aloud. "You need to move on with your life. She's gone," he added.

Signaling to the waiter, he downed his drink and ordered another. It's going to be another long night. There were several women across the bar who kept stealing glances his way, but he wasn't interested, had not been in a long time. Work was his only pleasure these days, but it was starting to get old.

The second drink helped, and he realized he could not get much done late in the evening. He would need his strength for the following day's activities, so he folded his notebook and picked up the letter from his great aunt he had received from an attorney in Nassau a month ago. He vaguely remembered her face, as he had not seen her for probably forty years. She died when he was a child. Even then he mainly remembered her special cakes with the icing on them that he loved so much, and the large kitchen with such wonderfully strange utensils in that old, Victorian house. He was quite shocked when the attorney for the trust had called.

"Your Aunt Clara selected you as trustee for an offshore trust before she died. She didn't want this letter delivered until you were forty-five, and it's yours now. Please come to Nassau, and let me hand deliver it to you as she requested."

"Dear Connor," the letter read, "I want to tell you about your relationship to Aaron Burr."

DELTA

By

L Todd Wood

Prologue

She was thirty-eight years old and a virgin. Her parents had seen to that. They had selected her when she was only ten to be the guardian of the flame. Her life was laid out in front of her before it even started. It had not been a bad life; in fact, it was quite pleasurable. She was worshipped and held a very high position in Roman society. She even had her own box at the Coliseum with the five other virgins. But, as with the clouds in the sky, things always change.

Julia and the five Vestal Virgins guarded the flame in the Temple of Vesta. The virgins and their ancestors had guarded the flame for a thousand years. The temple was a fifteen-meter-wide, circular edifice in the Foro Romano, supported by twenty Corinthian columns. It was one of the oldest structures in Rome and was used to store important records and business documents for safekeeping. There was an opening to the east pointing towards the sun, the origin of fire. The flame burned continuously inside. It was said that if the flame ever went out, Rome would fall. The year was 298 AD. Vesta was the goddess of fire, the goddess of the hearth—the fire that kept an ancient home alive. She was worshipped originally in the circular huts the Roman tribes built in the area, hence the circular design of the temple. The goddess kept Rome alive as long as they kept their covenant with her to keep the flame burning. At least, that was what the people were led to believe.

Julia also had a covenant with Rome, although not of her choosing. Her parents had offered her as a virgin to guard the flame when she was ten. The virgins came from very high-placed families in Roman society. It was an honor to have a daughter selected to guard the Temple of Vesta. In return for thirty years of celibacy, upon their fortieth birthday, the virgins were allowed to marry and received a huge dowry from the state. They had statues made in their likeness that were placed in the gardens around the temple. However, if a virgin broke her vow of celibacy to the Empire, the consequences were dire.

The Vestal Virgins lived in a multi-room structure right outside of the temple. The site was the most holy in Roman culture and was placed squarely in the center of Foro Romano, where it all began. This was where the first tribes of the ancient valley met to trade along the lowlands of the river. It was where Romulus was suckled by the she-wolf after being abandoned by his parents. Any free Roman citizen could take the fire to his home, and the temple therefore represented the hearth of Rome.

It was early evening when the visitor came to call on Julia. He was a younger man, a servant dressed in servant's clothes, and quite handsome. She met him at the gate to the temple grounds to talk after he had sent a request in to the College of the Vestals to speak with her. The senator's aide could come no further. "Tonight at midnight, Senator Thor will pay you a visit. He has something to give you, something that needs to be guarded, even from the emperor himself. This is the safest place in Rome. Please meet him." The visitor left without explaining further. Julia was left wondering at the gate for some time but finally retired to her room.

Julia was troubled. She would have to be very careful. This meeting was very dangerous for both her and the senator. She knew things were changing in Rome. The corruption was rampant. The emperor was claiming for himself more and more power. The Roman order and process that had survived for centuries was giving way to raw corruption and tyranny.

The Senate had long been relegated to the periphery. Originally the body was set up by the early Roman kings and came from the historical group of elders the tribes organized to help govern themselves. In fact, the word senate is derived from the Latin word senex, which means old man. Once Rome became a republic, the power of the Senate grew exponentially. However the republic was long gone. All power was now held by the emperor. No longer was he seen as an equal to the average citizen in Rome; he was a god. However, he was becoming more and more corrupt, cut off from communication with his subjects and events throughout the Empire. He received information filtered by his court with which he constantly feared revolt and death. His actions were not those of one concerned about the future of the Empire but of one concerned with staying in power. While he concentrated on giving out favors, the barbarians advanced to the north.

Night fell. At the appropriate time, Julia rose from her bed and left her chambers, moving as quietly as possible. She made her way out into the warm night. She could see the light from the flames of the hearth in the Temple of Vesta licking the ceiling of the ancient structure. She was scared. However, she trusted the senator and knew he was a good man; she would meet him despite the danger.

She made her way silently across the garden between the wading pools and stopped near the stone fence on the other side. Her white evening clothes stood out like a ghost under the full moon. The cicadas sang a rhythmic song of joy to the white orb in the sky. The Roman Forum was silent.

"Julia," a voice whispered. "I am here." She turned and walked toward the sound. The senator stepped from the shadows. "Thank you for coming," he said softly. He was old, probably over seventy, which was ancient for a Roman man. His eyes were flanked by deep crevices in his skin, and his hair was a wispy white. He walked with a pronounced stoop. He was dressed in a tunic made of expensive cloth with large, colorful stripes, identifying him as a senator.

"I came as you requested. What is so important? I cannot stay long," Julia declared.

"I don't have much time," he said and handed her a small, stone tube typically used to store documents. It was capped at both ends and sealed. "You must guard this with your life. It is the past and the future of Rome. Do not place it in the temple with all of the other royal documents. Keep it with you at all times. Tell no one. It is safe here I believe. No one will bother you. When you are older, pass it on to one of the other virgins with a sacred oath to guard it with her life as I request you to do."

She took the container. It was surprisingly light. There was a lanyard attached at both ends. She put the cord around her neck, and the scroll dangled between her breasts. She moved it under her night clothes so it could not be seen. "I will do as you ask," she replied, "because I believe you are a good man that wants what's best for Rome. I have seen you fight to restore Rome to its former glory and justice. I trust you." Julia had heard of the senator's reputation as being kind and wise, although they had never met in person. She looked him in the eyes one last time then looked around the courtyard, frightened that she would be discovered. "I must go."

With that reply she turned and walked back across the gardens. The senator disappeared into the night. What neither of them saw was another young girl, barely fourteen, also in a white night dress in the garden, hiding behind a column at the Temple of Vesta. She was Cornelia, one of the other five virgins. She had been guarding the flame through the night. Cornelia was still young but quite adamant in her opinion of herself and the importance of her role in Roman society. She was new to the temple and rather passionate about her duties. Cornelia was also a budding woman and felt subconsciously angry about not being able to talk to the young boys she frequently saw looking at her. She was jealous of the other girls in society and really quite angry about it. She knew that it was not permitted to meet male Romans without a chaperon, especially at night, and decided to take her anger out on Julia, as it was the only avenue she had, however misguided. Had Julia broken her vow of celibacy to the temple? She would need to report this to the authorities. She was certain she would be well rewarded by the emperor.

The next day, Julia rose late in the morning after a fitful sleep. She had not slept well after the meeting with the senator, and sleeping with the scroll draped around her neck would take some getting used to. She moved to the window and drew the curtain to let in some light. Strange, her morning servant was not next to her when she woke. That had never happened before. Her servant had taken care of her every need flawlessly for years. Since she had slept late, she was hungry. There was no breakfast by her bed either as she had grown accustomed to over the last twenty-eight years. A twinge of fear rose up her spine. She walked to the door to the outside chamber and opened it.

Her heart melted in terror as she saw the Praetorian guards outside of her sleeping quarters, waiting for her. The ten soldiers were in full ornamental battle gear and had no thoughts of allowing this girl to get away after the emperor's instructions. The emperor had a habit of decimating soldiers he surmised were not loyal. The practice consisted of killing one in ten men in a unit in order to ensure discipline. No, they would not let her get away. In fact they would enjoy this task.

"No, please, I can explain!" she shrieked and dropped to the floor, sobbing. Denouncing a virgin for incest against the state was a serious offense. The emperor used this opportunity shrewdly to blame this treason for his recent failures in battle and deflect blame from himself.

The guards picked her up off the ground and tied her hands behind her back. "It is too late for you; it has already been decided. You have broken your vow to Rome and the Temple of

Vesta." Julia screamed in horror, as she knew what was awaiting her. She wailed as they dragged her by the hair from her bedroom and out of the College of Virgins. The pain added to her fear but was nothing compared to what she was about to experience.

The soldiers carried her to the cobblestone road outside the temple grounds in the center of Foro Romano. The crowds had already gathered, as the word had spread fast of what was to happen. This was even better entertainment than the gladiators in the Coliseum. No one wanted to miss the show. They were used to the emperor providing routine ghoulish spectacles to divert attention from their miserable and declining living conditions. The crowd was excited.

First she was whipped by a thick cane fifty times. The back of her white clothes became stained with blood. She was close to unconsciousness but hoisted onto a funeral cart and tied to a stake emanating from the center. A pail of cold water was thrown in her face to wake her up in order to enjoy the procession. Soon she was again screaming in horror and shock at what was happening. She had done nothing wrong! She had been true to Rome; she no longer even had any sexual feelings. Those had vanished long ago. She had been true to her oath. But today it didn't matter.

The cart wound its way through the center of the ancient city and slowly made its way outside of the massive walls to the place where the dead were buried, to the Campus Sceleratus, a small rise near the gate. Roman citizens lined the streets to witness the spectacle. Some were empathetic and sad, others were enjoying the cruel procession and used the occasion to start another decadent binge of drinking, drugs, and sex. The corruption of the Roman ethos was almost complete.

Julia had fainted with shock in the now hot sun. Her head hung limp on her shoulder as her body was supported by the cords strapping her to the pole. Soon the procession stopped. Another bucket of cold water from the nearby aquifer was thrown on her to wake her up. She looked up and hoped she had awoken from a nightmare but stood in shock as she realized it was not the case.

Her parents and family were screaming and crying behind a wall of soldiers protecting the executioner. The wealthy family, once close to the emperor's court, would now be banished. Their lives changed forever. They would be lucky to escape with their lives and would soon be making hurried plans to flee the city.

The soldiers untied her from the cart and dragged her by her bound hands to the hillside below. The ropes around her wrists and the rocks on the ground cut into her skin. She pleaded with them to listen to the truth, but they ignored her. They led her to an open tomb. They stopped in front of the crypt, and a Roman judge walked up to her and began to speak.

"You have broken your sacred vow to Rome. You will now accept the consequences of your pleasure of the flesh." At this point, Julia was too weak to protest. The soldiers walked into the crypt and placed an oil lamp on one of the slabs next to a decaying body. The air smelled of death, as one of the bodies was fresh from burial a week before. The soldier adjusted the wick and lit the lamp. Beside the lamp he placed a loaf of bread and a cup of water. Then they brought Julia into the tomb and pushed her to the floor. She was mumbling in an incomprehensible manner.

The rock was then moved to close the tomb. The last vestige of light twinkled out as the stone was rolled across the opening. Julia's voice was drowned out to the outside world, and her screams whispered like death on the wind.

No one noticed the richly dressed man standing in the crowd. If they did notice, they did not speak to him. The power emanating from his stature made it clear he was not to be spoken to, although no one recognized him as a local. He was dressed in a way which was foreign to Roman society, but it was obvious he was a man of sophistication. If they had noticed him, they would have seen he was smiling.

One hundred years later, Emperor Theodosius I extinguished the fire in the hearth of the Temple of Vesta as he proclaimed it inconsistent with Christianity, now the official religion of Rome. A few years later, Rome fell to the barbarians.

Chapter One

The words just wouldn't come. He sat at the wooden table on the old, rickety, spindle chair, his eyes attempting to focus on the laptop. The chair creaked beneath him. He had been meaning to buy something new to sit on, but in reality he just couldn't part with an old friend. It had been two months, and it was now like they were married. His body had molded a depression in the soft wood of the seat. How could he get a new chair? It was not going to happen.

The words still wouldn't come. Sometimes when he started to write, the words gushed out of him like a hot geyser, not tonight. He leaned forward on his elbows into the table and stared at the blue and white screen. He began to make out the pixels in the coloring. The table swayed slightly below him with the force of his weight and screamed in pain. Nothing. Today was not going to be the day he made progress. He just didn't know where to take the story. He needed inspiration.

So inspiration it would be. Rafe stood up. He wavered slightly as he stood and grabbed the table to steady himself. Glancing at the bottle of Chianti on the table, he could see it was half empty. Another dead soldier stood next to it. He should have been really drunk, but he wasn't. A couple bottles of wine a day saw to that. His tolerance was impressive.

Next to the first bottle was a picture of his kids. I miss them, bad. He turned away and pushed the thought out of his mind. Actually, I'm the happiest I've been in a long time! And he really was. The divorce had been over for six months now. Oh, of course he still had the raging phone calls, usually in the evening when she was drunk. But the good thing was he didn't have to be in the same room anymore. He had been taught not to hit a woman. So he had taken it—for years. It almost destroyed him. No more.

Rafe made his way confidently to the balcony door as he had been doing for two months now and opened it. The smell of the sea embraced him like a foggy morning. But it was evening. The sun was setting. The sun was setting on Venice. His balcony overlooked one of the canals meandering off the main drag. He could hear the taxi boats plodding along, their engines sounding like a growling lion. It seemed they never stopped. Venice, like any major city, had an extensive public transport system, except hers was on water. Luckily his building was tall, taller than most around him, and his view was spectacular from the top floor. He could see the clock tower in St. Mark's Square in the distance. The balcony was quite large, and he had started a nice collection of herbs and other plants growing in the Venetian sunlight and salty air. It was a heavenly location for a writer. It was just what Rafe needed to find some peace. He just wanted to write and be left alone for a while.

He turned and made his way back across the main room to the exit and started down the several flights of stairs, emerging along the canal into the evening shortly after. It was going to be a beautiful night. The gondolas for hire were taking full advantage of the perfect conditions for a moonlit cruise. After a few twists and turns and five minutes later, he arrived at his favorite restaurant along the water. The nightlife here was fantastic. It was when the real Venetians came out to play, avoiding the horde of tourists during the day.

Rafe sat at a table in the outdoor seating area, and soon a waiter was describing to him in Italian the specials for the evening. He understood only half of what was said but shook his head in agreement. "Surprise me," he said in English. The waiter smiled and started shouting instructions to the chef as only an Italian could do. Soon the food starting coming and didn't seem to stop.

In spite of all his problems, and besides missing his kids terribly, Rafe really was happy. This place enthralled him. *Maybe I will never* leave Venice. The authentic Italian seafood meal went down easy, and the courses were never ending. He found himself apologizing to the overweight, female proprietor why he just couldn't eat anymore. He paid the bill and spent an hour wandering through the passageways of the floating city, marveling at the history. The walk helped to digest his meal. The best thing to do in Venice was to get lost. He was on an island for God's sake, so it wasn't really being lost. He could find his way back eventually. But the pleasure was in finding a new street and meeting new people and watching the Venetians do their thing in their element, which was the evening. Soon he was doing just that as he found himself chatting with a local businessman who owned a tobacco shop. He enjoyed a fine cigar and became fast friends with the gentleman. *This is how I always find inspiration.*

Eventually, he decided to go back to his flat and get some writing done. Maybe the evening stroll would stir his imagination. He could still see St. Mark's in the distance, and he oriented himself to the bell tower. Soon he would come out near his home. Rafe found himself walking along a foreign canal in a neighborhood he did not know. It was strangely quiet and almost deserted. He enjoyed times like these, finding new places in his new favorite city, listening to the noises of the night. Rafe reveled in the fact he had no schedule and no one telling him what to do. He was completely in control of his own destiny, and he loved it.

He gazed at the ornately decorated palaces lining the canal and tried to imagine the history of the owners hundreds of years ago. The parties they threw, the beautiful women who lived there, all of this danced through his mind. He casually stopped along one such palace, long since deserted due to the mold creeping up to the upper floors from the constant flooding. He paused to take in the structure. It was times like these that inspiration came.

Venice was sinking. Slowly, very slowly, but sinking just the same. The buildings were constructed on wooden pilings sunk into the mud and clay centuries before. The foundations of the city's structures rested on this wooden support. The earth delayed the process of decay, but slowly these pylons were deteriorating. Artesian wells sunk in the early twentieth century to feed local industry were discovered to be adding to the structural problems, hastening the sinking of the city's support. As the city's elevation shriveled, the floods came more often and the damage grew exponentially. Many of the palaces along the waterways were deserted, or at least the first floor, due to mold and other hazards from the encroaching sea.

The population of Venice was now mostly older, as families with children had moved out long ago because of the safety hazards and expense of living on the island. The Italian government had spent hundreds of millions of euros to stop the decomposition of the city but could only slow not alter nature's course. Seawater had a nasty way of eating into a foundation over time that no amount of human intervention could stop. The future of Venice was in doubt in the long run. Today, however, Rafe enjoyed the scenery and wondered about the past.

As the evening light dimmed, out of the corner of his eye, Rafe noticed a strange glow emanating from the base of the palace. It was an orange, fiery color wafting through the water like cream in a coffee. He walked over and looked closer. The strange, colored light angrily turned bright red and then was gone. He shrugged and kept walking. Must be the wine. Darkness set in for the rest of his trip home.

His head hurt but not too much. His body was used to the alcohol. He was terribly thirsty however. The sun was peeking through the venetian blinds and stabbing him in the eyes. He awoke but didn't want to move. This was his favorite part of the day. He could just lie in bed until he couldn't lie there anymore. Rafe reached for a glass of water on the nearby table and downed it quickly. Then he closed his eyes. I wonder what time it is. But, I don't really care.

Rafe Savaryn was a world traveler. He loved exploring different civilizations, new and old. He wrote books about those experiences and taught history at a small Ivy League school in the northeastern United States. He especially loved European history. His family had emigrated from the Ukraine during the previous generation, and he still felt he had roots in Eastern Europe. "If you don't know history, you're doomed to repeat it," he always told his incoming classes.

Rafe spent several months a year in different, far-off corners of the globe. Previously he brought his family, but on this trip he was alone, due to the divorce. He enjoyed finding places that no one in the West knew much about, places that experienced a deep history that had been lost to the ages. Learning about the past gave Rafe great pleasure, as it helped him understand the present. This was the secret of his books and why he had become such a successful writer.

One of his earliest memories as a child was running across an expansive, open terrazzo with a large statue in front of him. He was obliviously happy and his mother was chasing him from behind, calling for him. He remembered her explaining to him about the statue and how important it was to history. Rafe ignored her and kept running. He remembered reaching the statue and seeing a tall, bronzed man riding a horse. As he grew older, he had always wondered where that place was. Perhaps that is why I'm always searching and writing, hoping one day I'll run into that statue again. Perhaps that is where my curiosity for the past began.

But his favorite place in the world was Italy. And his favorite city in Italy was Venice. To live among the houses where the Italians had fled from the barbarians during the Dark Ages after the fall of the Western Roman Empire, and built a city on the marshy islands, was heavenly for him. He felt as if he dined with da Vinci when eating among the locals in the late evening. He reveled in the atmosphere. Today was going to be no different.

An hour later, his side began to ache from lying in bed, and Rafe sat up, throwing off the matted sheets. He walked to the balcony and once again threw open the doors. He breathed in the sea. It was a daily ritual he enjoyed. He checked on his herb garden and then walked to the bathroom. Rafe took a short, cold shower to revive himself, quickly dressed, grabbed his laptop, and headed out of his flat and down the stairs. Today was the perfect day to write. He enjoyed the exercise as he strolled through the waking city. Soon he was sitting at a table in St. Mark's square, the tourists and the pigeons milling all around him. The ideas came and he began to write....

Dreams of the Negev

A Short Story

by

L Todd Wood

Written while covering the Israeli, Gaza War of 2014

The siren started slowly but built quickly to a nerve-wracking crescendo, waking him rudely as the sunlight started to peak through the cheap, nylon curtains in the room. In an instant, he had a question to answer. Do I go to the shelter or not? The loud booms of the Iron Dome missile protection system shook the windows as the missiles found their targets, rockets fired at Tel Aviv by Hamas. It will all be over soon anyway, no time, he thought as he dug deeper into the covers for protection from the in-coming artillery. He was right. The sirens stopped momentarily. But, now he was awake. Groggily, he tried to piece together what was going on.

He knew he was in Israel, Tel Aviv to be exact, covering the war as a journalist. He had arrived several days earlier from the other conflict de jour, Ukraine, to report on the violence between Israel and Gaza for multiple news outlets. Having just turned forty years of age, his body no longer quickly adjusted to time differential when heading east. Although the sun was now brightly thrusting through the window shades like daggers as the Israeli day was starting, his body told him otherwise. Sleep, it said. He tried to get deeper into the covers. The cheap air conditioner in the low budget hotel had been running all night as the thermostat was broken. Even though outside the temperature hit thirty-five degrees Celsius, in his room, it was closer to fifteen.

He opened his eyes briefly. The sheet on the bed unfortunately had been kicked down to the foot of the mattress, he only had the synthetic bed cover over him and it wasn't enough. He was cold but he dared not move. The faux orange tile on the floor of the hotel room contrasted oddly with the tapestry hanging on the wall. It reminded him of a black velvet, hanging Elvis art piece one could buy on the side of the road in Memphis. The decor of the room was dated in the early seventies; however, everything was functional. He was thankful for that. Even the internet worked. The sounds were getting louder now outside as the stream of cars passing by his first floor window increased and the pedestrians walking towards the beach a few blocks away talked incessantly. Several dogs were barking. The same faded jeans and white shirt he had been wearing for a week sat rumpled on the floor. A have drunk glass of red wine stood next to the empty bottle on the bed stand. Another dead soldier, he thought.

He had been dreaming, that he was sure of. Lingering feelings of crime, pain, hurt, evil, abuse, and even death drifted through his clouded mind. He never knew why but those things were always there, subtly below the surface. But he also had a vague sense a door had opened somehow. It was as if he awoke too soon, that he was missing something, something important. That always happened when he wrote. He had stayed up late into the night, putting the finishing touches on a story. Writing was a gateway for him. It always led to other things. The dream was no exception.

For some reason, he also remembered it was his brother's birthday. His brother had passed away as a toddler when he was only four years old himself, from cancer. He had vague memories of him crawling across the floor to him on a yellow, ribbed, carpet. They weren't really memories, just flashes, snapshots of time stored somewhere in his brain. Strange the things that enter your mind sometimes. I really am cold. But, he didn't care and drifted off back to sleep.

He awoke to the sound of cats fighting. It was a horrible, screaming sound, like that of a woman being repeatedly stabbed. He rolled over in the sand and stared into the eyes of one of the felines who had walked over to him, searching for food. The cat's eyes were glowing a deep yellow, like that of the devil himself. He turned away, preferring not to return the animal's stare. His friend was dead, that he was sure of. There was no more breath coming from the body. He had taken a machine gun round to the chest. At least I don't have to listen to the sucking chest wound anymore, he thought to himself. The date was April 18, 1917 and he was in the Negev desert and he was cold. His body was shaking, attempting to ward off the chill. He relaxed as the sun began to peak over the horizon. At least I will die warm, he thought. The Gaza offensive had not gone well for the British. The Ottoman's were too dug in and well-defended. The Brits could not break their ranks. He had been cut off with his friend from the rest of his unit and they were pinned down behind a burnt out tank. As his friend was now dead, he was alone. When the light was strong enough for his enemy to see him, he would be finished off with artillery. The only thing left to do is write. At least I can enjoy the remaining few hours of my life. Writing was the only thing that brought him joy. He took out the few pieces of paper from his breast pocket along with a pencil and began scratching out a few sentences. For some reason, he wanted to finish the short story he had started a few days earlier. It was important for him to do that now. Even though it was highly likely no one would ever even know it existed, much less actually read it.

The birds were now circling overhead. They smelled the death of his friend. The blood had coagulated underneath him in the sand, creating a dark stain that had hardened in the heat. It was amazing how animals could pick up the scent of death from a long way away. The realization that they would pick his bones as well forced him to write faster. He was almost done. It was a love story, a story of two lovers reunited at the end of their lives. It would not be a story he would experience himself. He had long stopped thinking of his girlfriend. He had not seen or heard from her in over a year. His letters had not been returned. I guess it's better that way than to get a Dear John letter, he pondered.

He glanced up and saw the sun was now fully above the horizon and he was starting to sweat. I don't have much time now! He wrote faster. Eventually he peered over the small sand ridge in front of the hulk of the tank and saw activity on the other side. The artillery tubes were getting ready to fire. One of the spotters noticed his movement near the tank and he saw them point in his direction. It won't be long now. He wrote the final sentence, then turned on his back and stared up at the sky. Strange, the birds have gone. He heard the thump of the guns as the ground shook underneath him. Goodbye, he thought.

"Nyet!" he heard the man shout. His eyes fluttered open briefly and he realized he was still in the room under the nylon cover. The sun was now high in the sky outside as it was now midday in Tel Aviv. He could smell the Mediterranean ocean two blocks away in spite of the air conditioner, which was now straining to operate in the increased heat of the Israeli sun. A television was blasting in the lobby a few yards away with news of the war.

The Russian family had moved into the room next to him several days before and were very loud. They fought often, waking him from time to time as he slept. They were having another argument. He felt sorry for the daughter, who spent her time in the lounge chair in the hallway outside the hotel room, desperately trying to pass the time on her iPhone. She was approximately sixteen and had long blond hair and deeply tanned skin. She would be a real heartbreaker in a few years. There were many Russian Jews in Israel. The Jewish State was a natural place for Russian tourists to visit relatives who had immigrated after the fall of the Soviet Union. It had given him a chance to practice the language he had learned in college.

He thought about getting up, but his eyes still stung with fatigue. He rolled over, adjusted the pillows and drifted back to sleep.

The sentry stood on the ramparts of the fortress overlooking the desert sixty miles to the East of Gaza, and watched as the Roman siege ramp came closer and closer. Soon they would be here and he would die. There were only a few hours left. He had come to peace with his upcoming death. In fact, the whole settlement had decided to commit suicide before the Romans entered the fortress. The year was 74 A.D. and Caesar was angry. The Jews had revolted against Rome across the Levant and he wanted to make an example to the rest of the Roman Empire out of this last group of holdouts, perched upon the mountain in their citadel called Masada.

The world needs to remember us after we are gone, thought the sentry days before. For that reason, he had been writing every evening for the past two weeks, detailing the progress the Romans were making to overtake the fort and he's people's reaction to their upcoming death. He hid the scrolls in the temple, hoping they would be found long after the Romans had left.

He was one of the ten men chosen to kill all of the others. The job had been horrifyingly devastating to his soul. However, he had kept an eerie calm as he butchered men, women, and children alike, cutting their throats and letting the blood drain out of them. Now there were only the ten men remaining. Soon they would kill each other and the last man would kill himself. He was going to be that man. He would slit his own throat. But not yet. He had to finish the story first, the story of the Jewish revolt against the Romans. He wanted the world to know.

Below him, a thousand Jewish slaves, prisoners of war, helped build the ramp which the siege tower was now being slowly pushed upward. It had been three years that his people had held out in hope that somehow they would be spared. But alas, it was not to be. They will be here in a few hours. The siege tower pushed forward, inch by inch. He could see the eyes of the Roman soldiers, eager to ravage the population of the fort as they got closer.

He went to the temple with the last scroll and hurriedly wrote details of his last day. He wrote of his wife, whom he had killed. Her body lay in his home, where they had shared a wonderful last three years together. His children lay in bed with her. He wept for his youngest daughter, only two, when he had to cut her throat. As her father, he felt it was his duty to make sure she died fast. She had no forewarning of what he was about to do. He and his wife had made sure none of the children were aware of their fate before he took them outside one at a time and put the sharp knife under their chin. He wiped away the tears. There was no time for that now. He would see them again soon enough.

A bell rung. The hour had arrived. He picked up his sword and walked out into the sunlight to kill his friends.

The siren went off again. This time, he knew he was going nowhere. He had been in deep REM state and his body did not move. He didn't even open his eyes. Before he drifted back to sleep, one thought crossed his mind, I wonder how you sleep in war? Or can you ever sleep?

He dreaded seeing his parents, although the trip home was uneventful. Soon he was being led into the chamber where they waited for him. He straightened his spine, adjusted his clothing, and tried to look his best. Then he walked in.

"You are late," said his father. "We don't like to be kept waiting."

"You look terrible," said his mother. "Where did you get those clothes?" She motioned for a servant and barked, "Have him fitted immediately for some new clothing!"

"I tried to look my best," he said to deaf ears. The courtroom looked the same. There were lines of people from all over the galaxy waiting to see the Emperor and Empress. They did not have much time to speak to one of their children.

His mother softened a bit. "Come here and give me a hug," she cooed. "I have missed you. How is boarding school?"

"It's hard work," he replied, avoiding his mother's grasp. Two could play this game. "I'd like to see my brother."

"Your brother is out administering the outer planets. You will see him soon enough. When you have finished your studies! And only then! Since he left you he has been extremely busy, while you take your time finishing your degree at the university! What do you have to say for yourself?" his father boomed, the courtiers squeamishly trying to tend to his every need as his anger rose.

"I am working hard to finish father," he replied softly. "Well your writing has improved somewhat I have to say, judging from the reports the school has been sending me. Keep up the hard work and you will earn your rightful place on the throne. But it will not come easy." It was then he noticed a beautiful girl sitting to the right of his father. She had been very quiet but was looking at him strangely, with almost a morbid curiosity. His father saw him staring at her. "Ahhh," he said. "Meet Svetlana. When you return, she will be your queen. It has been decided. In ten years."

He looked at the girl and she turned her gaze to the floor and would not look him in the eye. But she had stolen a glance at him and the one thing he noticed was her deep blue eyes, as large as the ocean. She was strikingly gorgeous. A terrible fear he had never felt washed over him. "I suggest you finish your studies and hurry home to her," his father added with a smile on his face.

"Yes, father," he softly replied and backed out of the grand hall of the palace as his parents were distracted with other matters of state. His mind was spinning with apprehension. The girl was a new twist to his life, one that he hadn't expected. Quickly, his thoughts returned to his parents. At least that is over. They will forget about me for a while. The empire had to be administered. It had been that way all of his life. On the voyage back to the university, he started again to write. Maybe I'll make up a good story for Svetlana, he said to himself.

The knocking came softly at first. He thought he was dreaming or was the knocking coming from the room next door? But soon he realized someone actually was knocking on the door to his room. "Yes," he answered softly? The chill in the air made him shiver and he worked up the nerve to reach for the sheet and add to his covering on the bed.
"Do you want the room cleaned?" a man's voice asked.
"No, not today, thank you," he responded as loud as he could muster as he groggily sat up in bed.
"Ok, thank you." The voice was gone.
He pulled the covers off and threw his legs over the side of the bed. He reached for one of his shoes on the floor and threw it against the switch on the wall that controlled the air conditioning. Blissfully, the cold air stopped spewing from the device mounted high on the wall. He decided to get up anyway. He slipped on his jeans and the white shirt, splashed some water on his face and opened the door to walk outside and get some coffee in the lobby of the hotel.

As he walked to the front area of the establishment, he heard the Russian man next door screaming some profanity. He didn't understand the word, but understood the meaning. It wasn't a nice comment to his wife. He shook his head in pity for the man's family. It was then he noticed the girl was still there, busily typing on her iPhone as if she coulmake all of the bad energy from her parents go away. As he walked by, she looked up at him and smiled. She had huge blue eyes.

Lost Bastards

L Todd Wood

Preface

I didn't know what to think when I was contacted by the family of Richard Carpenter to write this book. However, the more I learned about the story, the more I was touched. I am humbled to have been asked to undertake this project. My only hope is that I have done the story justice. When you read this book, let it take you back to another time in America, almost seventy years ago. We had just fought and won the Second World War. We were tired of conflict and death. We just wanted to live in peace. There was much brightness ahead for America. We were the shining city on the hill.

But unfortunately, as we would soon learn, there was still evil in the world and it was on the march. It was called communism, which was just another word for totalitarianism. This evil would eventually kill several hundred million people before it was also vanquished. Actually, based on events we are seeing today, it wasn't completely eradicated. It only went dormant for a few decades, simply to reappear in our universities and media several decades later.

However, in the early 1950s, America just wanted to eat hot dogs, chase girls, and watch baseball. When evil did raise its head on the Korean Peninsula, America called for its warriors one more time. As always, they answered that call. They didn't cry. They didn't seek their safe spaces or demand trigger warnings. They just went, did their duty, died, or came home.

I'm going to open the door for you now to the Forgotten War. All I ask is that as you read, say a prayer for these brave men's souls. Honor them. On your journey to Hill 433, open your eyes, smell the gunpowder, hear the artillery, feel the machine gun fire raking the earth around you, feel the fear.

Honor them.

Prologue

It had been this way her whole life, as far back as she could remember. She was different from most others, and for some reason she could not understand, this was bad, in society's eyes. This difference made her disgusting, a criminal, a danger to German society. A danger that eventually Hitler decided needed to be exterminated.

Kunigunda (Gunda) Schuhlein (22 Jan 1929 – 16 Mar 1990) was the daughter of Johann Schuhlein (18 Apr 1893 – 27 Dec 1933) and Eugenie Amalie Jenieve Bauer (6 Nov 1894 – 25 Jun 1963). Gunda's father had been a German soldier in the first great world war. Her memories of him were vague. Really the only thing she remembered was that he was sick, always in bed, and always had trouble breathing or walking. Only later did she learn that it was due to the mustard gas in the trenches. He died young and left her mother and nine children destitute.

The fact that her father was a soldier kept the worst tendencies of German society away from her. If the authorities had known her mother was Roma, or a gypsy, she would have been killed with the others, shot, sent to the camps, whatever the Nazis felt like that day. Gunda's skin was dark, and became darker in the sunlight. The Roma were of Indian descent, having migrated up through central Asia and into Europe centuries before. She covered up as much as possible. She couldn't let her friends know the truth as the truth meant certain death.

She had heard of the camps. She had seen the horse drawn carts of the Roma herded by the police into a slum town near the garbage dump on the outskirts of town. She had heard of the forced sterilizations, the rapes, the killing, the stealing of anything these poor wretched souls owned, the death, the end of everything.

Her friends and family called her Die kleine Negeria, or in English, 'little niggar.' It was as if the Nazis stole her safety, her security, her self-confidence, even if they had not destroyed her body. Eventually the Nazis started classifying Roma based on physical characteristics as the church records did not list them as non-Aryan. All they recorded was that they were Christian, as all Roma were Catholic. Physical characteristics of pure, Aryan blood became vitally important. Gunda was constantly afraid her ethnic heritage would be found out. When the German youth were sent to work in the fields to support the war, she covered up as much as possible, deathly afraid of what the sun would do to her skin, as in making it darker.

She overcompensated to prove her Germanness. As the allied troops rolled into town at the end of World War II, she decided to try and help. Her friends had left her after hearing gunshots but Gunda spotted several abandoned German portable anti-tank rockets, or Panzerfaust, on the German side of the river after the bridges had been blown. She attempted to row the weapons across the river to German troops cutoff on the American-occupied side of the waterway. American forces opened fire, thinking she was a German soldier. She ducked and her German field cap, worn by all Hitler youth, fell off and they realized she was a female child. The boat was sunk. She stood on the shoreline, shaking her fist at the American invaders, her German blood boiling. She began throwing rocks at the Americans until she realized they were laughing at her, then walked off in frustration.

The other difference, that set her apart growing up was that she was poor, very poor. Hunger was a thing she kept by her bed every night, gnawing at her gut, interrupting her dreams of soup and bread. She never knew where her next meal was coming from. The house was always cold in winter.

She earned money as best she could. All of the children had to help. Starvation, death, and disease, were the alternatives.

She grew up during the Weimar Republic. As a child, the German Reichsmark collapsed as Germany attempted to pay war reparations with printed money. At the end of the First World War, the R-Mark was valued at four to the U.S. Dollar. Two years later, it was valued at over two million to one. The German treasury could not print the money fast enough to keep up with the rapid inflation. The victorious allies saddled Germany with a debt, and a guilt, they could never repay. Germany sank into a horrific depression, as did the United States. History would forever cite the Weimar Republic as an example of a currency crisis that led to political upheaval. This is the primary reason Hitler came to power. Germans were poor, destitute, and defeated. Hitler promised to change all that.

Gunda became creative with ways to make money. Since her father had passed, her grandfather would take young Kunigunda around the beer halls to empty the ashtrays into a bucket. These were massive, ornately decorated drinking establishments which would fill with large German men drinking copious amounts of beer and smoking. Occasionally she would receive a pfennig (German penny) or two for her efforts and an occasional smack from a drunk. Inflation was raging in Germany. The printing presses could not keep up with the demand for cash as the value of a mark plummeted. A hundred pfennigs might buy the family a loaf of bread.

Her grandfather and Gunda would sort through the bucket to pull out the bits of tobacco and cigarette papers to recycle. She became very adept with her small hands picking out the shreds of tobacco. Her grandfather would then hand make cigarettes to resell.

The poverty and the teasing made Gunda strong. This, in addition to her German upbringing, created a force of will inside of the girl who was turning slowly into a young woman, and an attractive one at that. In later years, she would attempt to pass on this will to survive to her children. Gunda survived the war. She survived the Nazis as the child of a gypsy. She became a woman.

As the American tanks rolled into the city of Bamberg, German residents hung white sheets of surrender from the windows. Gunda hid in fear in the basement of the apartment where her family lived. She was sixteen. As the rumble of the tank tracks shook the house, she dared to pull back the drapes and take a look at the Americans, whom she had heard so much about. There were hundreds of them in all types of military vehicles. One soldier turned to look at her. She froze in horror! He was a negro! They all were negroes! Gunda's town had been liberated by American negro troops in an ironic twist of fate.

She guessed the negro soldier was over two meters tall! He had a wide nose and huge lips which protruded beneath the steel helmet. He was chewing a large wad of tobacco and turned to look at her as he walked next to the half-track and passed her house. The soldier saw her looking out of the window and smiled as he spit tobacco her way. He had huge yellow stained teeth.

Gunda shook in terror and ran to the interior of the house. Her siblings teased her terribly, "Gunda, the negro is coming back for you! Little niggar!"

Gunda didn't leave the apartment for almost a month as she hid from her deepest fears and the large negro soldier.

Chapter One

The years after the end of World War II were a perilous time in history for all of mankind. The threat of a nuclear confrontation was front and center as the Soviets developed the bomb and began constructing the horrific Iron Curtain in Eastern Europe. The Berlin Airlift of 1948 was a case in point as Stalin cut off the German capital from resupply and only a year long display of American airpower saved the day.

The world was deathly afraid of the spread of communism which had overrun two of the largest countries on earth, the Soviet Union and China. The fear in Southeast Asia of the red scourge drove the decision making in Washington.

The situation on the Korean Peninsula had developed in a strange fashion. After the removal of imperial Japanese rule, Russian forces occupied the territory north of the 38th Parallel. Here they installed a Stalinist leader who outdid the Soviet leader in his ruthlessness, as if that was possible. The People's Republic of Korea was formed.

American troops occupied the South per an agreement struck in 1948 with the Soviets. A reluctant America backed a dictatorship in the Republic of Korea. Neither government on the peninsula recognized the other and both considered themselves the legitimate authority of all Korea. This stalemate remained until June 25, 1950 when 75,000 well-trained and well-equipped North Korean troops invaded the South and wreaked havoc. American troops quickly joined the conflict, per a United Nations Security Council Resolution, but to no avail as in barely two months U.N. forces were forced down to the Pusan Perimeter in a desperate bid to survive, much less repel the North. The mood in Washington was dark indeed. Communism was on the march.

East Berlin
Russian Sektor
1952

Corporal Carpenter laughed so hard the beer came out of his nose. It had been a while since he had laughed, he realized, as he caught his breath and cleaned his uniform shirt where the German beer had spilled down his chest. His buddy next to him, Corporal Whitehorse helped in this process, dabbing his U.S. Army enlisted shirt with a rag from the bar. "You made a mess of yourself, Carpenter. This is going to be hard to explain to your little German wife!"

Carpenter took a moment to look around the bar. The Russian soldiers and the Americans were still dancing, the beer swashing around the wooden floor of the small beer hall in the Russian sector of Berlin. The bartender, unsure at first at the prospect of Russian and American troops drinking together, now was enjoying making extra money on a slow night. He kept the beer flowing.

The object of Carpenter's amusement, a large Russian female soldier, had buried his other friend's head in her bosom. Ransom's head literally seemed to disappear. "Ona sovsem sletela s katushek!!! yelled a Russian enlisted man (she might be going off the rails!). Carpenter lay back in his chair and slapped his leg. "I won't tell Gunda about this, Whitehorse. There are some things that are better off not said!"

Corporal Carpenter didn't want to think about his wife, his sick daughter, or his future. No, he just wanted to keep drinking. He needed a break; he had decided to let go of the tension. I had been building inside of him. It was killing him, the stress of it all. He downed the rest of the beer and signaled the bartender for another. *Tonight I will just enjoy myself and tomorrow I will pay the price and get back to the grindstone.*

Carpenter reached up and felt his face and realized it was still swollen. The alcohol had dulled the pain but it wouldn't make the acute puffiness go down. That would just take time, and maybe some ice. "Yeah, Corporal Riney really put a whoopin on you Carpenter. Good thing we bet against you. I knew you weren't ready for that fight. I could see it in your eyes. And, it was a grudge match at that! You were going to fight no matter what to settle the matter once and for all with those guys! Even if you weren't ready. But, you were doing it just for the money! I knew you were going to lose. So all ends well. At least we have plenty of cash for this little night on the town. I could tell you needed a night out too, my friend. That's what friends do, take care of their buddies. So keep drinking and by the way, that little honey pot over there has her eye on you. Don't worry, what happens here stays here," Whitehorse said with a smile.

Earlier in the day, Carpenter had fought a hard fight with one Corporal Riney, as they both were part of the Army boxing league and had traveled to Berlin for a fight against another unit. It didn't go well as the fight was called after the third round. Carpenter had the face to prove it.

But the fight wasn't his biggest concern. Corporal Richard 'Dick' Carpenter had married a German, a big no-no in the post WWII U.S. Army. To show its displeasure, the military went so far as to refuse his wife and daughter's medical treatment at the post medical facilities. Their dependent status was not recognized. To make matters worse, his youngest daughter, just a toddler, was very sick. This caused immense financial pressure on Carpenter to create cash flow to pay for very expensive antibiotics. Boxing was an easy way to make money and to get special passes from time to time. However, this time it hadn't worked out as planned. Luckily, his friend had been smarter and he had money just the same.

Instead of bedding down after the fight as instructed, they had illegally made their way through an apartment complex near Check Point Alpha to bypass the guards and security to the Russian sector, a move strictly against the rules, one that could get them court martialed. The Berlin Wall was not fully built yet and if you were determined, you could still cross rather easily between east and west. The American dollar went a lot further in the Russian-controlled area of the German capital, for beer or for a short time with a German working girl. In addition, Carpenter and his friends wanted to see Berlin, even the Russian sector. U.S. or Russian officers would be none too thrilled however to find American soldiers drinking in a Russian-sektor bar. The Americans took their chances anyway and stumbled upon a hole-in-the-wall beer cellar with the light on.

Earlier in the evening, several Russian, enlisted soldiers had surprised Carpenter and his friends in the hole-in-the-wall tavern with possible trouble to ensue. However, a few greenbacks on the bar did the trick to calm things down. Now they were all the best of friends, something military camaraderie and a few beers tends to manufacture. The Russians even pulled out an accordion, another soldier a harmonica. Soon everyone was dancing and having a good time.

Carpenter felt a hand on his shoulder. The girl from across the room who had been eyeing him had worked up the courage to take matters into her own hands. She was probably desperate for money as well. Carpenter let her stay. For the time being, he thought.

"Aaahh...horosha padla!! Americanitz!" cried one of the drunk Russian soldiers, which meant *very beautiful whore, American!* Carpenter nervously laughed again. These guys were fun, too bad we were basically enemies, but soldiers of all nationalities understood things like women and booze. For now, they were brothers in arms.

Suddenly there was a cry from the doorway where some of the Russian soldiers had been keeping watch for anyone in their chain of command who might ruin the impromptu party. "Uhodim, capitan idet!" *My captain! My captain! Let's go! Let's Go!"* the Russian soldier shouted!

All of the drunken Americans immediately shook off their German girlfriends for the evening, grabbed their coats and fur hats and headed out the back door into the cold night to sneak back to the

American side. The Russian soldiers grabbed their weapons and went outside to meet their officer. The working girls were left frustratingly empty-handed.

Thirty minutes later the motley crew safely returned to Western Berlin without being detected. The men donned their coats and hats as the night chill began to sink in and the alcohol wore off. They stopped under a street lamp and Whitehorse lit up a cigarette.

"What the Hell do you have on Ransom?" Whitehorse yelled. Then a realization washed over his face and he howled, "You dumbass, you took a Russian's coat and hat!"

Ransom took off his hat and looked at the red star emblazoned on the forehead. "Damn, I thought this hat was too big. But the coat is sure warm!" he exclaimed.

Carpenter looked down and realized he had a Russian coat and hat on as well.

"What are we going to do now?" Whitehorse asked the others in the group.

"We sell them, for sure!" replied Carpenter. "We can make some nice money on the black market for those. We report ours stolen while on duty and get replacements."

"I have to admit you got it all figured out Carpenter," said Whitehorse.

"Now where to?" asked Ransom.

"To that little bar down the road, where else?" Carpenter responded. The men laughingly disappeared into the German night.

Hours later, and three bars later, Carpenter and the boys caught the red eye train back to Bamberg from Berlin. Boxing was now the last thing on his mind. He tried to catch some shut eye in the passenger car but it was no use. He would have to wait to get home before he would be able to sleep. The jostling and banging of the rail car simply wouldn't allow him to drift off. Carpenter's thoughts slowly came around to his family and the troubles he had tried so hard to forget the entire night.

Corporal Carpenter clumsily found his way home, the alcohol taking its toll on his senses. The sun was peeking its nose over the horizon. Luckily the streets were deserted at this time of the day as he neared his apartment. The recurring altercations with aggressive German youth had made his trips home from the post quite challenging as of late. He was relieved there would be no such combat this morning. His head would not have enjoyed it.

The pain of the recent beating with dehydration from a night of drinking combined to form a deadly pounding which he didn't want to share with the Hitler Youth at this time of day. Soon he reached the door to his building and made his way painfully up the stairs, wishing he had some aspirin and a glass of water.

Gunda met him at the door. She had been crying. Carpenter immediately felt guilty for spending the night out. *So selfish of me*, he thought to himself.

"Her fever is way too high! I've used all the medicine! We need more! The Doctor earlier said she was really sick. Dick, I'm worried! Do you have any money today?"

"Yes, I have a small amount for another couple days worth. It's okay. I'm home now." Gunda collapsed into his arms, exhausted after a night with no sleep taking care of Sieglinde. Carpenter carried her into the house and put his wife gently to bed. "I've got it now; go to sleep, Gunda," he said softly. She closed her eyes and moved no more as the exhaustion took hold of her.

Carpenter then went into the other bedroom and checked on his girls. Hanalaura, his adopted, older child, was sleeping soundly. Sieglinde, the two-year-old was wide awake and obviously in distress. He felt her forehead which was burning hot. She was wide awake but listless. Carpenter picked her up and cradled her in his strong arms, took her to the bath and bathed her in cool water to reduce her temperature. He would not sleep either that day and the stress returned with a vengeance, only now he had no sleep and a headache to go with it.

"Hang in there Siggie. Daddy's here now."

"   *My earliest memory, circa summer 1955 Büdigen, Germany. Dad was always bringing soldiers from his unit home for a good German meal, music and card games. Mom loved to cook and was always the life of the party.*

After one field maneuver, he brought home a fawn whose Mother had been killed. Dad loved animals. Mom named him Willie after her brother Wilhelm who never returned from the war. Quarters had basement caged storage areas and ours was empty as all our furniture was military quartermaster. We nursed and cared for Willie until he grew horns and kept butting Mom, he was our first pet. The photo was taken at the military game preserve where we took Willie. We'd visit him after church on Sunday with his favorite treats we had collected during the week."

Sieglinde Carpenter

Chapter Two

US Army Garrison Motor Pool
Erlangen, West Germany
October 1952

Carpenter squinted into the sunlight streaming across the tops of the trees as the clouds moved away and opened up a hole for the heat to burn through. It was seven o'clock in the morning and the air was crisp; he welcomed the heat from the sun's rays which bathed his face.

He stood at attention at the U.S. Army garrison motor pool, in Erlangen, West Germany, along with over two dozen other enlisted men. The men were organized into four sections. They formed up to wait for an announcement per the instruction of the command sergeant major; the content of this announcement they had no idea. But soldiers obey orders, so here they were, waiting. *It was always hurry up and wait in the U.S. Army,* Carpenter thought to himself. *I could use a cup of coffee right now.*

The sound of a U.S. Army jeep caught his ear, speeding in from the left, but he dared not turn and look to see who it was. A move like that at attention would invite a rebuke from the command sergeant and a week's worth of some unpleasant duty for sure. *We'll know soon enough.*

The jeep careened to a stop in front of the formation, an officer stood in the passenger's seat, his hands on the glass windshield. He turned to look at the enlisted men.

"At Ease! My name is First Lieutenant Sharp." he said to the men and then waited for them to relax. "I am told you are the best of the 1st Infantry Division. I am here to select as certain number of soldiers for a special mission. To be honest, I don't need all of you. So, over the next training cycle, you will prove to me which section is going to be the best at using those crew weapons..." He pointed towards a line of armored vehicles, smiling. The vehicles were M16 halftracks holding quad 50 caliber anti-aircraft weapons and fully tracked M19s holding dual 40mm cannons.

"*And*, to make things a little more interesting, the two sections that clobber the others in qualifications will get Christmas leave! The losers get to detail out all the vehicles and weapons for Christmas inspection."

There were shouts of excitement amongst the soldiers, who soon would be in competition for a coveted pass off the post for the holidays. Carpenter sensed a chance to make money and whispered to the man in formation in front of him, the same corporal who had beat him senseless in the recent boxing match. "Riney, you want to lose 20 bucks for top section?"

Riney, his hands folded behind him, flashed Carpenter four fingers, raising the bet to $40.

"I don't know," responded Carpenter in a hushed voice. He paused to think it over. "Okay. Forty bucks. It's a bet." Riney flashed a thumbs up, then the middle finger.

Staff Sergeant Mike Kowalski and Sergeant Al McCoy gave orders to their squads who mounted the vehicles and began preparing them to leave the motor vehicle compound. Carpenter and Whitehorse, under Kowalski's command, fell in line behind the Lieutenant's jeep as the convoy moved out. The jeep led the convoy to the firing range.

"You are either an idiot or desperate to make that bet with Riney," Whitehorse said to Carpenter as they maneuvered the vehicle down the post gravel road.

"I need the money."

"Now Ransom and I need to work our butts off for you. You will owe us Christmas dinner for this!"

"Deal done. Just help me get the cash. Siggie's really sick and desperately needs it! I'm scared."

Lieutenant Sharp stood in front of the now even further reduced number of enlisted men, once more formed up, this time on the firing range at the post. Two days had passed of intense weapons training and firing competition. Carpenter was especially nervous. Christmas with Gunda and the girls was imperative. Siggie was recovering but still needed a great deal of tender loving care. *I really need to win this thing.*

The officer's sergeant handed him a clipboard. He scanned the data and then addressed the men. "The results are in. And the results are clear. Kowalski's squad is number one and McCoy is number Two. Those guys get Christmas leave. The others get to GI the vehicles." Carpenter's group cheered while groans emanated from the losing sections. Carpenter relaxed. As they were dismissed to return to quarters, Carpenter jabbed Riney in the back and said, "Pony up Riney, you owe me forty bucks!"

"Yea, yea, okay, here you go." Riney dug into his pocket and produced the cash. "You won fair and square. But I'll be looking to win that back soon, Carpenter!"

"Any time, you know I'm up for it."

As they walked to the vehicles the command sergeant major called out, "You ladies enjoy your holidays. When you return in two days, we get to work. And, you find out what all of this is about. So enjoy your time off and get some rest. You're gonna need it!"

Whitehorse turned to Carpenter, "I don't like the sound of that."

"No, neither do I," Carpenter admitted out loud.

Ransom, unaware of their conversation, ran up and grabbed both of them around the neck. "Let the fun times begin! We're headed to your place for Christmas right Carpenter?"

Carpenter had met his wife Gunda two years earlier while on a weekend pass with a buddy to visit the Fränkische Schweiz (Bavaria's Switzerland) which was a beautiful mountain area near Bamberg. They got bored quickly with the stunning scenery, and decided to take the train back to Bamberg that Sunday morning. On the way to the train station, they went into a café for breakfast. The place was nearly deserted, with only a few older persons present. Right after they sat down, near the door, another older woman and what Carpenter viewed as a young girl came in. He made somewhat of a snide comment about not finding any women except seventy, and seventeen, not thinking that anyone spoke English. Someone approached their table, and he looked up to see the young girl. She spoke in English and said, "I beg your pardon, I am not seventeen, and you are very rude." With that she and the older woman left without ordering.

Carpenter fell in love at first sight. The two soldiers finished their breakfast, and went to the Bahnhof to catch the train back to Bamberg. The two women were on the platform, and boarded the same train as the two American soldiers. Carpenter did not see her again until he got off the train in Bamberg. He approached her there, and tried to make amends. *Man, this girl really has got a hold of me for some reason.* But she would give him nothing but a cold shoulder, and drove off in a Taxi.

After that, and for months, he looked all over the city for her, and was beginning to get depressed, thinking that he would never see her again. Having formed a friendship with his boxing coach, who was a Sergeant and lived off post with his wife in Quarters appropriated from the Germans, Carpenter was invited to his home for dinner. It was some kind of a special occasion, and they were having Goose for the evening meal. He nearly fainted when he walked through their door, and discovered that Gunda was their maid. He was overjoyed, and spent a considerable amount of time that evening getting under her feet, as she tried to go about her work. She finally put him out of his misery, and agreed to a date the next day. As an aside, the goose as very rich, and made him sicker than a dog; he threw up several times on the way back to the Barracks. The very next day he started to court Gunda in earnest, and it was only a couple of months until she said yes. The two love birds tried to get permission to marry, but neither the Americans, nor the Germans would allow them to do so, without waiting months, and doing a significant amount of paperwork.

In early February 1950, Carpenter took a furlough, and the two drove over to Bern Switzerland and got married on February 6th. Then they took a honeymoon trip through Northern Italy, Southern France, and into Spain. They wanted to see Paris, so they headed north through France. That was a big mistake, as the French were very rude, because Gunda was a German, and traveling on a German Passport. They spent only one day and night in Paris, and drove back to Germany. They never returned to France.

I was a very young child and my towering father was always a beacon of safety and security. It was Easter and I was on an Easter Egg hunt struggling through grass that was tall to me with dozens of others about my age. From his glorious height he would softly call my name then point and I would run/stumble with my large basket until I found a colorful egg and claim the prize that was now mine.

A time later I was risen from my small height and posted on his great chest of honor and held firmly in his firm arms. He told me he was proud of all the eggs I had found & I was happy in the moment. Then he pointed at a young girl with her mother. We knelt. I remember him saying something but I was shocked/confused when he instructed me to take two of my own eggs and place them in her basket. I felt it was wrong, they were mine! But I loved my father.

Then I remember looking at the girl's face and seeing sudden happiness. I looked up and saw my father was smiling, and looking around the girl was smiling, her mother was smiling and I found myself smiling too.

Again the great pleasure of being lifted unto Olympus, being in warm and secure arms and knowing all was well.

John R. Carpenter

Chapter Three

After their marriage, Dick and Gunda had returned to army life. He was frequently restricted to the post or placed on temporary duty in the field. It was around this time that the war on the Korean Peninsula broke out. Carpenter was assigned as a clerk to the battalion sergeant major and was also frequently the battalion commander's driver. During these long periods of restriction to base or deployed on exercises, Carpenter took the time to become extremely knowledgeable on weapons, particularly crew-served anti-aircraft systems. He spent hours and hours alone on at night or on the weekends, learning about his new passion. This personal quest and hunger for weapons expertise is what led to him being 'volunteered' for the secret mission to Korea. It was also during this period, while Private Carpenter was frequently deployed, that Gunda was raped and became pregnant. A poor, single, German girl in American-occupied Germany was an easy target. It was the second time she had been taken advantage of. She broke the news to him, probably one night over tears, when he returned from one of his frequent temporary duty assignments. After processing the information, Private Carpenter made a decision. He loved Gunda deeply and would accept the child as his own. The two of them made a pact. They would never tell the child the truth. She would always be 'their daughter.' American troops were always coming and going in 1950s Germany. Siggie would never have the chance to even find out who her real father was. Whether or not this was the best course of action, would remain to be seen. After DNA tests in later years, Siggie found out she was not Carpenter's biological child. It caused her great distress and a feeling of 'not belonging.' Gunda and Dick went to their deaths without revealing the truth.

In November of 1950, due to his weapons expertise, Carpenter was sent on temporary duty to a new weapons school in another part of Germany.

> "Gunda had a daughter from a previous relationship with an American soldier. When the war ended, American forces occupied Bamberg. Gunda was just 18, and trying to survive. She stayed at home, and looked for work, which was nearly nonexistent for a young woman. In early 1946 she met an American soldier, who got her drunk, and then took advantage of her. They subsequently established a relationship which lasted for about six months, until the soldier shipped out. She named the child after her Grandmother. When I first met her she was four years old, a lovely, but very spoiled child. At first I did not know how to relate to Laura, I loved her mother, but Laura did not want anything to do with me. So we established a very strained relationship with very little interaction between us. However, I began to feel affection for her, and was able to slowly improve the relationship. When her baby sister (Linda) arrived, that broke the ice, and our relationship steadily improved, and my love for her grew. She became my own daughter."

Richard Carpenter, Memoirs

Gunda gave birth to Siggie two months premature on December 29th, 1950. She was born with the assistance of a Hebamme (midwife) in Gunda's parents apartment as the American authorities still did not recognize Gunda or her daughter Hanalaura as Carpenter's dependents. Carpenter and Gunda had been living with her parents in Bamberg, Germany. Carpenter, who had not been home in weeks, was granted leave by his section commander who took pity on him. He arrived home on New Year's Day in 1951.

The doctor was called after her birth because Siggie was born so premature. No one thought she would survive.

However, the doctor and the midwife rigged a homemade incubator and Siggie miraculously survived. She steadily grew stronger.

"Linda was originally named Sieglinde Margareta in German. The German authorities would not accept Linda Margaret as her name. It was not on their list of acceptable names. Later when she, Laura, and John became naturalized citizens we changed her name to Linda Margaret. Linda was named after a German Aunt Sieglinde, and an American Aunt Margaret. We thought it important to recognize the two different cultures that had come together in her birth."

Richard Carpenter, Memoirs

Carpenter remained on temporary duty at the weapons school and rarely saw his family. In October of 1951, he was returned to his original post in Bamberg and reunited with the girls. He was overjoyed.

"During my absence the clerical position I held in the battalion had been filled by another soldier. They needed a clerk in the regimental personnel office, and I got the assignment. My job was to do all the paperwork clearances for soldiers whose tour was ending, and who were returning to the United States. It was strictly an 8:00 am to 5:00 PM, and I loved it. It gave me I lots of time to spend with my family.

"It didn't take long for me to realize that many soldiers were not able to get a full clearance to leave, because they had cars registered in their

names, and had not disposed of them. Most of the cars were being held in Germany Repair Shops for payment of the repair bills. So I worked out a system with a friend of mine, Whitehorse, (a mechanic) to buy the cars for a pittance. The soldiers were happy. They got to go home. The Repair Shops were happy. They were able to dispose of an American Automobile that was costing them storage, and to which they could not acquire title. Whitehorse and I were happy as we were making quite a bit of money from the system. We also made a friend, who was a military police desk sergeant. He gave us a temporary registration for each car which was good for 90 days, but did not show up on the official records. That way, when we sold the cars to other soldiers, it appeared that title had been transferred directly from the soldier who had gone home.

"Another part of the deal was the black market. Each American Registered Vehicle was able to receive a 100 gallon gas coupon book each month. There were several American Gas Stations at the Exchange Facilities where we could get gas in exchange for the coupons. The books cost $10.00, or 10 cents a gallon. Whitehorse owned a converted jeep, that had a 100 gallon gas tank. As soon as we received the temporary registration, we would buy a gas coupon book, and then fill his gas tank. With a full gas tank we would then visit the German repair facility where the car was located, and strike a deal. Gas on the German economy was very expensive, over four dollars a gallon. In every instance we were able to swap gasoline to pay the repair bill, and take possession of the car. Whitehorse would then get the car into selling condition and we would park it near the regimental exchange complex with a "For Sale" sign on it. We had no problem in disposing of two or three cars each month and this resulted in a real financial bonanza for each of us, even after we paid off everyone. I would estimate that during that time I was getting $500.00 each month for my part in the endeavor. I wish I could have kept it up forever. I stayed in this assignment for well over a year, until the deal fell apart with the departure of my buddy, and the military police desk sergeant., who rotated back to the States. I was still a private first class. I had not really put any serious thought into getting promoted, and making a career of the service. But, I had become addicted to the *extra money and was looking for a way to improve my salary. To be promoted to corporal, I had to attend the regimental noncommissioned officers academy. So I volunteered, and in May of 1952 I was assigned to* the academy. It was a four week course and I had no problem passing it. On graduation, I was promoted to Corporal."

Richard Carpenter, Memoirs

Upon leaving the academy, Corporal Carpenter was assigned as a section leader, weapons platoon, 60mm mortars, A Company, of the 1st Battalion. He again spent weeks in the field, away from his family. To rectify the situation, he tried out for the regimental rifle team. With all of his weapons expertise, he was accepted easily and was assigned to this new special duty assignment with all kinds of free time to spend with Gunda and the girls. Carpenter was nothing, if not creative and persistent, to make sure he was the best father possible, in his own way.

The earliest memory of my father—we had just come back from Germany. We were watching the station wagon being lifted off the boat. It was a sight to see. Then the cable broke, needless to say down came the car!

We ended up spending the week in New York. We saw the sights including the Statue of Liberty. The parks I remember were all street like, Made out of asphalt. After a week, we were on our way to California. So many stops along the way. Historical; Little Big Horn, Gettysburg, Paul Bunyan. It was fun as a kid. Siggie usually sat in the back because she got car sick. She thought it was great; she didn't have to pass snacks or drinks that mom packed. John, Rich and I along with mom and dad. Dad mainly drove at night and slept during the day. He always got a motel with a swimming pool. Kept us kids busy! We saw relatives along the way. My aunt Annie, my mother's sister. Grandma Braaten, dad's mom, she lived on a farm. I remember her flowers being so tall or maybe it was me being so short. I am not sure which it was. LOL. We made it to San Diego in 1966. We stayed with my Uncle Toby, Aunt Edith, Marjorie, and Chuck until my parents bought the house on Twin Lake in La Mesa. Precious memories of family get togethers, birthdays, thanksgiving and Christmas. The many times trying to find Rich who always seemed to find the pond and him being naked as a jaybird.

Ruth Carpenter

After the first two months of the conflict on the Korean Peninsula, U.N. forces, 88% comprised of American troops, were pushed down to the Pusan Perimeter; the conflict looked lost. However, General MacArthur landed new forces in a daring amphibious assault at Inchon and encircled the enemy, forcing them back up to the Yalu River. At that point, the Chinese entered the war, supported by the Soviet Union. U.N. forces retreated south to the 38th Parallel and the fight became a war of attrition.

December 1952
Parade Ground
Erlangen, West Germany

Carpenter once again stood at attention. There was no banter in the air this early morning. The holidays were over and they were once more formed up waiting on the Lieutenant. *No one is laughing this morning. No, this time it is serious.* He shivered in the cold German morning, in spite of his field jacket.

There were just shy of twenty of them now from the original group of soldiers. They were the ones that had proved their skills and impressed the officers. However, a couple other men had been added to their motley crew, a medic and radar specialist, upping the obvious danger level for the mission. None of the men were oblivious to these new developments. All that was left was for the Lieutenant to drop the other shoe, and tell them where they were headed, although most of them already knew.

Once again the jeep roared up to the formation and screeched to a stop; Lieutenant Sharp was again standing in the passenger seat, for effect. He had a smile on his face.

"I got a bad feeling when an officer smiles like that," Whitehorse whispered to Carpenter.

"Yea, what the Hell have we got ourselves into?"

The Lieutenant spoke, "Gentlemen. From this moment on you are restricted to post. You are not to leave quarters without permission. You are not to communicate with anyone outside this post. Is that understood?"

"Yes, Sir," was the uniform response from the enlisted soldiers of the detachment.

"You men have been selected, due to your superior skills with the crew-served, anti-aircraft weapons we have been training on for the last few days. You are the best of the best. Your country needs you and I will be proud to lead you into battle. Yes, we are going into combat. We are going to Korea. We will be inserted into the middle of combat operations under cover as an anti-aircraft unit. We will be testing a new technology, battlefield radar, a technology that will give us an edge in the war, and against our enemies all over the world. We obviously don't want the Chicoms to know we have this capability to pick them out and target them on the battlefield, so this is an extremely sensitive mission. We are to test and perfect this technology in combat conditions. This technology could literally turn the tide of the war. I trust you will do your duty and I know I can count on you..."

Sergeant First Class Quincy, the detachment sergeant, looked over at Whitehorse. Although they were all friends, Quincy had put his sergeant hat on and now was signaling the other enlisted guys in the formation to shut the fuck up. Quincy was a career man who saw combat at the Battle of the Bulge. The squad sergeants Kowalsky, who was also a combat veteran, and McCoy took the hint and made a facial expression to the other men to keep it down while the Lieutenant was speaking.

"I don't like this one bit," Carpenter said under his breath. He had the look of death on his face, like all the blood had drained from his head to his feet. "What the Hell is he stressing combat for? I've got a sick girl at home I have to take care of! What does he mean we can't leave the post?"

At that point, the Lieutenant started introducing new members of the team. First there were the radar operators who were trained on the new equipment. Then attention turned to a man who had joined the rear of the formation. He had a red cross armband, a helmet with the red cross, and was carrying a medical kit. "This is Private First Class Casper. He will be our combat medic."

That was when the realization hit the squad that they were going into harm's way. Carpenter wasn't worried about himself. He was worried about his family. *How will I get money to the girls? How will I even get word to them that I am shipping out?*

The Lieutenant kept talking. As he talked, Carpenter noticed armed guards surrounding their tent compound. "None of you can leave this area," he heard the Lieutenant say. *This is fucking serious,* he thought to himself.

"As we assembled with other volunteers, we were immediately isolated in a tent complex, and guards were placed around our compound. The next morning a signal corps major, and an artillery lieutenant briefed us on the assignment, and told us it was Top Secret. We were not to

discuss it, under any circumstances with anyone outside of the assembled group. The assignment was to form a test unit to explore the potential of a new anti-vehicle, anti-personnel field radar system under combat conditions. As a cover, in addition to the radar, we were being assigned the equipment, and weapons of an anti-aircraft battery. This included four half tracked vehicles. Two mounted with quad fifties, and two mounted with twin forties. We were to become proficient with both the radar, and the weapons."

Richard Carpenter, Memoirs

The lieutenant continued, "Radar was the ultimate wonder weapon at the start of the last World War. The Brits used it to channel their limited air power to where the Germans were flying into England. By the end of the war, it seems that everyone had radar. Even the Krauts had a radar which could locate Russian tanks coming at them … little good it did them. Since then radar has become more sophisticated and smaller. As you know we have radar that can see and track incoming artillery rounds for counter-battery fire. In the States, I have helped develop a new generation of radar that can see soldiers in the field at night, in fog, and even if they are camouflaged. We can see them coming and hit them before they know we are there. We will be conducting our training at the old German tank range at Tagelow near Erlangen … When we are ready, I will be proud to lead you men to Korea for a 3 month tour for combat testing. Thank you. I thank you. Your country thanks you. Now you will be sent to your individual squads for more in-depth training on the equipment. Sergeant?"

"Dismissed!" said Sergeant Quincy.

Carpenter walked briskly up to Sergeant Quincy from behind as he walked back to the trucks, then tapped him firmly on the shoulder.

The man turned around to face him. "Sergeant! ... I have less than a year left and I am married. And..."

Quincy cut him off, "I read your file Carpenter. According to the Army, you are not married to any *Nazi* yet."

A look of rage washed over Carpenter's face. He tensed up as if he might punch Quincy, which would be an offense worthy of a court martial. Whitehorse stepped forward and put his hand on Carpenter's shoulder. Ransom and Kowalski also moved closer to restrain Carpenter if need be.

"If your dependent application gets approved by division, then we will deal with it. And *only* then. You should have gotten more than a slight slap on the wrist for fraternizing with a ... German national. You are officially single just like every swinging dick out here. You volunteered, now don't come whining to me soldier," Quincy adds. He then storms off, angry himself.

Kowalski steps in front of Carpenter, blocking the view of the noncommissioned officer walking away. "Don't worry, all AA units in a combat zone are stationed behind the battle lines. That is Army SOP. And don't forget you get combat pay!" He smiled, trying to calm Carpenter down. "And besides, the war may be over before we even get there."

Ransom spoke up, "Who volunteered for Korea?"

"None of us did," replied one of the radar specialists.

"I sure the hell didn't."

"Me neither. I didn't volunteer for anything. I was assigned. This is bull shit," added other members of the detachment.

Kowalski, one of the squad NCOs jumped in, "Enough ladies. You either volunteered or got volunteered. Shit happens! Deal with it. Now, get over it."

McCoy added, "Time to get on the trucks. Grab your gear and let's go. Move it!"

Our training started immediately with artillery officers, and NCO's from the division artillery units stationed in Erlangen training us on the vehicles, and weapons. The Major, and the Lieutenant did all of the training on the radar systems. We were all experienced soldiers, and it did not take long for us to become an cohesive unit.

We trained day, and night until mid-February 1953. Then we had a test of our skills; we were sent to the field in a nearby training area. As part of aggressor forces, facing an attacking infantry regiment, our mission was to detect all the enemy movements, and classify them for theaggressor forces commander. To accomplish this we had to split up into four teams. Each team centered upon one radar set, and one half track vehicle, protected by an infantry platoon.

We passed the test with flying colors. In every instance of troop, or vehicle movements, our teams were able to detect them, in particular at night. Our reports to the aggressor commander allowed him to shift forces, and meet every movement of the Regiment, For the regiment, it was a disaster, for us a celebration, In early March we were advised that we had completed our training, and were being shipped to another location. We had to box up all I of our equipment, and personal items, and get them ready for the move. It only took us a couple of days, and we were alerted to move in mid-March.

Richard Carpenter, Memoirs

Tangelow Test Range
West Germany
1953

Carpenter walked out of the tent carrying a rolled-up sleeping bag and headed for the deuce-and-a-half pulling a trailer as the detachment prepared to move out. Whitehorse was busy packing the unit's gear. The guards around their compound were especially tense this evening, as if they knew the day was not normal and change brought risk. They kept an eye out for any odd occurrences around the compound, as ifs the North Koreans themselves were on the prowl in Germany. "You know, we've been guarded here like virgins in a whorehouse," Carpenter lamented. This has been the tightest security I have ever seen. All my efforts to send a letter or call have been thwarted. I really miss my wife and kids. My wife is probably thinking I just up and disappeared by now. Sergeant Quincy found out that my dependent request still is in limbo. So, if anything happens to me in Korea, my wife and kids will get nothing! The worst thing is there is not a f'in thing I can do about it. Gunda needs money for Siggie and I'm f'ing stuck here. Unreal. She could die if she doesn't get medicine!"

Sergeant Kowalski yelled out, "Carpenter, Whitehorse! You guys ride with the equipment! Hurry up! All aboard! Next stop is Frankfurt's Rhein-Main Air Force base!" The MPs helped Carpenter and Whitehorse into the back of the covered truck and took seats beside them. Slowly the convoy moved out onto the autobahn to transport the men and equipment to the airfield for the flight eastward. Whitehorse took out a pack of cards to try and take Carpenter's mind off the situation. It was no use, he looked as sad as a puppy separated from his mother for the first time. The military policemen were nervous, looking out the back of the truck as they caressed their M-1 carbines with rounds in the chamber. *I'm tired of this top secret crap*, Carpenter thought to himself as he tried to visualize his family and what was going on at home. *I have no idea if I will ever see them again.*

Suddenly the truck downshifted and began to slow down. The massive vehicle then drove onto the side of the road and eventually stopped. The two younger MPs in under the tarp in the rear grabbed their weapons. The MP sergeant smiles at all of the men and says, "Relax, stopping as scheduled."

"Carpenter! Get your butt out here! Now!" yells Sergeant Kowalski.

Carpenter scrambled out the back of the truck and saw Kowalski and the MP sergeant grinning like they just took candy from a baby. Kowalski handed Carpenter a wad of money. "If anyone asks, we had bad fuel," Kowalski says. He then grabbed Carpenter and turned him so he could see towards the front of the truck. There, standing next to a vehicle parked on the side of the road was his wife, Gunda.

"It's medicine money for the baby. You got five minutes, Daddy," said the MP sergeant with a grin on his face.

Carpenter rushed forward and grabbed Gunda in a warm embrace. He didn't want to let go. "You're going to war?" she asked incredulously.

Carpenter handed her the wad of money and quickly took off his watch and ring. "Sell these if you have to, but take care of Siggie. I'll be back for these, if I can, I promise!"

Gunda buried her head in his shoulder and weeps. Carpenter pulled out his wallet and emptied it of money as well. Then he hugged her one last time.

"Almost brings a tear to your eye, doesn't it" said the military policeman from afar near the military vehicle.

"Yes, that it sure does," replied Kowalski.

Carpenter forced them apart and then sadly walked back to the truck and hopped in the back. Gunda was left watching them as they drive away, stunned.

However, Carpenter was overjoyed and humbled at the camaraderie of his fellow soldiers. He felt like a giant weight had been lifted off his shoulders. In fact, he was speechless, and didn't utter a word until they were loaded on the plane at Rhein-Main.

We were trucked to the Frankfurt Rein Main Air base, where we spent a couple of days in isolation. Not able to go anywhere unescorted by senior NCO's, or our Lieutenant. In late March we boarded an air force cargo airplane, a big Globe Master. Our first stop was Gander Newfoundland, and the next Fort Sill Oklahoma. At Fort Sill we spent a couple of days learning about some improvements that were being made to our radar equipment. Then we again boarded the same air force cargo plane. We stopped in Alaska long enough to refuel, and then flew directly into Kimpo Airfield in Korea. We all pretty much knew where we were going, but we were not told until we left Fort Sill. We arrived in Korea on the 1st of April (April Fools Day) 1953.

Richard Carpenter, Memoirs

Chapter Four

Carpenter and the unit arrived at Kimpo Airfield in Korea and immediately were driven with their equipment by truck to the north side of the airfield. There were tents waiting for them and they bedded down for the night after establishing guard duty for the equipment and a security perimeter for the entire group. The first thing they noticed was the smell, and the hulks of destroyed aircraft which had been pushed into the grass and left to rot in the hot sun.

Kimpo Airfield was positioned west of the city of Seoul and lay in a vast plain at the foot of the mountains to the north. Rice paddies surrounded the flat surface of the field and were fertilized with human waste. Kimpo had changed hands several times during the war and General MacArthur inspected the troops at the field in 1953 after the U.S. Army had pushed the Chinese back north to the 38th Parallel. The men of Carpenter's detachment still were of the opinion that their little 'excursion' into the warzone would be brief and unexciting. They were very wrong.

The men were inserted into the Korean conflict at the behest of the U.S. Army Security Agency. This unit was responsible for signal intelligence collection as well as electronic countermeasures. It was the successor to Army intelligence operations during WWI. The ASA reported to the National Security Agency or NSA. In 1977 the unit was merged with the U.S. Army's Military Component to form the United States Army Intelligence and Security Command.

Corporal Carpenter and the detachment were once more in formation outside their tents at Kimpo Airfield. It was morning but the sun was already beaming in an attempt to burn off the overnight cooler temperatures. Carpenter had his field jacket on and was as comfortable as he could be considering he was about to go to war. The Lieutenant once again walked out to brief them on the coming day's events.

"Gentlemen, we are being redeployed up on the line. We won't be fully engaged in combat as our position will be approximately one mile south of the forward line of troops. We will be bedded down with a Republic of Korea, or ROK, anti-aircraft artillery unit of the ROK Capital division, assigned to the American corps. That sector has been fairly quiet and it should give us a good chance to test out the equipment. However, we will be in a war zone so take care of your buddy next to you and be prepared for combat at all times with a moment's notice. That is all, load and prepare your gear for the drive north!"

The convoy to transport the detachment's men and equipment consisted of two trucks with trailers and a jeep with a trailer as well. The progress up into the mountains was slow as the roads were damaged from the war and not well maintained. "I don't want to break an axle in one of these ditches," Ransom said to Carpenter as he steered one of the heavy trucks.

As the convoy drove through a village, the children came out to beg. They saw only the very young and very old. Many rice fields were being planted. Only occasionally did they see the debris of war. They stopped at an armed checkpoint of very serious looking ROK troops and the convoy's papers were checked.

As they progressed closer to the MLR (Main Line of Resistance), they passed through a deserted bullet ridden village and paused at a control point before starting the drive up a hill at the orders of Korean MPs. A truck with wounded and dead ROKs was seen coming from the front. The wounded ROKs glared at the Americans as they passed the stopped American convoy. The men's attention was then directed off to the side of the road by loud voices where several Koreans were standing blindfolded. With three quick orders in Korean, a firing squad readied, aimed and fired. As the convoy started up the hill, a

ROK MP Officer walked the line of those shot and calmly shot each one again in the head.

Eventually they arrived at the ROK position after dark and quickly unloaded their equipment and supplies into a large bunker on the top of Hill 433, which is now located in the Demilitarized Zone or DMZ, which separates North and South Korea. The ROK troops showed the men a portion of the bunker complex and they bedded down for the night. Machine gun fire and the rolling thumps of artillery could be heard in the distance. The Lieutenant cautioned the men again to keep their weapons at the ready. Guards were posted and the men spent their second night in-country and their first of many nights on Hill 433.

"The next morning we got a good look at the unit, and the position we were in. It appeared to be just over a mile from the front lines. With binoculars, and the artillery spotter scopes we were able to trace much of the friendly lines, into no man's land, and in one valley a little bit of the Chinese lines. The position looked pretty good; the batteries' four half-tracks were well dug in, and well spaced. A series of trenches connected everything together. The position area looked to be about half of a football field in size. In the center of the position, and on the South side was the large bunker where we had spent the night. The only other Americans there were a forward air controller team, an Army sergeant, and two other enlisted men. The FAC team's Lieutenant had been wounded and evacuated, and was never replaced while we were there."

Richard Carpenter, Memoirs

The men did not sleep well in their new surroundings. Carpenter woke early and made his way up the trench from the bunker to the top level, then stepped into the fresh, morning air.

The fifty square foot space was a communications, command and observation area. Only about three feet of the structure protruded from ground level, and was very heavily sandbagged. The Lieutenant was observing the enemy positions over a mile away, using binoculars. The sound of fighting could be heard, although it was less intense than the previous evening. It seemed both sides needed sleep before the killing began again.

"I can see a lot of activity on the Chinese side." He handed the binoculars to Carpenter and pointed north east. "See, to the right of that valley, along the ridge, you can see enemy activity. The rest of their lines are hidden."

Carpenter raised the glasses to his eye as the sun broke over the ridge and attempted to locate what the LT was talking about. Finally he spotted what Lieutenant Sharp had seen, his first look at the enemy. There were a few dozen men scurrying around a fortified position. It looked as if they were attempting to move a gun emplacement. "Yes, I see them," Carpenter replied. He handed the binoculars back to the junior officer.

Carpenter took the moment to look around. It had been very dark when they arrived the previous evening and now in the daylight, he wanted to get a look at his surroundings and understand the lay of the land. As he turned and walked back down the trench, Whitehorse and Ransom met him halfway.

"Quite the operation they have going here. Did you take a look downstairs?" asked Whitehorse.

"No, I didn't. Let's do that now. What do you say?" Carpenter responded.

The men continued down the tunnel which led from the upper observation deck and soon were in the second level of the bunker. There were several rooms hewn out of the rock which were used primarily to house troops. The facility was obviously an abandoned mine which had been converted into a bunker complex. The actual underground system was huge and included four levels. The American detachment was boarded in one of these rooms which included enough cots for all of the GIs. Many of the men were still sleeping and Carpenter, Ransom, and Whitehorse quietly walked past them to the lower level. Electric lights glowed weakly above them and provided enough light to make the trek downward into the depths. Soon they exited the tunnel into another cavern which was not as refined as the upper levels but functional. It mainly consisted of a food storage area and a makeshift kitchen. Bags of rice lined the walls and the smell of dried fish permeated the space.

Carpenter almost stumbled over a very narrow railroad rail and he blurted out, "An old mine tunnel!" A few ROK soldiers ahead of them looked back curiously and realized the American was talking to himself and not to them. The 3rd level was under the boarding area and on the low end he could see where the tunnel had collapsed. "That must have been the original entrance to the mine." Carpenter walked slightly uphill toward the back end of the chamber. Old mining equipment and an ore car were long abandoned in the opening. He saw more sacks of rice and dried fish. As he turned to explore further, he heard dripping water and was amazed to find a cistern of water built near the collapsed end of the tunnel.

Whitehorse responded, "Someone planned this very well." The Americans looked up and saw water dripping from above into the cistern.

"Must be a couple hundred gallons," said Carpenter.

"Three hundred at least," said Whitehorse.

Ransom dipped his finger into the water, "It is cold and it's clear."

Carpenter and Whitehorse were examining the cistern when Ransom noticed a small Buddhist shrine and statue against the wall. He picked up the statue. "Look what I found! A fat little man!" Beside the statue was a small bowl with pieces of rock candy inside. Before Carpenter or Whitehorse could say anything, Ransom picked up a piece of candy and popped it in his mouth. A sudden cry of anger in Korean from across the room alarmed the men. A group of armed ROK soldiers suddenly confronted the three GIs, hands on